Edith Adams

OMNIBUS

Zazu Pitts (left), an American movie actress, joins in a cooking demonstration with Marianne Linnell as Edith Adams, on 21 October 1952. Linnell holds the *Thirteenth Prize Cook Book*.

Edith Adams

OMNIBUS

Compiled by Elizabeth Driver

whitecap

Acknowledgments

Whitecap Books and Elizabeth Driver thank the *Vancouver Sun* for permitting Edith Adams to come to life again in this omnibus. They are also grateful to the generous *Sun* readers who lent their Edith Adams cookbooks and shared their stories.

Proofread by Lesley Cameron

Printed and bound in Canada

Library and Archives Canada Cataloguing in Publication

Adams, Edith
    Edith Adams omnibus / compiled by Elizabeth Driver.

Includes index.
ISBN 1-55285-613-5

    1. Cookery. I. Driver, Elizabeth II. Title.

TX715.6.A367 2004   641.5   C2004-904632-2

The publisher acknowledges the financial support of the Government of Canada through the Book Publishing Industry Development Program for our publishing activities.

Please note that the ingredients, methods, and cooking times listed in this book are for the kitchen appliances and techniques in use from the 1920s to the 1950s. Current equipment and supplies may produce different results that are inconsistent with today's food safety guidelines.

All illustrations in this book are reproduced with the permission of the *Vancouver Sun*, the copy-right owner. Elizabeth Driver and Whitecap Books thank the following individuals and institutions for supplying photographs or allowing material in their collections to be photographed for the illustrations: Joyce Ansley, 12th and 13th annuals; Norma Bean, 6th and 9th annuals; Thelma Bell, *The Vancouver Sun $100.00 Cook Book*; Stella Kay, 5th annual; Joan B. Smith, *The Vancouver Sun $100.00 Cook Book*, 9th, 12th, and 13th annuals; Wendy Turner, 3rd, 4th, and 6th annuals. Robert Linnell, pp. 2, 35, 39, 87, 91, 146, 155, 166, 190; Legislative Library, Victoria, B.C., p. 6; University of British Columbia Archives, Vancouver, p. 11; Vancouver Museum, pp. 43, 99, 119, 159; *Vancouver Sun*, pp. 194, 198, 206, 219.

Although recipe contributors' street addresses appeared in the original Edith Adams cookbooks, Whitecap Books has not included them in this omnibus to protect the privacy of contributors and their families.

Contents

The first Edith Adams column, "Rhubarb Is Best Dessert for Spring," appeared in the *Vancouver Sun* on 4 April, 1924, p 17. One week later, on April 11, the newspaper christened the "Edith Adam's Cookery Page" with the banner headline, pictured above.

Edith Adams
British Columbia's Kitchen Oracle

By Elizabeth Driver

In 1999 Edith Adams, Vancouver's very own cooking expert and household advisor, disappeared completely from the pages of the Sun *newspaper after seventy-five years of service. She began to slip out of the public eye as her contributions to the food pages became less frequent. No ceremony marked her departure. Yet, British Columbians remember her with affection, and the recipes she featured in her columns remain favourites in many homes, where instructions for Lazy Daisy Cake (p. 198) or Limey Bride's Sausage Batter (p. 191) are found in faded clippings or dog-eared newsprint copies of the* Sun*'s annual Edith Adams cookbooks.*

As a tribute to this culinary icon and as a permanent record of her legacy, the *Edith Adams Omnibus* brings together hundreds of treasured recipes, selected from the first thirteen issues of the Edith Adams "prize" cookbooks produced by the *Sun* almost every year, from the mid-1930s to 1950.

But who was Edith Adams and what made her so famous for so long? Mathematically minded readers will already be calculating her age at retirement—at least ninety-five years old, because she made her debut on April 4, 1924 (some articles have incorrectly counted from the founding of the newspaper in 1912). The truth is that Edith Adams was a fictitious character played by a series of food editors and their assistants. Her name was coined by the *Sun*'s Circulation Manager, Herb Gates, and it had the typographical advan-tage for newspaper headings of no descending letters.[1]

The first women to fill the role of Edith Adams are unknown, but in 1947 Marianne Pearson Linnell took on the job, assisted by Myrtle Patterson Gregory and Eileen Norman. Others who followed Linnell included Judy Ruddell, Barbara McQuade, Eve Johnson, and Murray McMillan. In the recollection of one *Sun* reader, Joan le Nobel, who responded to an appeal by Whitecap Books for information for the omnibus, "The fact that [Edith Adams] didn't actually exist ... was not really publicized, but it was not exactly a secret, either, and there was a woman—Marion[2]—who stood in for her (sort of) at the Cottage."

Edith may have been imaginary, but British Columbians entered into her world as if it were real. They wrote to her and telephoned,

Edith Adams was local and therefore close to the people and the seasons of British Columbia. Another aspect that made her special was that she interacted with her readers.

with queries on all manner of household subjects, from cooking and cleaning to etiquette and interior decorating; and from 1947, when the newspaper opened the Edith Adams Cottage in the *Sun* Building, with its own private door at 510 Beatty Street, they visited the Cottage to watch her lead cooking classes. When the newspaper began to print photographs of Linnell at the Cottage, the captions sometimes identified her as (unmarried) Miss Edith Adams, not as Linnell.

Although most *Sun* readers likely understood that the person they saw in the photograph or at the Cottage demonstrating a recipe was an employee with a private life separate from Edith, they willingly participated in the make-believe. Sometimes there were awkward moments, because several staff members answered the phone as Edith and a caller might notice a different voice and comment, "Oh, I spoke to you yesterday, but you're not the same person."[3] Eve Johnson recalls that telephone conversations as Edith were occasionally surreal: "[W]hen the phone rang an especially long time, more than one caller said [to me]: 'Oh, I hope I didn't get you out of the garden.'"[4] When the *Sun* hired

McMillan, the newspaper's first male food editor, it became untenable for him to continue answering, "This is she."[5] So ended Edith's three-quarters of a century as the province's kitchen oracle.

From today's perspective, it seems odd that the women of British Columbia embraced the fiction of Edith Adams, but the *Sun* newspaper was at the forefront of a continent-wide trend in corporate advertising. In the United States, the persona of Betty Crocker had been invented by the Washburn Crosby Co. (now General Mills Inc.) in 1921, just three years before Edith. In Canada, Anna Lee Scott, another creation, represented the Maple Leaf Milling Co. on cookbooks from 1924, the same year as Edith's start, and there were later idealized figures, such as Martha Logan for Swift Canadian Co. and Rita Martin for Robin Hood Flour Mills, both launched in the 1930s, plus Brenda York for the Maple Leaf Milling Co., beginning in 1947. These national characters offered trustworthy advice, but Edith Adams was local and therefore close to the people and the seasons of British Columbia.

Another aspect that made her special was that she interacted with her readers, not only by answering questions, but by soliciting their recipes and reproducing them in the cooking pages, so that she was perfectly in tune with the needs of the province's home cooks. Newspapers in other Canadian cities featured food writers under their real names or under a pseudonym specific to an individual, but only the *Vancouver Sun* devised a fictional character to direct its food department. In this respect, Edith Adams was unique in Canada.

From the beginning, Edith spoke directly to her readers. Her first cooking column, for example, celebrated the early spring harvest of "lowly backyard rhubarb" anticipated the upcoming crop of luscious British Columbia strawberries, and encouraged Vancouverites to frequent "the downtown markets, including the curb market on Pacific Avenue," where they would find lettuce, green onions, radishes, celery, and tomatoes to "add a dash of color to the dinner table." Recipes for B.C. fish and shellfish, fresh or canned, appeared regularly. She also understood the need for economy in the kitchen, especially during the Depression and the World War II–period, when rationing restricted purchases of meat, sugar, and butter. The casserole dishes, especially, reflected families' small budgets and the limited ingredients available, whether because of those difficult times or the winter season.

The *Sun* had offered prizes for readers' recipes before Edith's first appearance, but from April 1924 Edith set the challenges and dispensed the awards. The answer to "Can You Feed a Family of Four on $1 a Day?" on her second page won $5; a few months later, a recipe for B.C. small fruits netted $3. Eventually, she gave out a dollar daily for each "reader's prize recipe." The lure of the financial reward and the pride of having one's recipe printed in the newspaper was irresistible.

The attraction increased when the *Sun* began publishing Edith's selection of the best prize recipes in an annual cookbook—what an honour it was for a homemaker to have her recipe chosen! Each year, British Columbians eagerly awaited the next annual issue of the prize recipes, some keen to see whether their recipes were included, others just happy to have their own copy of the latest Edith Adams cookbook for reference in the kitchen. "These little books were almost like Bibles during the war," writes Mrs Eileen Heiland, another one of the many people who responded to Whitecap's appeal for information. She adds that her friends enjoyed discussing which recipes they had used.

In another letter, Marion Linn recounts how she participated in the recipe contest, from her home in Nanaimo: "In that era I was a new mother ... Many of the recipes which I submitted brought the $1 cheques in the mail and were printed in the paper of course. It was fun. My variation of the Sausage-Noodle Casserole is in the 13th annual book [p. 214]. I still make that casserole and make it in the same pyrex dish used in 1948. We had it for dinner last week in fact."

Rita Morin sent Whitecap her memories of growing up in the 1940s, in a logging community on St Mary's Bay, Senora Island, about 65 miles north of Campbell River, where food came in once a month: "The [food] order was

Prize-winning recipes printed on the *Edith Adams* cooking page merited a try; those picked for the annual prize cookbook were guaranteed good!

written [by my mother] and sent to Woodward's Food Floor in Vancouver and would arrive—hopefully all of it—in order to be able to make the recipes that had been identified in the Edith Adams' cookbook as looking very promising to try out on her young family."

Like Rita's mother, Marion Linn also relied on Edith Adams and the prize cookbooks: "Edith Adams taught me how to can fruit and make pickles and relishes, which I still do today. I also learned to make fruitcake, which was my husband's favorite, and there were always 'Cry Baby' cookies [p. 201] in the cookie jar for the children and Lazy Daisy or Crazy Chocolate Cake [p. 198] for desserts… all made with recipes from Edith Adams."

In another letter, Jean Astbury's daughters describe their mother's resourcefulness throughout the 1930s and 1940s, when she grew, harvested, and preserved all the accompaniments for the family meals, without the aid of a refrigerator for storage. Jean began collecting the Edith Adams prize cookbooks from the first issue and surely turned to them for canning ideas.

Women who were lucky enough to own electric refrigerators—a new appliance in Canadian homes in the 1930s—would have delighted in preparing the fashionable ice-box

cookies and cakes. Prize-winning recipes printed on the Edith Adams cooking page merited a try; those picked for the annual prize cookbook were guaranteed good!

The *Edith Adams Omnibus* presents the first thirteen numbers of the prize cookbooks in the order in which they were published; however, since the texts for the first and second annuals were nearly identical,[6] there are actually twelve sections in the omnibus. Each annual's year of publication appears at the start of each section. With the exception of the twelfth and thirteenth numbers, which are copyrighted 1948 and 1950, the *Sun* did not date the cookbooks; however, publication announcements in the newspaper pinpoint most years (the dates for the first/second and fourth annuals are approximate).

The arrangement of the recipes generally follows the original text, and the instructions are faithfully reproduced, including such charming phrases as "remove from fire" for remove from heat. The only changes have been occasionally to re-order the list of ingredients to match the order of preparation, a helpful modern convention, and to correct a few typographical errors. You can use the omnibus in two ways: Browse each section, or turn to the index to find recipes by type.

The selection includes recipes using locally grown or harvested foods (orchard fruits; salal berries in Wild Berry Pie, p. 204; salmon; wild game), dishes typical of the province's British heritage (Steak and Kidney Pie, p. 36; Haddie Scrambled Egg, p. 22), an early attempt at Asian food (Si-Yong Choi, p. 17), and a wealth of good cookies and cakes, from traditional Christmas baking to Tomato Soup Cake, p. 47, based on a commercial product. There's a wide variety of jams and pickles, but no canning instructions have been reprinted because the processing methods are out of date.

Where bread recipes call for 1 yeast cake, substitute 15 mL (one 8-g package or 1 tbsp.) of dry yeast (traditional, not fast-rising); at the stage where the dry yeast is dissolved in lukewarm liquid, first add 2 mL ($^1/_2$ tsp.) sugar to the liquid to help the yeast grow (if not already stipulated in the recipe).

The salads lack today's variety, and it's clear that Edith's readers favoured the gelatine type—not a 21st-century taste.

Cooking in British Columbia has evolved, but there's still much to enjoy in the *Edith Adams Omnibus*. Preparing and eating these favourite foods is a powerful way to connect with the past and share memories around the table. As Marion Linn recalls about her life in the era of Edith Adams: "The dollars were few, the entertainments were simple, the friends were many and faithful. It wasn't the best of times, but it was good times and nice to remember."

Housewives telephoned the Edith Adams Cottage with their cooking questions. In 1950 two assistants answer a call: Phyllis Marie Atrill (left) and Shirley Pinchin (right), winners of the Vancouver Sun Service Fellowship in Home Economics.

End Notes

1. *Sun Spots* (*Vancouver Sun* in-house periodical) (February 1947).

2. Linnell was called Marion at birth, but changed her name to Marianne in later life, so Joan le Nobel remembers correctly.

3. Nathalie Cooke, "Getting the Mix Just Right for the Canadian Home Baker," *Essays on Canadian Writing* No. 78 (Winter 2003), p. 208. In this article Cooke explores how Canada's "fictional food figures" of the early to mid-20th century helped to "feminize and humanize the food industry" (p. 192).

4. Eve Johnson, *Five Star Food*, Vancouver: Pacific Press, 1993, p. 8.

5. Cooke, p. 208.

6. There is one small, but distinguishing, difference in the texts of the first and second annuals, in the introductory letter "To Our Readers" on p. 1. In the first annual, reproduced in the omnibus, the letter refers to "this $100 Cook Book—so called because of the hundred prize recipes included in its contents"; in the second annual, the letter refers to "this second edition of our $100 Cook Book—so called..." Demand for the first annual prompted the newspaper to reprint it. Subsequently, a decision was made to produce a new collection of recipes, numbered as the third. The first annual is rare: There are no known copies in public institutions and only one privately held copy surfaced during production of the omnibus.

The Vancouver Sun
$100.00 Cook Book

circa 1934

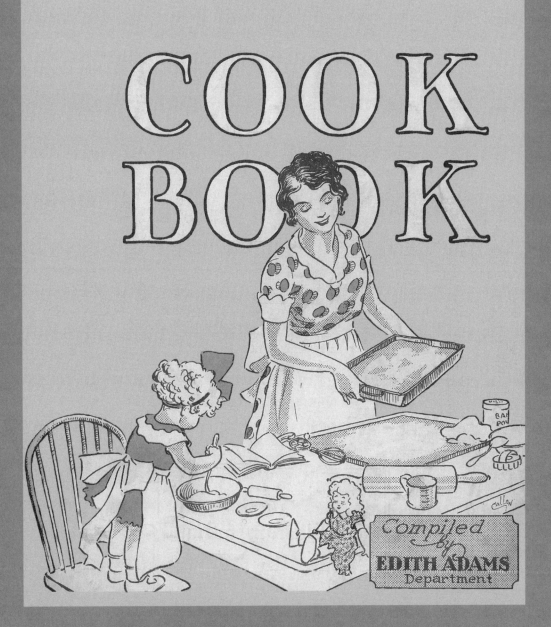

TO OUR READERS:

In keeping with the custom of The Vancouver Sun to offer to its readers services over and above those found within its daily pages, this $100 Cook Book—so called because of the hundred prize recipes included in its contents—has been compiled and arranged for the use of the housewife whose duties and activities are those of the average homemaker.

Edith Adams, whose Cookery Page appears Friday of each week in The Vancouver Sun, has given considerable thought and preparation to the placing of the recipes.

The arrangement is the natural one in which the foods appear on the table. For instance, appetizers—suggestions to capture and stimulate any faint or jaded appetites—are followed by soups; bread and muffins; meats—and with meats we think of fish and fowl; vegetables; salads and dressings; and a large classification of desserts, cakes, cookies, pastry, puddings and all manner of "finishing off sweets."

Under the heading of beverages are not only tea and coffee recipes but scores of delectable wines and cordials.

In the miscellaneous pages are grouped candy, canning and preserving, cheese dishes, egg dishes and suggestions for children's menus and parties.

Abbreviations are used: A capital T for tablespoon, a small t for teaspoon, c for cup.

Edith Adams is continually at your service, and may be reached by telephone or letter.

THE VANCOUVER SUN

Appetizers

Oyster Cocktail

- 8 small raw oysters
- 1 tablespoon tomato catsup
- ½ tablespoon vinegar or lemon juice
  Salt
- 2 drops Tabasco sauce
- 1 teaspoon celery, chopped
- ½ teaspoon Worcestershire sauce

Mix ingredients, chill thoroughly, and serve in cocktail glasses or cases made from green peppers placed on a bed of crushed ice.

Tomato Juice Cocktail

- 1 cup tomato juice
- 1 tablespoon mild vinegar
- 2 teaspoons sugar
- 1 tablespoon lemon juice
  Tiny bit of bay leaf
- 1 slice onion, making 1 teaspoon when grated or chopped
- 1 bruised celery stalk

Mix ingredients, let stand 15 minutes and strain through cheesecloth. Chill and serve in small glasses.

Canape Suggestions

Anchovy butter, lobster butter, sardine butter, watercress butter, parsley butter, caviar, cheese, chopped olives and red or green pepper, pate-de-foie-gras, salmon.

Three Fruit Cocktail

- 5 tablespoons grapefruit juice
- 2 tablespoons orange juice
- 1 tablespoon lemon juice
  Few grains salt
- ½ cup charged water
- 4 sprigs mint
- 2 level tablespoons sugar syrup
  Crushed ice

Mix ingredients thoroughly in a cocktail shaker. Put crushed ice in four cocktail glasses, pour in mixture, and serve at once. Garnish each glass with a sprig of mint.

Soups

Clam Chowder

- 1 onion
- 6 slices bacon
- 1 can minced clams
- 1 potato
- 1 carrot
- 1 pint milk
- 1 tomato

Dice onion and bacon and fry well. Add juice of clams. Dice the potato and carrot. Add to the first mixture and cook for 15 minutes. Heat milk, clams and tomato in separate pan, but do not boil. Combine two mixtures and serve at once. This is sufficient for three people.

From Mrs. H.G. Brown, Vancouver.

Vegetable Soup (Mother's)

- 1 large soup bone
- ½ cup pearl barley
- 1 cup dried peas (previously soaked overnight)
- 2 medium onions
- 2 medium carrots
- ½ medium turnip (cut into small pieces)
  Salt and pepper to taste

Wash the bone. Cover with 2 quarts of hot water or part stock. Add rest of the ingredients and boil gently for at least 3 hours. Skim off any fat. Serve with crackers or bread and butter.

From R.V. Peasland, Victoria.

Pea Soup

- 1 quart peas
- 3 carrots
- 4 onions
- 1 head of celery
  Sweet herbs
  Spring parsley
  Small toast cubes
  Dried mint

This soup should be made with liquor in which any kind of meat has been boiled, but the liquor of salt pork gives it a more savoury flavour.

Wash the peas and put them into a pot with the bones and the carrots that have been thinly sliced. Simmer gently for about an hour. Then add the onions cut in thin slices, a head of celery, a few sweet herbs and a few sprigs of parsley chopped fine. Let the whole stew gently for three hours. Stir now and then. Press the whole through a colander with a spoon, season with pepper and salt. Put it over the fire again to have it quite hot. Serve it up with small cubes of toast and some dried mint rubbed fine.

From Florence Boye, Victoria.

Si-Yong Choi (Watercress Soup)

- 1 lb. lean beef
  Small piece ginger root
- ½ lb. tender watercress
- 2 eggs well beaten
  Few string beans

Shred about one-quarter of the beef in one tablespoon of vegetable oil and 1¼ teaspoons of sugar and let soak for 15 minutes.

Use remaining beef to make one quart of soup stock, straining soup until it is clear. Fry shredded beef in vegetable oil and cover with chopped ginger. Add watercress and soup stock and bring to a boil. Remove from fire and add beaten egg. Cook again for 5 minutes, and add cooked beans and season with salt and pepper.

From Ramona Carter, North Vancouver.

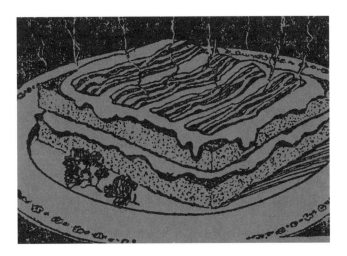

Breads and Sandwiches

White Bread

- 1 tablespoon lard or other shortening
- 2 tablespoons sugar
- 2½ teaspoons salt
- 1 cup scalded milk
- 1 cup boiling water
- 1 yeast cake dissolved in cup lukewarm water
- 6 cups sifted bread flour

Put shortening, sugar and salt in large bowl without lip or in top of large double boiler. Add liquid. When lukewarm, add dissolved yeast cake and 3 cups flour. Mix thoroughly with knife or spoon. Add 2 cups flour, mix with knife, and add remaining flour gradually, using just enough to prevent sticking.

Turn on floured board or cloth, leaving a clean bowl. Knead until mixture is smooth and elastic to the touch and bubbles may be seen under the surface. Return to bowl, cover with clean cloth and board or tin cover. Let rise until double in bulk.

Cut down. Toss on slightly floured board or pastry cloth, knead, shape and place in greased pans, having pans nearly half full. Cover, let rise to double in bulk. Bake 15 minutes in hot oven (425°), then reduce to moderately hot (375°) and bake 30 to 35 minutes longer.

One or two tablespoons butter may be added for a richer bread or for biscuits and rolls.

Entire Wheat Bread

- 1 cake yeast
- 2 tablespoons sugar
- 1 tablespoon shortening
- 3 cups lukewarm water
  About 2 quarts whole wheat flour
- 2 tablespoons salt

Work the yeast and sugar together with the back of a spoon, add these to the lukewarm mixture in which the shortening has been dissolved, then pour the mixture into a hollow in the centre of the flour, which has been mixed with salt. Beat in a portion of the flour, and as soon as stiff enough to handle, knead to a smooth dough, remembering that owing to the larger amount of gluten in whole wheat flour, it must be kept softer than white bread. Cover and put away in a warm place to rise four or five hours. Divide into portions, knead slightly and place in greased bread pans to rise until double in bulk. Bake from 45 to 60 minutes, temperature 350° for first 15 minutes, then increase to 375°, reducing to 350° for the last 15 minutes of baking.

Toasted Cheese and Bacon Sandwich

- ¾ pound Chateau cheese
- 3 eggs beaten until light
- 1½ teaspoons table sauce
- ¾ teaspoon salt
- ½ teaspoon paprika
  Few grains cayenne
- 8 slices of bread
- ¾ pound bacon, sliced very thin

Put the cheese through a sieve or food chopper. Combine the first 6 ingredients, and mix well. Spread on bread. Cut the bacon same length as bread. Cover cheese with bacon and bake 8 to 10 minutes under gas flame or in a hot oven. [Note: Chateau was a brand name; use cheddar.]

Asparagus Rolls

Cut buttered fresh bread into thin slices, cut off the crusts. Wrap one asparagus stalk, the length of a slice in each piece of bread. The stalks must be seasoned with salt and pepper, or they may be dipped quickly into French dressing just before being wrapped.

Salmon Sandwiches

- 1 small can salmon
- ¼ cup mayonnaise
- 2 tbsp. minced cucumber pickle

Flake the salmon and mix with mayonnaise and pickle. Spread on thinly sliced bread and butter and cover with another slice which does not require butter.

Apple Butter

Butter white or whole wheat bread, sliced very thin. Spread apple butter, then a thin slice of cold ham seasoned with a little prepared mustard, and top with another slice of bread spread with apple butter.

Cucumber

Place slices of peeled cucumber in cold water to crisp, slice bread very thin and spread with butter. Place sliced cucumber on bread and cover with thick salad dressing. Place a lettuce leaf over salad dressing. Cover with second slices of bread and serve.

Cream butter before spreading when making sandwiches; it is quicker.

Meats

Chili Con Carne

- 1 medium sized onion chopped
- 3 tablespoons butter
- 1½ pounds ground round steak or hamburg
- 2 cups canned red kidney beans
- 2 cups canned tomatoes
- 1 teaspoon salt
  Pepper to taste
- ¼ teaspoon sugar
- 1 teaspoon chili powder

Brown the onion slightly in the butter, then turn into it the ground meat. Cover, but stir occasionally until the meat also is nicely browned. Add the beans, rinsed of their liquor, and the tomatoes. Season with salt, pepper, sugar and chili powder.

Cook the mixture slowly for one hour, tightly covered. Water may be added if it seems too thick. Serve piping hot.

From Mrs. L.O. Lamson, Upper Sumas.

Deviled Round Steak with Mushrooms

- 1½ lbs. round steak cut 1½ inches thick
- 1 teaspoon mustard
- 3 tablespoons melted butter
- 1 teaspoon Worcestershire sauce
- 1 teaspoon salt
- ½ teaspoon pepper
- ¼ teaspoon paprika
- 1 teaspoon onion, chopped
- 3 tablespoons lemon juice
  As many mushrooms as desired

Score steak deeply on both sides and spread the mustard. Mix the next seven ingredients well and marinate the steak thoroughly. Brown the steak in a hot skillet on both sides. Brown mushrooms at the same time in the butter in another skillet. Add one cup of hot water to sauce in which steak was marinated and pour over steak and mushrooms. Cover and cook slowly for one hour.

This is delicious without the mushrooms, too.

From Mrs. M. Shiles, New Westminster.

Stuffed Meat Loaf

Loaf:
- 1½ lbs. round steak minced
- 1 egg well beaten
- ½ cup milk
- 1 tsp. salt
- ½ tsp. pepper
- 1 tbsp. Worcestershire sauce

Stuffing:
- 1 cup soft bread crumbs
- Salt
- ½ tbsp. sage
- 1 tbsp. grated onion
- ½ tsp. pepper
- 4 tbsp. melted fat

Sauce (optional):
- Tomato or Mushroom Sauce

Combine meat, egg, milk, salt, pepper and sauce. Line sides and bottom of a loaf pan with about three-fourths of this mixture. Make a stuffing with the bread crumbs, salt, sage, pepper, grated onion, fat and remaining meat mixture. Cook in a hot oven 50 to 60 minutes. Serve with tomato or mushroom sauce.

From Mrs. Peter Green, South Wellington.

Baked Ham with Jelly

Cover the ham with water and after bringing to the boiling point reduce the heat and allow it to simmer 25 minutes to the pound.

Let cool slightly in the water. Then pull off the skin and cut away some of the fat. Spread with brown sugar, insert cloves about one inch apart.

Bake in roasting pan for 30 minutes in a moderate oven. Remove from the oven and spread thickly with tart grape or apple jelly and bake 30 minutes longer, or until well glazed. Serve hot or cold.

From Mrs. H.W. Pollock, Vancouver.

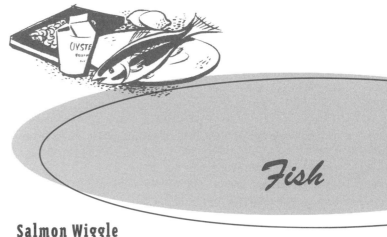

Fish

Salmon Wiggle
- 1½ tablespoons butter
- 2 tablespoons flour
- 1 cup milk
- 1 cup liquid from salmon
- 2 teaspoons salt
- 1 teaspoon lemon juice
- Dash of red pepper
- 1 can salmon
- 1 can peas

Make a white sauce of first four ingredients. Add seasoning. Stir until creamy. Add the salmon and peas and cook three minutes. Serve on buttered toast. This will serve six.

From Mrs. N. Montgomery, loco.

Halibut Baked in Milk
- ⅔ teaspoon salt
- ¼ teaspoon pepper
- 3 tablespoons flour
- 2 pounds halibut
- 2 tablespoons minced parsley
- 1 teaspoon onion juice
- 2 cups milk

Mix the salt, pepper and flour and roll the fish in this. Lay it in a casserole, sprinkle over with parsley and onion juice, and pour the milk around it. Bake, covered about ¾ of an hour, temperature 350°F. Serve in casserole.

Fried Oysters
- 24 large oysters
- ½ cup bread crumbs
- 1 teaspoon salt
- ⅛ teaspoon pepper
- 1 egg

Clean and drain the oysters. Roll in bread crumbs, seasoned with salt and pepper. Let stand 15 minutes or more. Then dip in beaten egg, roll in crumbs again. Let stand again, 15 minutes or more in cool place. Fry one minute or until a golden brown in deep fat. Drain on paper. Serve on hot platter, garnished with parsley. These are good served with French fried potatoes.

Baked Salmon and Corn Pie

1 pound tin Clover Leaf salmon
1 tin white corn
2 cups white sauce
  Seasonings
2 cups mashed potatoes

Turn out salmon, free from skin and bones and flake lightly. Mix with equal quantity of canned corn and combine with white sauce. Season with salt and pepper, adding a little finely minced green pepper or a grating of onion.

Turn mixture into a buttered baking dish, drop fluffy mashed potatoes over the top by spoonfuls. Brush the top with melted butter. Bake in a moderate oven until golden brown on the surface.

Fowl

Creamed Chicken

2 tablespoons fat
2 tablespoons flour
1 cup milk or cream
  Salt and pepper
1 tablespoon chopped parsley
2 cups cooked chicken
1 egg yolk

Make a white sauce of the fat, flour and milk. Season with salt and pepper. Add parsley and chicken and cook until the sauce is thoroughly hot again. Beat the egg yolk, adding 2 tablespoons milk and pour into the mixture. Cook 2 minutes, stirring constantly. Creamed chicken may be varied in a number of ways, by substituting mushrooms or chopped cooked eggs for part of the chicken or by adding chopped pimento or olives.

Stuffed Chicken

2 cups bread crumbs
1 small onion, cut fine
4 tablespoons melted fat, bacon
½ teaspoon salt
⅛ teaspoon pepper
1 slice chopped bacon
1 teaspoon poultry seasoning

Mix all together with 1 tablespoon cold milk or part of an egg. Dress, clean and stuff the chicken. Rub chicken well with butter, salt and pepper. Cover with a well greased thick paper, and place in roasting pan with plenty of basting. Set in hot oven. Temp. 450° to 500°, then reduce heat to 375°F. Time, 1 hour and 30 mins. if 4 lbs. chicken. Baste well with hot fat, just before serving.

Scalloped Chicken

2 cups cooked celery
1 cup diced chicken
3 tablespoons chopped pimento
1½ cups cream sauce, seasonings
½ cup dried crumbs

Wash and scrape celery and cut in short pieces. Cover with boiling water, cook till tender, drain, reserving the stock for half the liquor in the sauce. Mix celery, chicken (which may be canned) and pimento and put into casserole alternately with the sauce. Cover with crumbs, dot with butter, and cook 15 minutes in hot oven.

Chicken Gumbo

1 onion finely chopped
4 tbsp. butter
1 quart chicken stock
½ green pepper, finely chopped
1 c. cooked or canned okra
2 tsp. salt
¼ tsp. pepper
1 to 2 c. canned tomatoes

Cook onion in butter 5 minutes, stirring constantly. Add to stock with remaining ingredients. Bring to boiling point and simmer 40 minutes.

Vegetables, Salads

Cheese and Celery Puffs

- 1 ounce butter
- 1½ ounces flour
- ¼ pint water
- 1 egg
- 1 yolk of egg
- 2 ounces grated cheese
- 1 small heart of celery
- Pepper and salt to taste
- Fat for frying

Melt the butter in pan, add flour and water. Stir until it boils. Cook well for five or ten minutes, then let cool. Add egg and yolk of the other egg, grated cheese, chopped celery, pepper and salt to taste. Mix all together. Then drop mixture from a teaspoon into the hot fat and fry until nicely browned.

From Mrs. J. Wheeler, Lumby, Vancouver Island.

Beauty Salad

- 1 package raspberry Jell-O
- 1 pint boiling water
- ¼ teaspoon salt
- 2 bananas, diced
- 1 tablespoon lemon juice
- ½ cup walnut meats, finely cut

Dissolve Jell-O in boiling water. Add salt. Turn into individual moulds, filling them one-fourth full. Chill. Sprinkle bananas with lemon juice. When Jell-O is firm, arrange a layer of bananas on Jell-O. Sprinkle with nuts. Add another layer of Jell-O. Chill. When firm, fill mould with remaining Jell-O. Chill until firm. Unmould on crisp lettuce. Garnish with mayonnaise. Serves eight.

Pear Salad with Ginger Mayonnaise

- 3 cups pears, diced
- 1½ tablespoons lemon juice
- Dash of salt
- 4 tablespoons chopped preserved ginger and syrup
- ⅓ cup mayonnaise
- ⅓ cup cream, whipped

Sprinkle pears with lemon juice and salt. Toss lightly together with dressing made by folding ginger and mayonnaise into whipped cream. Serve on crisp lettuce. Serves six.

Waldorf Salad

- 1½ cups celery, diced
- 3 tablespoons lemon juice
- 2 tablespoons sugar
- Dash of salt
- 1½ cups apples, diced
- ⅓ cup mayonnaise
- ⅓ cup cream, whipped

Crisp celery by allowing it to stand in ice water. Drain and dry thoroughly. Add lemon juice, sugar and salt to apples, and chill for 10 minutes. Add celery. Toss lightly together with dressing made by folding mayonnaise into whipped cream. Arrange crisp lettuce in salad bowl and pile salad lightly in it. Garnish with strips of pimento and halves of English walnuts. If red apples are used, leave the skin on half of them. Serves six.

Egg Dishes and Omelets

Baked Eggs in Tomato Sauce

- 2 c. cooked tomatoes
- 1 onion (small)
- ½ t. salt
- 2 t. sugar
- Pepper
- 2 T. butter
- 2 T. flour
- 6 eggs
- Grated cheese

Cook tomatoes, onion, salt, sugar and pepper together for 20 minutes. Press the pulp through a sieve, discarding seeds. Melt butter, add flour and mix well. Add the tomato juice slowly and bring to the boiling point, stirring constantly. Pour the sauce into six individual baking dishes. Break the eggs, one at a time into a cup and slip carefully into each dish. Sprinkle with cheese. Bake in a moderate oven 15 minutes or until eggs are set.

From Mrs. L. Roberts, Vancouver.

Omelet Espagnole

      2 T. butter
      1 Spanish onion, chopped
      1 t. salt
      5 eggs
      ¼ t. pepper
      5 T. water

Melt the butter in the omelet pan and fry the onion in it very slowly until soft and golden-brown. Add salt to the egg whites and beat them until stiff. Beat the yolks until thick and add the pepper and water. Fold carefully together, adding a tablespoon of cooked onion; the remainder should be set aside in a warm place. Pour the egg mixture into the omelet pan, cover, and cook very slowly till firm throughout and golden on the bottom. Spread the remaining onion over the cooked omelet, fold over, turn onto a hot platter and garnish with parsley.

From Miss Myrtle Roberts, Vancouver.

Haddie Scrambled Egg

      6 tablespoons shortening
      8 eggs
      ¾ cup milk
   Or ⅜ cup evaporated milk, with ⅜ cup water
      1 cup cooked, flaked haddie
         Pepper
         Toast and tomato sauce

Melt the butter, dripping or fine shortening in a frying pan. Beat the eggs slightly and combine with the milk; pour into the hot fat and cook slowly, stirring well—I like to use a limber spatula, which keeps the egg well scraped from the bottom of the pan. When mixture begins to thicken, add the cooked fish, flaked with a silver fork and freed from skin and bone. Cook to consistency of thick custard. Serve on hot buttered toast.

Well seasoned tomato sauce is an appetizing addition. You can make your own sauce or heat canned tomato sauce or undiluted canned tomato soup for the purpose.

Orange Omelet

      1 egg
         Grated rind of ⅓ of an orange
      1 tablespoon orange juice
      2 teaspoons powdered sugar
      ½ cup butter

Beat the yolk of the egg and add the orange rind and juice. Add the sugar. Fold in the beaten white and cook as a plain omelet. Fold the omelet. Sprinkle thickly with powdered sugar.

Cookies and Cakes

Preserved Ginger Cookies

      ¾ c. butter
      2 c. brown sugar
      2 eggs well beaten
      ½ t. soda
   1½ t. baking powder
   3½ c. flour
   1¼ c. milk
      ½ c. finely cut preserved ginger

Cream butter and add sugar gradually, beating well. Stir in the eggs. Mix and sift twice the soda, baking powder and flour. Add to the egg mixture alternately with milk. Mix thoroughly, add ginger and form into a roll. Let stand in the ice-box overnight to chill. In the morning slice thin. Bake in a moderate oven.

From Mrs. N. Maggiora, Nanaimo.

Sugar Cookies

      ⅞ cup butter
      2 cups sugar
      2 eggs beaten light
      5 cups flour (about)
      1 teaspoon soda
      1 teaspoon salt
      1 cup sour milk
      1 teaspoon flavour

Cookies made with sour milk are more tender and delicate. Cream butter and add sugar, blend well until smooth, then add beaten eggs and flavour, then flour sifted with soda and salt, alternate with milk until about 4 cups used, then add flour until enough to roll out.

Sprinkle with sugar and bake in hot oven about 10 minutes.

Doughnuts

2½	tablespoons butter
1	cup sugar
3	eggs, beaten until light
1	cup milk
3½ to 4	cups flour
4	teaspoons baking powder
1½	teaspoons salt
¼	teaspoon cinnamon
¼	teaspoon grated nutmeg

Cream butter and add half the sugar. Add remaining sugar to eggs and milk and combine mixtures. Add 3½ cups flour, mixed and sifted with baking powder, salt and spices; then enough more flour to make dough stiff enough to roll. Shape and fry.

Doughnuts should come quickly to top of fat, brown on one side, then be turned to brown on other. Avoid turning more than once. They must be kept at a uniform temperature (370 deg.). If too cold, doughnuts will absorb fat. If too hot, doughnuts will brown before sufficiently risen.

Apple Sauce Cake

½	cup butter
1	cup sugar
1	teaspoon soda
1	cup cold, unsweetened apple sauce
1	cup raisins, cut finely
1	teaspoon cinnamon
1	cup nuts, cut finely
½	teaspoon powdered cloves
2	cups flour

Cream butter, add sugar gradually. Add soda to apple sauce and add to butter and sugar. Add other ingredients and bake in buttered and floured pan 40 minutes in moderate oven.

Pies, Puddings

The Queen of Raisin Pies

½	c. chopped raisins
½	c. chopped currants
1	c. sour cream
1	c. sugar
	Pinch of salt
½	t. baking soda
1	t. cinnamon
¼	t. cloves
1	egg white
1	egg yolk

Put in double boiler the above ingredients with the exception of the egg yolk. Save egg white for icing. Cook until thickened, remove from fire and add egg yolk. Fill pie-shell and make a meringue of beaten egg white and add ¼ teaspoon baking powder, 2 teaspoons sugar and five drops of vanilla extract. Cover pie and brown in quick oven.

From Mrs. Andrew Hoflin, La Glace, Alberta.

Apple Pie with Cheese Crust

      1 cup sugar
      1 teaspoon cinnamon
      ¼ teaspoon salt
 4 to 6 tart apples
      1 tablespoon butter

Mix sugar, cinnamon and salt. Pare and slice apples thinly. Arrange on pie crust, sprinkle sugar over the top and dot with butter. Cover with a cheese crust made by spreading grated cheese on half the pastry to be used for the top crust, then folding other half of crust over and rolling out as usual. Bake at 425°F for 30 to 35 minutes.

The proportions used in this pastry are 1½ cups flour to ½-cup shortening, ½-tsp. salt and ice cold water to make a dough.

Pumpkin Pie

      2 eggs
    1½ cups milk
      ½ cup sugar
      1 tablespoon flour
      1 teaspoon salt
      ½ teaspoon nutmeg
      1 teaspoon ginger
      ½ teaspoon cinnamon
      2 cups canned pumpkin

Line a large pie plate with pastry, having a fluted edge. Beat the eggs well, add the milk, sugar, flour, salt, nutmeg, ginger, cinnamon and pumpkin and combine thoroughly. Pour into pastry-lined plate. Bake at 450°F for 15 to 20 minutes to set the rim, then reduce to between 350° to 375°F for 30 minutes. This recipe makes one large pie or two small ones.

Lemon Pudding

      1 c. sugar
      1 T. flour
      1 T. butter
      1 lemon-rind and juice
      2 eggs beaten separately
      2 cups milk

Mix the sugar, flour, butter and grated rind and juice of lemon together with the egg yolks. Add the milk. Lastly add the stiffly beaten egg whites.

Put in a buttered bowl and set in a pan of hot water and bake three-quarters of an hour. Be very careful not to brown too quickly.

From Mrs. J.D. Lawrence, Prince Rupert.

Plain Baked Custard

      3 cups cold milk
      3 eggs slightly beaten
      ⅓ cup sugar
      ⅛ tsp. salt
      ½ tsp. flavouring

Combine the ingredients. Transfer to six medium-sized custard cups. Stand in a pan of warm water and bake (Temp. 350°F.) until firm in the centre and browned on top, about 30 minutes, or, if baked in a large dish, allow 45 minutes.

Preserving and Pickling

Mixed Pickles

      1 qt. chopped cabbage
      1 qt. celery
      2 c. green peppers
      1 c. red peppers
      2 c. lima or string beans
      2 c. onions
      2 c. red tomatoes (not too ripe)
      ½ c. cooking salt
      3 c. brown sugar
      4 T. dry mustard
      1 T. tumeric powder
      6 c. cider vinegar

Chop all the vegetables but not too fine. Mix and put them in a stone jar or earthen bowl and cover with the salt. Then cover with a plate and press down. Next morning drain. Put sugar, mustard and tumeric in the vinegar, and add to the drained vegetables. Boil slowly one and one-half hours. Seal in wide mouth sterilized bottles. When cold dip in melted wax and put into a cool dry place for winter use.

From Mrs. Annie Delaney, Sullivan.

Crabapple Chutney

    7   lbs. crabapples
    1   qt. brown vinegar
    3½ lbs. brown sugar
    2   T. ground cinnamon
    2   T. ground cloves
    2   T. ground allspice
    1   T. salt

Cook crabapples with just enough water to keep them from burning until they are soft enough to press through a sieve. Remove from the fire and press through a sieve. Add vinegar, sugar, spices and salt. Cook one hour and thirty minutes longer. Seal while hot.

From Mrs. T.S. Armstrong, Dundarave.

Grape Fruit Marmalade

    2   large oranges
    1   grape fruit
    2   lemons
    12 cups water
    2   sticks cinnamon bark
    5   lbs. sugar

Wash the fruit, quarter and remove seeds and cores. Cut into small pieces and put through food chopper. Put into large granite kettle and add the water. Let stand twenty-four hours. Add cinnamon bark. Boil two hours and remove the bark. Add the sugar and boil until jellied. When cool pour into jars and cover with paraffin.

From S.S. Lloyd, Bushnell, Florida.

Rhubarb and Pineapple Jam

Cut 4 pounds rhubarb into small pieces, add 2 lbs. of sugar and let stand overnight. In the morning put 2 lbs. sugar into preserving kettle, add the rhubarb juice and a tin of pineapple cut into small pieces, also juice from pineapple, boil 10 minutes and then add the rhubarb and boil for 20 minutes. Pour into jars and cover in the usual way.

From Jean Skelley, Vancouver.

Candies

Date Balls

- 2 cups stoned dates
- ⅔ cup chopped nuts
- 1 tbsp. minced preserved ginger
- 1 tbsp. ginger syrup
  Desiccated coconut

Pass the dates, nuts and ginger twice through the food chopper; moisten with the syrup; form into balls with the hands and roll in coconut.

Sweet Almond Paste (Marzipan)

- ¼ lb. confectioner's sugar
- ½ tsp. salt
- ¼ lb. blanched almonds, ground
- 1 egg white, beaten

Mix thoroughly and knead smooth. If too stiff it may be softened with a little orange flower water or lemon juice, but not much can be safely used. Let it stand 24 hours, then shape. This is often made into fruit or vegetable shapes, coloured with vegetable colouring and provided with angelica stems. It may be rolled into balls, then rolled in cocoa or grated chocolate.

Lanark Toffee

- 1 cup sugar
- 1 cup cream
- ⅛ tsp. vanilla

Melt the sugar over a slow heat with the cream. Let it come gradually to the boil, stirring constantly. Cook to 244 degrees, being very careful that it does not burn. Remove from fire, stir in vanilla and pour on buttered tins. Cut in squares.

Butter Taffy

- 2 cups light brown sugar
- ¼ cup molasses
- 2 tbsp. vinegar
- 2 tbsp. water
  Pinch of salt
- ¼ cup butter
- 2 tsp. vanilla

Boil first five ingredients until, when tried in cold water, the mixture will become brittle. When nearly done, add butter, and just before turning into greased pan, vanilla. Cool. Mark in squares.

Fill Your Apartments
Without Delay

Ever noticed what section of the paper is the most popular this time of year? Look around you—the Apartment-To-Rent columns are read on every side. Everybody wants to move—to change—to find something different. They pore over the Apartment-To-Rent columns! You can attract scores of people, if you advertise in The Vancouver Sun.

Read and Use

SUN Classified ADS
TRINITY 4111

Edith Adams Prize Winners Third Annual Cook Book

1935

Edith Adams

Prize Winners

THIRD ANNUAL

Cook Book

The Vancouver Sun

Once again The Vancouver Sun is happy to accede to the demand of its readers and to present herewith its Third Annual Cook Book. This Cook Book does not aspire to be a complete compendium of home cooking but is a selection from the many thousands submitted by Vancouver Sun readers.

It is, as its name implies, a collection of prize winning dishes devised by some of the most successful home cooks of British Columbia and carefully tested out in scientific culinary laboratories.

The young homemaker need not expect to find here that complete knowledge of cookery that is essential to a bright career in the family kitchen.

But housewives who are at a loss for new preparations to tempt jaded appetites will find in these pages a wealth of tasty dishes that will sharpen and renew the family's table zest.

This Prize Winners' Cook Book is presented to you with The Vancouver Sun's compliments, as the concrete result of a year's successful kitchen experimentation on the part of British Columbia's most deft and inventive housewives.

Edith Adams.

Edith Adams, the Cookery Editor of the Vancouver Sun offers a daily prize of $1 for the best recipe submitted by readers

Cakes

Orange Sponge Cake

Complete Dessert in Itself

    3 eggs
    ¼ teaspoon Gillett's cream of tartar
    1 cup granulated sugar
    2 teaspoons orange rind
    ⅓ cup orange juice
    1½ cups pastry flour
    1½ teaspoons Magic baking powder
    ¼ teaspoon salt

Separate eggs; beat whites and cream of tartar until stiff. Add yolks one at a time, beating well before addition of each yolk. Add sugar gradually, still beating with egg beater. Remove beater. Add grated rind and orange juice. Fold in flour sifted with baking powder and salt.

Bake in two layer cake pans in moderate oven of 325°F for 20 to 25 minutes.

Spread orange cream filling between layers.

Orange Cream Filling:

    ¼ cup sugar
    1½ tablespoons flour
    ¼ teaspoon salt
    2 teaspoons grated orange rind
    ½ cup orange juice
    2 teaspoons butter
    1 egg yolk
    1 teaspoon lemon juice

Put sugar, flour and salt in top of double boiler and mix. Add orange rind and juice. Add butter and egg yolk. Cook until smooth and thick. Remove from fire and add lemon juice.

Cover top and sides with Seven-Minute Frosting. Sprinkle coconut over all.

Note: If you don't like coconut, grate a little orange rind on the frosting before it cools.

Mrs. Joe Johnson, New Westminster, won a prize for this scrumptious cake.

Honey Crust Cake

    ¼ cup butter
    ½ cup sugar
    2 egg yolks
    ¼ teaspoon salt
    ⅔ cup flour
    1 teaspoon baking powder
    ¼ cup milk
    ½ teaspoon vanilla

Cream butter with sugar and egg yolks until fluffy. Add sifted ingredients alternately with the milk.

Add flavouring and pour into greased square cake pan (7 x 7 inches). Bake in moderate oven of 350 deg. F. for about 20 minutes.

Cool, then spread with:

Honey Crust:

    ⅔ cup honey
    1 tablespoon butter
    ¾ cup chopped nuts

Bring the honey and butter to the boil. Cook slowly for 5 minutes. Cool and spread half over top of cake. Sprinkle with nuts and then glaze the top with remaining honey mixture.

This cake is even more delicious if split in two layers before honey crust is put on and a filling of sweetened whipped cream is spread in between.

The prize went to Mrs. K. Hansen, Vancouver.

Coffee Spice Cake

    2 cups flour
    2 teaspoons baking powder
    ¼ teaspoon salt
    ⅛ teaspoon ginger
    1½ teaspoons cinnamon
    ¼ teaspoon cloves
    ¼ teaspoon nutmeg
    ½ cup butter or other shortening
    1 cup sugar
    2 well beaten eggs
    3 teaspoons molasses
    7 tablespoons cold coffee

Sift flour once and measure before adding baking powder, salt and spices. Sift together three times.

Cream butter thoroughly adding sugar gradually. Cream until light and fluffy. Add eggs and molasses and beat well. Add flour alternately with coffee, a small amount at a time. Beat after each addition.

Bake in 2 nine-inch layer pans for 25 minutes, or for 40 minutes in an 8-inch square tin at 375°F.

Cool and cover with the following frosting:

    3 tablespoons butter
    2 cups sifted powdered sugar
       Dash of salt
    ¼ teaspoon vanilla
    2 tablespoons strong coffee

Cream butter and add sugar, salt and vanilla. Beat until light and fluffy. Add coffee slowly until consistency to spread.

Note: For a decided coffee flavour use double strength coffee, that is 4 level tablespoons coffee to 1 cup of water.

This delicious spice cake won a prize for Miss Alice Mix, South Westminster.

Banana Cake

½ cup butter
1 ⅛ cups sugar
2 eggs
⅛ teaspoon salt
1 teaspoon baking powder
2 cups flour
2 large bananas
½ cup chopped nuts
1 teaspoon vinegar
¾ cup Nestle's milk
or ½ cup milk and ¼ cup water
1 teaspoon vanilla
1 teaspoon soda

Cream butter and add sugar, adding the eggs, saving one white for icing if you wish. Add salt and baking powder and flour, which has been sifted four times. Crush bananas with fork, add nuts and last of all put vinegar in milk, vanilla and water with soda and add to the mixture.

Bake in moderate oven for 1 hour, if a loaf tin is used, and about 50 minutes if baked in layers.

Cover with "7-minute" icing, made with brown sugar.

This prize went to Miss E. Reid, Trail.

Cookies

Soft Molasses Cookies

4½ cups sifted flour
1 teaspoon baking soda
3 teaspoons ginger
1 teaspoon salt
1 cup butter, or other shortening
1 cup sifted brown sugar, firmly packed
2 eggs well beaten
¾ cup molasses
¾ cup sour milk

Sift flour once and measure. Add baking soda, ginger and salt and sift again. Work the butter with spoon until creamy. Add sugar, gradually, beating after each addition until light and fluffy. Add eggs, molasses and sifted dry ingredients alternately with milk, beating after each addition.

Chill for one hour or more. Then turn onto floured board and roll to quarter-inch thickness. Cut with scalloped cookie cutter. Bake in 375 deg. F. oven for 12 minutes.

This popular cookie recipe won a prize for Mrs. H. Ritchie, Albion.

Jam-Encased Cookies

½ cup butter
¾ cup rice flour
¼ teaspoon salt
½ cup sugar
¾ cup pastry flour
1 teaspoon baking powder
1 egg
Milk
Raspberry jam

Rub butter into the mixed and sifted dry ingredients. Mix into a stiff paste with the egg yolk and a little milk (about 2 tablespoons).

Divide into balls. Hollow each and insert a little raspberry jam. Close up and drip in the white of egg. Flatten a little.

Bake in a hot oven of 400°F. for about 15 to 20 minutes.

Note: They will crack and show jam through.

Mr. H.G. Bailey, Vancouver, sent in this recipe.

Hermits

    1   cup butter
    1½ cups sugar
    ½   cup molasses
    3   eggs
    1½ teaspoons baking powder
        Flour (about 3½ cups)
    ½   teaspoon nutmeg
    ½   teaspoon cloves
    1   teaspoon cinnamon
    ½   cup milk
    1   cup chopped dates
    1   cup raisins
    1   cup chopped walnuts

Cream the butter, sugar and molasses together. Add the eggs one at a time and beat well. Add the sifted dry ingredients alternately with the milk. Then the floured fruit and nuts.

Drop from a fork onto an oiled pan. Bake in a 375 deg. F. oven.

The prize for this recipe went to Mrs. W.H. Mattie, Oliver.

Rolled Oat and Coconut Fingers

    ¾   cup butter
    3   tablespoons syrup
    3   tablespoons sugar
    2½ cups rolled oats
    1½ cups fine coconut
    1   teaspoon ground ginger
    ½   teaspoon salt

Melt butter and syrup before adding to the other ingredients, which have been well mixed together.

Press into a shallow greased tin. Bake in a 325°F oven till a pale brown or about 35 minutes.

Cut into fingers before it is quite cool.

Note: Made with 4 cups rolled oats, instead of coconut, these cookies are very nice for the children. The flavour is improved if allowed to stand 24 hours before wanted.

This recipe has won a prize for Mrs. J. Clegg, Port Alberni.

Breads

Apple Corn Bread

    1   cup bread flour
    2½ teaspoons baking powder
    ⅓   teaspoon salt
    ½   cup cornmeal
    ⅓   cup shortening
    ¼   cup sugar
    1   egg yolk
    ¼   cup molasses
    ¼   teaspoon soda
    ¾   cup milk
    1   egg white
        Apples, sugar, and cinnamon

Sift flour, baking powder and salt before adding the cornmeal. Cream the shortening and sugar, then add the egg yolk. Stir the soda into the molasses, then add to shortening mixture. Add the dry ingredients alternately with the milk.

Fold in the stiffly beaten egg white.

Pour the mixture into a shallow, well-greased pan. Place apples, pared, cored and cut in eights, in rows on batter. Sprinkle with a mixture of sugar and cinnamon. Bake in a 375 deg. F. oven for 25 to 30 minutes.

To serve, cut in squares and serve with cream or pudding sauce.

This can be served as a dessert with cream or with butter as a bread.

It won a prize for Miss Catherine Gilfillan, North Vancouver.

Ginger Cheese Muffins

    2   cups flour (measured after sifting three times)
    3   teaspoons baking powder
    ½   teaspoon ginger
    ½   teaspoon salt
    1   egg
    ½   cup milk
    ½   cup molasses
    4   tablespoons melted butter
    ⅔   cup grated cheese
    1   teaspoon vanilla

Sift flour, baking powder, ginger and salt. Beat egg and add milk gradually, then molasses. Add to dry ingredients. Then add butter. Lastly fold in cheese and vanilla.

Half fill muffin tins and bake in 375°F oven for 15 to 20 minutes.

Serve hot with butter.

The prize for these tasty muffins went to Mrs. J.R. Williams, Vancouver.

Date and Nut Loaf

    1   teaspoon soda
    1   cup cut dates
    1   cup boiling water
    ¾   cup brown sugar
    1   tablespoon shortening
    ¼   teaspoon salt
    1   egg unbeaten
    ½   cup chopped walnuts
    1½ cups flour

Sprinkle the soda over the dates and pour over the boiling water.

Cream sugar, shortening, salt and egg together. Add nuts, dates and flour.

Turn into a bread pan and bake in a moderate oven, 350°F, for 45 minutes.

This moist loaf recipe, sent in by Mrs. J. Ross Polson, North Vancouver, is excellent to take on picnics.

Cheese Straws

    1   tablespoon butter
    ⅔   cup pastry flour
    ¼   teaspoon salt
           Few grains cayenne
    ⅛   teaspoon pepper
    1   cup grated cheese
    1   cup soft bread crumbs
    4 to 6 tablespoons milk

Soft moist crumbs from the inside of a loaf of fresh bread are wanted for the cheese straws. The amount of milk varies with the moisture of the crumbs.

Cream the butter in a mixing bowl. Add the flour which has been sifted with the salt, cayenne and pepper. Mix the grated cheese and soft crumbs which have been packed solid in the cup, into the butter and flour mixture. When all is well mixed add the milk gradually until the mixture leaves sides of the bowl.

Roll to a quarter-inch sheet, and cut into strips a half-inch wide and six inches long. Bake in a moderate oven of 375°F until crisp and brown.

This ideal salad accompaniment won a prize for Mrs. Henry Casher, Vancouver.

Marianne Linnell, as Edith Adams (top of stairs, dressed in white), welcomes members of the Ambassadors of Britain Chapter of the Imperial Order Daughters of the Empire, who have come to enroll in the first "School for Brides" starting 23 April 1947.

Entrees

Steak and Kidney Pie

 2   beef kidneys
 2   teaspoons salt
 ½   teaspoon pepper
 2   tablespoons chopped parsley
 2   tablespoons vinegar
 2   teaspoons Worcestershire sauce
 1½ tablespoons melted fat
 2   pounds round steak
 1   medium onion
 2   tablespoons dripping
 3 or 4 cups water or stock
 3 or 4 tablespoons flour

Wash the kidneys in cold water. Scald and remove the skin. Split and cut out the veins, cords and fat. Soak in cold water for 30 minutes. Drain and cut into small cubes.

Combine the salt, pepper, parsley, vinegar, sauce and melted fat. Add the cubed kidneys, stir well and allow to stand for 30 minutes.

Cut the beef steak into cubes. Chop the onion and add both to dripping in the pan. Heat until the meat is seared on all sides and the onion is lightly browned. Add the kidneys with dressing in which they were standing. Brown slightly. Add the water or stock, cover and simmer until the meat is tender, or about 1½ to 2 hours. Add more liquid during the cooking if necessary.

Put the meat into a casserole or meat-pie dish. Thicken the liquid in a pan with the flour which has been mixed to a paste with a little cold water. Pour it over the meat in the casserole.

Cover with pastry or biscuit dough and bake in hot or 450 deg. F. oven until the crust is nicely browned, about 20 to 30 minutes.

This will serve 8 persons.

This popular hot dish won a prize for Miss Hilda Anderson, Union Bay.

Cheese Fondue

 7   slices buttered bread (or one-half loaf)
 1   cup grated cheese
 2   cups milk
 2   eggs
 ½   teaspoon salt
     Dash cayenne
 ¼   teaspoon mustard

Put bread in layers in a buttered baking dish alternately with the cheese. Mix all the other ingredients together and pour the mixture over the bread and cheese. Place baking dish in pan of hot water and bake in a moderate oven until firm, or about 30 minutes.

This ideal Lenten dish recipe won a prize for Miss D. Campbell, Victoria.

Scotch Broth

 ¼   lb. dried green peas
 ½   lb. mutton
 ¼   lb. pot barley

Soak the peas overnight.

The neck is very suitable for this soup. Cover the mutton with cold water in a large stew pot. Throw in one tablespoon of salt. Bring to the boil and simmer for 1 hour.

Add the following:

 2   large carrots diced
 1   small turnip diced
 3   leeks thinly sliced
 1   small cabbage shredded

When the mutton has simmered until almost tender add the vegetables including the peas and barley. Simmer for at least another hour.

Chop a few sprigs of parsley and grate one medium sized carrot. Stir gently into the soup. Simmer 15 minutes and serve.

Note: This is a very old Scottish recipe, and is a meal in itself.

To ensure the peas being tender we suggest adding them to the mutton at the first of the cooking.

This well made Scotch broth is a real treat. It won a prize for Mrs. C.B. Tremayne, Vancouver.

Parsnip Balls

 2   tablespoons butter
 1   teaspoon salt
     Dash of pepper
 2   tablespoons cream or top milk
 2   eggs
     Bread crumbs

Wash, peel and boil sufficient parsnips to make 2 cups when mashed.

When tender, drain and mash them with the butter, salt, pepper and cream. Mix all well together. Put in a pan on the stove and stir till bubbling. Remove the pan and mix in one beaten egg. Put away to cool.

Shape into balls, coat them with remaining beaten egg and bread crumbs. Fry a crisp brown in hot, deep fat at temperature of 375 to 385 degrees F.

Mrs. E.M. Oliver, New Westminster, won a prize with this recipe.

Puddings

Glorified Rice

Dissolve 1 package of raspberry jelly powder in 1 cup of boiling water. Add 1 cup pineapple juice and set aside until congealed. Then beat with egg beater to consistency of heavy cream.

Fold in the following:

    2   cups cooked rice
    ¾   cup crushed pineapple
    4   tablespoons sugar
        Few grains salt
    1   cup whipping cream

Beat all together and set aside to harden. Serve with whipped cream and garnish with cherries.

This dessert can be prepared in advance to avoid last-minute preparations. This won a prize for Mrs. W.J. Stokes, Burnaby.

Peach Dumpling

    1½ cups pastry flour
    3   teaspoons baking powder
    ½   teaspoon salt
    5   tablespoons shortening
    ½   cup milk
    6   good sized peaches
    6   tablespoons white sugar

Sift together the flour, baking powder and salt. Rub in the shortening lightly, and add just enough milk to make a soft dough.

Roll out to about one-eighth inch thick on slightly floured board. Divide dough into six equal parts and put skinned peach on each. Sprinkle with sugar and moisten edges of dough and fold up around peach, pressing tightly over the top of fruit.

Place in greased baking pan, sprinkle a little more sugar over each and place a piece of butter on top of each dumpling. Put in oven and bake 10 minutes at 450°F, then reduce heat to 375°F for 20 minutes more.

Serve with whipped cream, hard sauce or lemon sauce.

This substantial dessert recipe was submitted by Miss H.E. McTaggart, Vancouver.

Orange Sponge Pudding

    1   tablespoon butter
    1   cup sugar
    3   tablespoons flour
    2   egg yolks
        Juice and rind of 1 orange and ½ lemon
        (⅓ cup juice)
    1   cup milk
    2   stiffly beaten egg whites

Cream butter and sugar. Add flour and mix well. Then add egg yolks, juice and rind of orange and lemon juice and the milk. Beat well. Fold in the egg whites.

Bake in a buttered dish in a pan of hot water for 45 minutes at 350 deg. F., or until it forms a sauce on the bottom and nice sponge on top.

This is an excellent dessert for an oven dinner and won a prize for Mrs. Codorin, Ocean Falls.

Red Glace Apples

    2   cups sugar
    1   cup water
    ½   cup corn syrup
    1   teaspoon red colouring
    ½   teaspoon cinnamon flavouring
    12 apples
    12 skewers

Cook sugar, water and syrup until it forms a real hard ball in water.

Remove from fire and add red colouring and cinnamon. Put apples on wooden skewers and dip into the hot syrup. Drain well and place on a well-greased pan to cool.

Note: We recommend dipping the apples immediately the syrup is ready. We also found this syrup sufficient only for 5 or 6 medium to large apples.

Glazed apples make you think of Autumn and Halloween. This recipe won a prize for Miss Muriel Nicholls, Vancouver.

Relishes

Pickled Green Tomatoes

Peel enough small green tomatoes that will be covered when you prepare 3 pints of water and ⅓ cup salt. Drop the tomatoes into the water and cook until tender, but not soft. Then drain well.

Boil 4 cups of white sugar in 1 quart of white wine vinegar. Put 2 tablespoons of mixed spices in a little cotton bag and boil with the vinegar solution. Pour this over the drained tomatoes and let stand overnight.

In the morning, pour vinegar off and boil with the spices until it is a thick syrup.

Put tomatoes in sealers and pour cooled syrup over the tomatoes and seal.

Note: It will require about 4 pounds of tomatoes for this recipe. According to our usual method, we diluted the vinegar by one-quarter, that is, 3 cups of vinegar and 1 cup of water.

This exceptionally good tomato pickle recipe came from Mrs. Barrett, Vancouver.

Spiced Cranberries

       5 lbs. cranberries
    3½ lbs. brown sugar
       2 cups vinegar
       2 tablespoons ground cinnamon
       2 tablespoons ground allspice
       1 tablespoon cloves

Boil all together for two hours. Seal in sterile jars. This will make 8 to 10 pints.

Note: This is a nice change from the ordinary stewed cranberries to serve with cold meats.

Very nice to have on hand for special occasions.

This cold meat relish won a prize for Mrs. Ed. E. Hill, Vancouver.

Pickled Orange Slices

Boil 6 medium-sized oranges in water until tender. Change the water three times and use one teaspoon of salt in the first water.

Cool and slice into quarter-inch slices, leaving on the peel.

Boil the following together for 5 minutes:

       2 cups sugar
       1 cup white vinegar
     ½ cup corn syrup
     12 bruised coriander seeds
       1 stick cinnamon
     12 cloves
     ¾ cup water

Place the orange slices in a casserole. Cover with the syrup and bake in a moderate oven of 350 deg. F. until the oranges are clear, or about 30 minutes.

Store in sterilized jars or crock.

This excellent accompaniment for roast fowl won a prize for Mrs. G.F. Clark, Vancouver.

Apple and Ginger Chutney

     15 large sour apples
       4 sweet green peppers
       1 small chili pepper
       3 medium onions
       1 cup preserved ginger with syrup
       1 cup seeded raisins
       3 cups vinegar
       1 cup water
       2 tablespoons white mustard seed
     ¼ teaspoon whole cloves
       1 teaspoon allspice berries
       1 small bay leaf
    1½ cups brown sugar
       1 teaspoon ground ginger
       2 tablespoons salt

Pare, core and chop apples. Remove seeds from peppers and chop with onions. Cut ginger into small pieces.

Mix apples, peppers, onions, raisins, vinegar and water. Tie the whole spices in a bag and add.

Simmer gently for 2 hours. Add the sugar, ground ginger and salt. Continue boiling until of the desired thickness. Bottle while hot in sterile jars.

This recipe has won a prize of $1 for Mrs. J.C. Robey, Vancouver.

The *Vancouver Sun* reported the visit of June Whitley (left) to Marianne Linnell (right) at the Edith Adams Cottage on 16 November 1948: "Three years ago June used to help Edith Adams by answering cooking calls from her secretarial desk in the *Sun*'s editorial rooms. Now she's an actress in Hollywood ..."

Edith Adam's Prize Winners 4th Annual Cook Book

circa 1937

The Vancouver Sun is happy to once again accede to the demands of its readers and to present herewith its Fourth Annual Cook Book.

This Cook Book does not aspire to be a complete compendium of home cooking, but is a selection from the many thousands submitted by Vancouver Sun readers.

It is a collection of prize-winning recipes devised by some of the most successful home cooks of British Columbia and carefully tested in scientific laboratories.

Homemakers who are confronted with the preparation of three meals a day will find in these pages a wealth of tasty dishes that will sharpen and renew the family's table zest.

This Prize Winners' Cook Book is presented to you with The Vancouver Sun's compliments, as the concrete result of successful kitchen experimentation on the part of British Columbia's most deft and inventive housewives.

Edith Adams.

Cakes

Jubilee Cake

- ⅞ cup butter
- ⅔ cup sugar
- 4 eggs
- ⅓ cup almonds, blanched and chopped
- 2½ cups flour
- 1 teaspoon baking powder
- ½ teaspoon salt
- 1 cup seedless raisins
- 1⅓ cups currants
- ⅓ cup orange and lemon peel, cut fine
- 2 tablespoons orange juice

Decorate with:
- ⅓ cup almonds, blanched and split
- ⅓ cup citron, cut in thin slices and strips
- ⅓ cup candied cherries, cut in pieces

Cream butter and sugar, add the eggs one at a time and beat five minutes after adding each. Stir in chopped almonds. Sift flour with baking powder and salt and mix with the fruit before adding to the creamed mixture. Add orange and lemon peel mixed with orange juice.

Pour into a paper lined tin and decorate with the blanched almonds, citron and cherries.

Bake in a 375 degree F. oven for 10 minutes, then reduce heat to 350 degrees F. and continue baking for 45 to 50 minutes.

This cake won a prize during Vancouver's Golden Jubilee. **It won a prize for Miss Hazel Thomas, Vancouver.**

Cherry Cake

- 1 pound butter
- 2 cups fine fruit sugar
- 8 eggs
- 4 cups pastry flour
- 2 teaspoons baking powder
- ½ teaspoon salt
- 1½ cups or more of chopped glaced cherries
- ¼ teaspoon cinnamon
- ¼ teaspoon nutmeg

Cream butter and sugar. Add 1 egg at a time creaming well

after each addition. Add the flour which has been sifted with the baking powder and salt. Flour the cherries and add. Pour in paper-lined loaf tins and sprinkle with cinnamon and nutmeg. Bake 1½ hours at 350 degrees F.

This is really a pound cake with cherries. This is rather a large cake so you might want to make just half this amount.

It won a prize for Mrs. Victor Vavallin, Trail.

Pineapple Turnover

- 1½ cups flour
- ½ teaspoon salt
- 1 teaspoon baking powder
- 1 cup sugar
- 3 egg yolks
- 3 egg whites
- ½ cup pineapple juice

Sift together the flour, salt and baking powder. Beat half of the sugar into the egg yolks and half into the egg whites before folding the two mixtures together. Fold in the sifted dry ingredients alternately with the pineapple juice. Put this batter over the following:

- 2 tablespoons butter
- 1 cup brown sugar
  Pineapple slices
  Nuts

Melt the butter in a cake pan and add the brown sugar. Spread to completely cover the bottom of the cake pan. Arrange the slices of pineapple on top and place nuts between the slices. Cover with the batter and bake in a 350 degrees F. oven for about 40 to 45 minutes. Turn out immediately and serve with a liquid sauce or whipped cream.

This delicious and attractive sponge cake dessert can be made with apricots, prunes or peaches.

This recipe won a prize for Mrs. W. Giguere, Vancouver.

Tomato Soup Cake

    4   tablespoons butter
    1   cup sugar
    2   egg yolks
    2   cups bread flour
    1   teaspoon allspice
    1   teaspoon cinnamon
    1   teaspoon soda
    2   teaspoons baking powder
    1   can tomato soup
    1   cup chopped nut meats
    1   cup raisins

Cream butter, add sugar and egg yolks unbeaten. Sift together the flour, spices, soda and baking powder three times. Add tomato soup alternately with the sifted ingredients to the first mixture. Fold in the nuts and raisins and bake in a moderate oven of 350 degrees F. for about 35 to 40 minutes.

This tomato soup cake has a delicious flavour.

It won a prize for Miss M. Mannering, New Westminster.

Cookies

Granny's Ginger Cookies

    1   cup shortening
    1   cup brown sugar
    1   cup cooking molasses
    2   teaspoons baking soda
    ½   cup milk
    2   eggs
    1   teaspoon salt
    4   teaspoons ground ginger
    4   cups flour

Cream shortening, sugar and molasses together until smooth. Dissolve soda in the milk and add to creamed mixture. Add beaten eggs, beating mixture all the while. Have salt, ginger and flour sifted together and add slowly.

Roll out thin and cut with rather large cookie cutter.

Miss Allice M. Parry, Victoria, won a prize for this recipe.

Ice-Box Cookies

    ½   cup brown sugar
    ½   cup white sugar
    1   cup butter
    1   egg
    2   tablespoons orange juice
        Grated rind of 1 orange
    2¾ cups flour
    ¼   teaspoon soda
    ½   cup blanched almonds

Cream together the sugars and butter. Add the egg well beaten, the orange juice and rind. Last add the sifted flour and soda and then the shredded almonds.

Form into a roll and wrap in waxed paper. Chill in the refrigerator overnight, or until firm enough to slice thin.

Bake in a moderate oven of 375 degrees F. for 8 to 10 minutes.

Everyone will like these crisp flavourful cookies that won a prize for Miss Marvel Bratin, Chilliwack.

Sandies

        ¾ cup butter
        5 tablespoons confectioner's sugar
        2 cups sifted flour
        ¼ teaspoon salt
        2 tablespoons ice water
        1 cup coarsely ground pecans

Cream the butter well before adding the confectioner's sugar, flour, salt and ice water.

Flour the hands and pinch off small pieces of the dough and roll to the size of your little finger, then roll in the ground pecans. Arrange cookies an inch apart on an oily cookie sheet.

Bake in a 325 degrees F. oven till delicately browned, or about 20 minutes.

To further glorify these "Sandies" we suggest rolling them in powdered sugar when they are still hot. They won a prize for Miss E.M. Ritchie, Vancouver.

Shortbread

        3 ounces sugar (¼ cup)
        5 ounces butter (10 tablespoons)
        6 ounces flour (1½ cups)
        2 ounces rice flour (¼ cup)
           Few grains salt

Beat the sugar and butter to a cream before adding the flours and salt. Use the hand to work in all the flour. Roll to three-quarters of an inch thick and cut in desired shapes.

Bake in a slow oven of 325 degrees F. for about 30 minutes.

Shortbread is a general favourite particularly so at Christmas time. Its goodness depends on the flavour of the butter. So be sure the butter is sweet and fresh.

Miss M. Sinclair, Vancouver, won a prize for this recipe.

Pumpkin Cookies

        1¼ cups brown sugar
        ½ cup shortening
        2 eggs, well beaten
        1½ cups cooked pumpkin
        1 teaspoon vanilla
        1 teaspoon lemon extract
        2½ cups flour
        4 teaspoons baking powder
        ½ teaspoon salt
        ½ teaspoon ginger
        ½ teaspoon nutmeg
        ½ teaspoon cinnamon
        1 cup raisins
        1 cup chopped nuts

Cream the sugar and shortening. Add the eggs, pumpkin and flavourings and blend thoroughly. Sift flour, baking powder and spices before combining with the creamed mixture. Add the fruit and nuts.

Drop from the tip of a teaspoon onto a well oiled baking sheet. Bake 15 minutes in a 375 degrees F. oven.

These orange coloured spice cookies won a prize for Mrs. Nellie McDonald, Vancouver.

Desserts

Pumpkin Custard

Beat 2 eggs slightly before beating in ⅔ cups of brown sugar, 1 teaspoon powdered ginger, 1 teaspoon cinnamon, ⅓ teaspoon allspice and ½ teaspoon salt. Add 1½ cups drained pumpkin and stir in 2 cups scalded milk.

Turn into a wet mould or individual moulds and oven-poach at 350°F. for 50 minutes, or until firm.

Chill and unmould on serving plates. Top each serving with whipped cream and garnish with finely chopped candied ginger.

Here is another recipe that proves good things other than pie can be made from pumpkin. This recipe won a prize for Mrs. Nellie McDonald, Vancouver.

Lemon Curd

    3 lemons
    3 eggs
    6 tablespoons butter
    ½ pound castor sugar

Grate the lemon rinds. Squeeze the juice and strain. Beat eggs slightly and add the other ingredients.

Put in a saucepan and cook over a low fire, stirring constantly, until thick but do not let mixture boil.

There are so many uses for Lemon Curd that most housewives keep it on hand most of the time.

This won a prize for Mrs. C.W. Friend, Vancouver.

Stuffed Peaches

Take large halves of peaches and drain well. Arrange the halves on a serving plate and into each half put a very little of the syrup from preserved ginger.

Whip one cup of cream stiff. Sweeten to taste and add three tablespoons of finely-chopped preserved ginger and ½ cup of chopped nuts.

Fill the hollow of the peaches with the cream mixture and garnish with slices of ginger and nuts.

If ginger is taboo with you we suggest substituting citron in its place.

This won a prize for Mrs. Alvin Gregory, Vancouver.

Gooseberry Amber

    2 tablespoons butter
    1 pound gooseberries
    ½ pound icing sugar (1⅓ cups)
    3 tablespoons fine cake or bread crumbs
    3 eggs

Melt the butter in a saucepan. Add fruit and sugar and cook gently until a thick pulp, or about 20 minutes. Then stir in the crumbs. Beat the yolks of eggs and mix them with the pulp. Butter a deep pie dish, pour in the mixture and bake in a moderate oven of 350°F for 25 minutes or until the mixture is set.

Beat the egg whites stiff, add 6 tablespoons granulated sugar. Spread over the top of the pudding and bake 15 minutes in a moderate oven or until a golden brown.

This won a prize for Mrs. McHugh, Vancouver.

Coffee Cream Torte

Beat 6 egg whites stiff, add ¾ cup sugar and ⅔ cup unbleached ground almonds. Put into two pie pans or one large cake tin. Bake 20 minutes in a slow oven of about 300°F. Then cover with the following filling:

    ¾ cup sugar
    ½ tablespoon cornstarch
    ¼ teaspoon salt
    6 egg yolks
    ¾ cup strong coffee
    ½ cup butter

Mix sugar, cornstarch and salt. Add beaten egg yolks and coffee. Beat over a low fire until thickened. Add butter and cool. Pour over baked meringue and sprinkle with chopped blanched and toasted almonds.

This won a prize for Mrs. P. Schnoor, New Westminster.

Jams, Jellies, Marmalades

Sliced Apple Jelly

    4 quarts of apples
    6 cups vinegar
    2 cups water
    ½ teaspoon cloves
    ¼ teaspoon grated nutmeg
    1 stick cinnamon or 1 ounce of ground cinnamon
    2 lemon slices

Wash the apples and cut in slices. Cook until tender in the vinegar and water with the spices and lemon slices. The apples should be just barely covered with the liquid.

Drain through a jelly bag. Measure the juice and boil for 15 to 20 minutes before adding the sugar in the proportion of 3 cups of sugar to 4 cups of juice. Boil rapidly for 3 minutes longer or until it jells when tried on a cold plate.

Make some of this jelly to serve with your roast pork or ham. It won a prize for Mrs. Mary Finlayson, Sunnyside, Ioco.

Jewel Jam

    2 cups cranberries
    2 cups water
    4 cups chopped apples
    4 cups chopped quinces
    5 cups sugar

Cook the cranberries in the water with the skins and cores of the apples. Drain through a jelly bag. To the strained juice add the chopped apples and quinces.

Cook for 5 minutes and add 5 cups of sugar. Cook until thick and clear. Bottle and seal.

This jam is bright and clear and has a nippy flavour. The recipe won a prize for Miss Martha Vander Hock, Abbotsford.

Cantaloupe Marmalade

    4 oranges
    6 cantaloupes
    1 tin crushed pineapple

Grate the oranges and cut the pulp fine. Peel the cantaloupes and remove the seeds before cutting the pulp into small cubes.

Mix together with the pineapple and measure. To each cup of fruit add 1 cup of sugar. Boil the fruit for 1 hour before adding the sugar.

Boil again for about 10 minutes or until jam-like consistency. Bottle in hot sterile jars.

The cantaloupes really predominate the flavour of this unusual marmalade.

The recipe won a prize for Mrs. Tom Edmonson, Agassiz.

Breakfast Marmalade

    1 orange
    1 lemon
    1 grapefruit

Cut the fruit by hand or put through the food chopper. Add 10 cups of water and let boil for 1 hour. Then add 10 cups sugar and boil another hour or to the desired thickness has been obtained.

Bottle and seal.

This makes a fair amount of delicious marmalade at a surprisingly low price.

The recipe won a prize for Mrs. A.G. Manzer, Duncan.

Strawberry Jam

    2 boxes fresh strawberries
    5 cups sugar
    ½ cup lemon juice

Wash and clean the berries and leave whole. Add the sugar and let stand for 4 hours. Boil for 10 minutes before adding the lemon juice. Continue boiling for another 10 minutes. Bottle in small, hot, sterile bottles and cover with melted wax.

This jam has the loveliest bright red colour. The lemon juice is responsible for the colour and also it helps the jellying.

Mrs. H.S. Scott, Vancouver, won a prize for this recipe.

Fisherman's Pancakes

Make a batter of the following:
- 1 egg, beaten
- ⅓ cup milk
- ¾ cup flour
- ½ teaspoon salt
- 1 teaspoon baking powder

Into this well-beaten batter fold:
- 1 cup cooked salmon, boned and flaked
- 1 slice of cooked and minced bacon

Fry on a slightly oiled griddle until bubbly, turn and fry to a golden brown. Serve at once.

Here is a pancake recipe which is ideal to serve at lunch time if your breakfasters have time for only toast and coffee in the morning. It is also a good way to use up any left over cooked salmon. This won a prize for Mrs. J.W. Lloyd, Nanoose.

Crab Cutlets

- 2 tablespoons butter
- 2 tablespoons flour
- Pepper and salt to taste
- ¾ cup rich milk
- 1 cup crab meat
- Dash of cayenne
- Few drops of onion juice
- Fine bread crumbs

Prepare a white sauce of the butter, flour, pepper, salt and milk. Add the flaked crab, cayenne and onion juice. Spread the mixture on a platter to become cold. Then mould into small chops, dipping in the fine crumbs, then in seasoned evaporated milk and again in the crumbs.

Fry in deep fat and serve immediately after they are thoroughly drained on absorbent paper.

These cutlets or croquettes have a very nice texture and flavour. They won a prize for Mrs. David H. Drummond, Lynn Creek.

Ovenized Salmon

- 1½ pounds salmon
- 2 tablespoons butter
- Pepper and salt
- ½ cup hot water

Place the salmon in a casserole or covered dish. Put pieces of butter on top and season with salt and pepper. Pour water over all and bake 15 to 20 minutes depending on the thickness in a modest oven of 350°F. Baste and turn the fish over and bake another 15 minutes longer.

Serve hot with parsley sauce and green peas.

Any left over salmon cooked in this way is delicious in salad with sliced cucumbers. This recipe won a prize for Mrs. A.E. Spall, Chilliwack.

Fish

Lenten Fish Pie

- 1 pound cod
- 2 tablespoons butter
- 2 tablespoons flour
- ½ pint milk
- 1 teaspoon salt
- ¼ teaspoon pepper
- 1 tablespoon chopped parsley
- Mashed potatoes

Boil the fish in a little water until it is tender. Drain and separate into flakes.

Make a white sauce by melting the butter, adding the flour and gradually stirring in the milk. Stir constantly to prevent lumping. Add the salt, pepper, chopped parsley and flaked fish.

Spread this creamed mixture in a well-buttered pie dish and cover with a generous layer of fluffy mashed potatoes. Bake in a moderate oven of 350°F for about 30 minutes or until thoroughly heated and a delicate brown on top.

Fish, owing to its mineral and vitamin content, should be included in the diet at least once a week. This is an economical dish and one that will utilize left-over mashed potatoes. It won a prize for Mrs. H. Longden, Nanaimo.

Meats

Rice and Pork Cooked with Kraut

- 1 pound of pork steak
- ½ cup brown rice
- Seasonings
- Butter
- 1 small onion
- 1 13-oz. can of sour kraut

Grind the pork and add to the rice, together with the salt and pepper. Work together and make into 6 meat balls.

Put some butter in a pan and add the meat balls and a small onion sliced. Fry until slightly browned before adding the kraut and 1 cup of water. Cook slowly for about 1½ hours.

Here is a hearty dish for hearty appetites. It is easily made and it won a prize for Mrs. M. Acherbach, Vancouver.

Indian Pie

- 2 cups dry bread crumbs
- 1 cup stock or milk
- 1 pound cooked meat
- 2 onions
- 1 apple
- ½ cup raisins
- 1 tablespoon curry powder
- Salt
- 4 tablespoons beef dripping
- 2 eggs

Soak the crumbs in the stock or milk. Mince the meat, onions and apple and mix well with the crumbs, adding the raisins, curry powder, salt and dripping. Add the beaten eggs last.

Put the mixture in a greased loaf pan and bake for about 40 minutes in a moderate oven of 350 degrees F.

Here is a dish that has the savour of the Orient. Yet it is made of everyday ingredients which every housewife has on hand. This recipe won a prize for Mrs. F.M. Taylor, North Vancouver.

Red Flannel Hash

- 1 cup cooked beets
- 2 cups cooked potatoes
- 1 cup cooked carrots
- 1 cup corned beef
- 1 medium onion
- ½ teaspoon salt
- ⅛ teaspoon pepper

Put the above ingredients through a food chopper. The mixture can be varied according to ingredients on hand, but be sure to have enough beets to keep the mixture a bright red. Season and if the mixture is too dry add a little gravy, white sauce or milk.

Turn into a greased casserole and place in a moderate oven and bake until it is hot. Or if you like, brown it in a frying pan in some hot dripping and fold over like an omelette.

This is an inexpensive way to serve a colourful and flavourful hash. This recipe won a prize for Mrs. A. Dickinson, Victoria.

Yorkshire Pudding

- 2 eggs
- ½ cup flour
- ½ teaspoon salt
- 1 cup milk
- ¼ cup beef dripping

Beat eggs, flour, salt and milk until smooth. Have the dripping hot in a roasting pan before putting in the batter. Bake 20 to 30 minutes in a hot oven of 400° to 425°F.

There is no better accompaniment for roast beef than Yorkshire pudding. This recipe won a prize for Mrs. G. Earnshaw, New Westminster.

Pastries

Hot Water Pastry

    1 cup shortening
    ½ cup boiling water

Stir together until creamy then add:

    3 cups pastry flour
    1 teaspoon baking powder
    ½ teaspoon salt

Sift together the dry ingredients before adding to the hot water mixture. Cool and allow to chill thoroughly before rolling.

    Don't let the making of pastry defeat you, try this fool-proof recipe. It won a prize for Miss Jean C. Archibald, Vancouver.

Cranberry Mince Tarts

    1½ cups cooked and sweetened cranberry sauce
    2 cups mince meat
       Pie crust

Mix together the mince meat and cranberry sauce. If dry mince meat is used break into pieces and place in saucepan with 1½ cups water and cook for 3 minutes, stirring constantly until lumps are broken. Cool and add cranberries.

    Put into individual pie tins lined with pastry. Place strips over the top to form lattice tops.

    Bake in a hot oven of 450°F for about 18 to 20 minutes.

    This amount will make about sixteen large tarts.

    If you have some left-over cranberry sauce from the holiday be sure and try mixing it with mince meat for tarts.

    This delicious and most unusual combination won a prize for Mrs. F.P. Colpitts, Hollyburn.

Scotch Currant Bun

    ½ cup butter
    1½ cups flour
    ½ teaspoon baking powder
       Cold water

Cut the shortening into the dry ingredients and mix to a paste with a little cold water. Roll thin.

    Grease the inside of a cake pan and line it neatly with the paste, reserving a piece for the top.

Filling:

    4 cups sifted flour
    1½ teaspoons cinnamon
    ½ teaspoon ginger
    ½ teaspoon black pepper
    1½ teaspoons allspice
    2 cups sugar
    1 teaspoon soda
    ½ teaspoon cream of tartar
    1 pound currants
    1 pound seedless raisins
    ¼ pound almonds
    1 pound sultanas
    1 pound mixed and chopped peel
    3 eggs
    ⅓ cup milk

Sift dry ingredients together. Add fruit and nuts. Make moist with eggs and enough sweet milk to moisten, or about ⅓ cup.

    Pack into the pastry lined tin and cover with paste. Moisten edges to fasten it and prick top with a fork.

    Brush top with egg and bake in a moderate oven of 350°F for 1½ hours. Then reduce to 325°F and continue cooking about 1½ hours longer.

    Like all spicy cakes, the flavour of this bun improves on standing. It won a prize for Mrs. K. Hansen, Vancouver.

Relishes

Fruit Chutney

    3 pounds plums
    1 pound green apples
    2 ounces ginger
    1 ounce garlic
    1 Spanish onion, chopped
    3 cups brown sugar
    1 teaspoon salt
    1 green pepper
    1 teaspoon cayenne pepper
    6 cloves
    1 pint white vinegar

Cut the plums from the stones before combining with the other ingredients. Boil slowly until thick, or about 2 hours. Stir frequently.

Bottle in hot sterile jars.

The plums give this relish a most unusual flavour. This recipe won a prize for Miss Maude Hallander, Vancouver.

Homemade H.P. Sauce

    12 large pears
    16 large onions
    24 ripe tomatoes
     4 cups brown sugar
     4 cups cider vinegar
     4 teaspoons cloves
     5 teaspoons salt
     1 teaspoon pepper

Chop the pears, onions and tomatoes, or put through the food chopper. Boil until soft and press through a fine sieve. Add the sugar, vinegar, cloves, salt and cook slowly for 3 hours. Stir in the pepper and pour into sterile bottles.

This spicy sauce won a prize for Mrs. H. Briggs, Vancouver.

Bread and Butter Pickles

    5 medium sized cucumbers
    3 medium sized onions
    ¼ cup salt
    1 cup vinegar
    1 cup water
    1 teaspoon celery seed
    1 teaspoon mustard seed
    ¾ cup sugar
    ¼ teaspoon turmeric

Wash the cucumbers and slice in thin slices without peeling. Peel and slice the onions. Combine the onions and cucumbers with the salt. Let stand for 2 hours and drain well.

Heat the vinegar, water, celery and mustard seeds, sugar and turmeric to the boiling point before adding the vegetables. Heat through but do not overcook or you will not have crisp pickles. Pack in hot sterile jars.

Judging from the numerous requests for this recipe it must be the most popular homemade pickle. Mrs. H.E. Moffatt, Vancouver, won a dollar for it.

Corn Relish

     1 tablespoon mustard
     4 tablespoons flour
     1 tablespoon turmeric
     4 cups brown sugar
     ¼ cup salt
    1¼ quarts white wine vinegar
     6 cucumbers
     1 bunch of celery
    10 onions
     2 red peppers
    12 ears of corn

Make a paste of the mustard, flour, turmeric, sugar and salt. Use some of the vinegar to moisten.

Cut the cucumbers, celery, onions and red peppers quite fine. Add the corn which has been cut from the cobs.

Cover with the above sauce and bring to the boil and simmer for 30 minutes before bottling in hot sterile jars.

Corn relish is especially appetizing when served with pot roast. This recipe won a prize for Miss E.M. Ritchie.

Sweet Mustard Pickles

- 1 large cauliflower
- 2 dozen small cucumbers
- 1 pound small brown skinned onions
- 1 head celery
- 1 pound green beans

Cut these into suitable pieces and sprinkle by layers with salt and leave overnight. Drain in the morning and let cold water run over them and drain well again.

Make a **dressing** of:

- 4 tablespoons dry mustard
- 1 quart brown malt vinegar
- 2 tablespoons turmeric powder
- Dash of cayenne pepper
- 4 cups white vinegar
- 1 cup flour

Add the vegetables and simmer for about 10 minutes, stirring frequently. Pour into hot sterile jars and seal.

The delightful aroma when you are making this will make you think of the ham or beef that will accompany this relish, at serving time, in the future.

This won a prize for Mrs. A.J. King, Vancouver.

Salads

Shrimps in Tomato Aspic

- 3 tablespoons cold water
- 2 tablespoons gelatin
- 2 cups tomato juice
- 6 whole shrimps

Soften the gelatin in cold water and dissolve in the hot tomato juice. Strain and cool.

As it begins to thicken pour a little in the bottom of 6 individual moulds. Press several whole shrimps into the bottom of each mould.

Add the following to the remaining jelly:

- ½ cup chopped shrimps
- ½ cup chopped cucumber
- ¼ cup mayonnaise
- ½ teaspoon salt
- Dash of cayenne

Fill the moulds with this mixture and chill until firm. Unmould on lettuce and serve immediately.

This tasty recipe was submitted by Miss Kathryn Peck, Vancouver.

Fruit Salad Dressing

- 2 eggs
- ¼ cup sugar
- Few grains salt
- ¼ cup pineapple juice
- ¼ cup lemon juice
- 1 cup whipped cream

Beat eggs before adding the sugar, salt, pineapple and lemon juice. Cook in a double boiler, stirring constantly until thickened. Then set aside to cool. Whip the cream and fold into the mixture just before serving.

This dressing is ideal to serve with fruit salads. It won a prize for Mrs. Jack Paul, Boston Bar.

Salmon Macaroni Salad

        2   cups cooked macaroni
        1   pound of cooked salmon
       12   small radishes
    8 or 10   small green onions
        1   head of lettuce
            Mayonnaise
            Salt and pepper
            Dash of paprika

Break macaroni into small pieces and cook in rapidly boiling salted water. When tender drain and rinse with cold water to remove excess starch.

Bone and flake the salmon and add to the macaroni together with the sliced radishes, chopped green onions and some of the lettuce finely shredded.

Moisten with sufficient mayonnaise to bind the ingredients together. Season with salt and pepper and garnish with lettuce and paprika.

This nourishing salad recipe won a prize for Miss Phyllis Harris, Carvolth Road, Milner.

Health Salad

        2   young carrots, grated
        1   cup diced celery
        1   cup shredded cabbage
        1   cup finely cut dandelion leaves
        1   large apple, diced
       ¼   cup chopped walnuts
            Salt to taste

Just before serving, toss lightly together with sufficient salad dressing or mayonnaise to moisten.

Arrange on individual plates and place a little salad dressing in the centre. Garnish with choice dandelion leaves and thin strips of pimento.

Serve with cubes of cream cheese and whole wheat bread.

Salads should have an important place in the menus the year around, but in the spring when appetites are apt to be a trifle jaded, they must be especially appealing. The use of dandelion greens in salad is a good way to get your daily green vegetable.

This recipe won a prize for Mrs. R.P. Forst, Abbotsford.

Sweets

Never Fail Creamy Fudge

        2   cups brown sugar
        3   tablespoons flour
       1½   teaspoons baking powder
       ¼   teaspoon salt
       ½   cup milk
        2   tablespoons butter
            Flavouring
       ½   cup nut meats

Mix sugar, flour, baking powder and salt together. Stir in the milk. When the sugar is dissolved add the butter and boil slowly for 30 minutes, or to the soft ball stage. Add the flavouring and nuts and let cool before beating until thick. Pour into a buttered pan and mark into squares.

A box or dish of home-made candy is always welcome. This recipe won a prize for Mrs. A. Armitage, Vancouver.

Delicious Chocolate Fudge

        2   cups white sugar
        2   squares unsweetened chocolate
       ½   cup milk
        2   tablespoons syrup
        1   tablespoon butter
        1   teaspoon vanilla
       ½   cup chopped nuts (if desired)

Mix the sugar, chocolate, milk and syrup together and cook until it forms a soft ball. Stir occasionally to prevent burning. Add the butter and vanilla and allow it to cool thoroughly before beating. Beat until the glossy appearance disappears and add the nuts. Pour into a buttered pan and mark in squares.

This popular fudge recipe won a prize for Miss Lena Vanderhock, Abbotsford.

Honey Taffy

½ cup strained honey
1½ cups white sugar
¾ cup water
2 tablespoons butter
½ teaspoon vanilla

Heat honey, sugar and water, stirring until sugar is dissolved. Cook until mixture makes a hard ball when dropped in cold water or when it reaches 265 degrees on a candy thermometer. Then add the butter and vanilla.

Pour on oiled pan and cool until it can be handled. Pull until creamy and hard. Cut into half-inch pieces with a knife or scissors and dust lightly with powdered sugar.

The whole family, especially the children, will enjoy a taffy pull. This recipe won a prize for Mrs. Steve Sullivan, Tupper Creek.

Date Dainties

2 cups sugar
½ cup milk
1 egg white
¼ cup walnuts
¼ cup cherries
½ teaspoon almond flavouring
⅛ teaspoon salt
   Pitted dates

Cook the sugar and milk together for 15 minutes, or until a soft ball forms in cold water. Stir slowly into the egg white which has been beaten stiff. Continue beating until the mixture thickens, then add the chopped nuts, chopped cherries and flavouring.

Fill the centre of pitted dates with the mixture and dip in fine coconut.

Here's the ideal gift for a convalescent friend, or for a special surprise for your family. It won a prize for Mrs. Haines, Vancouver.

Soups

Split Pea and Vegetable Soup

3 good large cups split peas
1 teaspoon soda
1 large onion
2 medium carrots
1 potato
3 thin slices of bacon
   Salt and pepper to taste

Take the split peas and put in boiling water to cover, with the soda, and cook fast until the peas are soft but not mushy. Remove from the heat and wash thoroughly till all trace of the soda has disappeared.

Cover the peas again with boiling water and allow to stand while preparing the other ingredients. Cut the onion, carrots, potato and bacon into small pieces. Add to the peas and boil for about 3 hours, or until the mixture is a thick creamy soup.

This economical and delicious soup recipe won a prize for Mrs. H. Davis, Alert Bay.

Beet and Cabbage Soup

1 red beet
1 small onion
2 cups shredded cabbage
1 tablespoon butter
2 teaspoons salt
   Pepper
1 tablespoon vinegar
½ cup rich milk or cream

Shred or chop the vegetables before simmering in sufficient water to cover. Add the butter and seasonings when nearly done.

Just before serving, stir in the vinegar and cream. Add water to make about 1½ quarts in all.

Chopped parsley is a tasty addition. It can be added with the butter and seasonings.

This won a prize for Mrs. Harry Boedak, New Westminster.

Barley and Cheese Soup

1 meaty soup bone
2 cups barley
½ cup tomato catsup
1 teaspoon celery salt
2 onions
1 potato
2 carrots
½ teaspoon pepper
1 teaspoon salt
1 cup noodles
½ cup grated cheese

Cook a soup bone with very little fat. Put it into a large pot with sufficient water to cover. Add the barley and boil until the meat falls from the bone.

Strain the liquid and add the vegetables which have been grated and the seasonings. Continue boiling until the vegetables are cooked.

About 20 minutes before serving time add the noodles and keep the soup simmering. At serving time stir in the cheese, or sprinkle it on top of serving.

This nourishing soup won a prize for Mrs. H.J. Davis, Englewood.

Lentil Soup

1 onion
2 stalks celery
1 carrot
3 tablespoons butter
1 cup lentils
1 can evaporated milk, or 1 quart fresh milk
2 teaspoons salt
¼ teaspoon pepper

Cut onion, celery and carrot into small pieces. Fry in butter for about 15 minutes before adding the lentils which have been thoroughly washed. Add sufficient water to cover and cook until all is tender, then rub through a sieve.

Return to the heat and add the milk and seasonings and bring to the boil, adding sufficient milk to make about 2 quarts.

A bowl of this hot steaming soup, a crisp salad with a roll or muffin and some stewed fruit makes an excellent lunch for child or adult.

This recipe won a prize for Mrs. J.E. McGregor, Kimberley.

Eat Wisely and Cheaply

Owing to the numerous requests for all or a portion of this service, we are including them in this, our Fourth Annual Cook Book.

"Eat Wisely and Cheaply" was written for The Vancouver Sun by Miss Nora H. Miles of Cranbrook.

Miss Miles is a graduate of McGill University, Montreal, in Home Economics and later did post graduate work at the Infants' Hospital, Vincent Square, London.

These articles deal with low-cost menus and have been worked out with the thought of balanced foods.

The purpose of this series is to prove that malnutrition can be avoided even on a limited food budget. These menus both nourishing and interesting for the small sum of 17c per day per person.

Remember, over-eating and poorly-balanced meals are large contributors to poor health, which in turn lowers the resistance to disease germs. A full stomach isn't always a well-fed or well-treated one.

Miss Nora H. Miles

That's Your Dividend!

When the trifling sum you spend on one of our Want Ads brings you results beyond your warmest expectations—that's your dividend on a wise investment in advertising value.

CALL WANT AD HEADQUARTERS
TRINITY 4111

If you need a good cook, or any other kind of domestic help, any season of the year, we suggest that you let a little ad in our Help Wanted Columns bring you just the houseworker you want. Be sure to advertise where results are immediate and most satisfactory. Call Want Ad Headquarters NOW! Trinity 4111.

The writer with the world's largest reader audience

OF all the writers in the world, the one with the most readers is not Bernard Shaw or any other of the famous ones. More people read and look for the writings of this wise lady of vast experience and boundless sympathy than those of any other writer. Her column of advice and answers to human problems goes to sixty million readers in thousands of periodicals in every corner of the world. Dorothy Dix understandingly bridges the gap between youth and maturity, sanely rationalizes the relations of men and women, and the Sun is proud to include her writings among its daily features.

•

DOROTHY DIX in Vancouver SUN

•

Phone Trinity 4111 for Delivery

Prize Winners 5th Annual Cook Book

1938

PRIZE WINNERS

5TH ANNUAL

COOK BOOK

by Edith Adams

THE VANCOUVER SUN.

Wilson

IN PRESENTING this, the Fifth Annual Cook Book, The Vancouver Sun is happy to accede once again to the demands of its readers.

As with previous editions, this does not aspire to be a complete cook book, but is a selection from the prize-winning recipes published daily in The Vancouver Sun within the past year.

These prize-winning recipes, which were selected from many thousand submitted by Vancouver Sun readers, have been carefully tested in scientific laboratories.

In arranging the sequence of the recipes, we begin with soups, then entrees or luncheon dishes, vegetable dishes, salads, breads, desserts, which include cakes, cookies, pastries and puddings, and so on; thus endeavouring to assist homemakers with the preparation of three meals a day. In these pages the homemaker will find a wealth of tasty dishes that will sharpen and renew the family's table zest.

We would call attention to the daily prize recipes as they appear in The Vancouver Sun and also the weekly cookery section which appears every Thursday.

This Fifth Annual Prize-Winners' Cook Book is presented to you with our compliments, and is the direct creation of our capable and inventive housewives of British Columbia.

Edith Adams.

Cookery Editor,
THE VANCOUVER SUN.

Soups

Super-Soup

    1   mutton shank
    3   pints cold water
    2   teaspoons salt
    ½   cup pearl barley
    1   large tin tomatoes
    1   large onion
    1   cup chopped carrot
    1   cup grated carrot
    2   cups celery tops
        Dash of pepper

Bring shank slowly to boil with salt. Add barley and another pint of hot water. Simmer gently for 2 hours before adding the tomatoes, chopped onion, carrots, celery tops and pepper. Simmer for another 2 hours, adding a little water frequently. Celery seed may be used if there is no fresh celery on hand.

This substantial soup is on the order of Scotch broth. It won a prize for Mrs. A. Telford, Vancouver

Grandfather's Potato Soup

    3   potatoes
    1   tablespoon butter
        Salt and pepper
    1   teaspoon nutmeg
    1   teaspoon sugar
    1   tablespoon mustard
    1   cup milk
    1   cup water
    1   tablespoon grated carrot

Cut the potatoes into small pieces and boil until soft. Drain and mash with a fork and add butter and seasonings. Beat to a cream before adding milk and water. Add the grated carrot and simmer until the carrot is cooked.

Some might want to reduce the amount of spice in this soup, which won a prize for Mrs. John Craigh, Langley Prairie.

Squash Soup

        Squash
    2 or 3 small onions
    ¼   teaspoon thyme (optional)
        Salt and pepper to taste
        Lump of butter
        Milk

Peel squash and cut in pieces. Boil with finely-cut onions in a small amount of water until tender. Mash and add seasonings, butter and milk. Heat to boiling point and serve immediately.

This soup should be fairly thick and is very filling for a supper dish. Marrow could be used instead of squash. This golden coloured soup won a prize for Mrs. A. Wittier, Naramata.

Beet Soup

Peel and cut into narrow strips the following vegetables:

    1   carrot
    1   large onion
        Few celery leaves
    1   carrot
    1   cup shredded cabbage
        Add the following:
        Salt and pepper
    2   tablespoons butter
    1   can tomato juice
    5   cups cold water

Put in soup pot and boil gently until vegetables are done. Serve immediately.

This flavourful soup won a prize for Mrs. L. Arthur, Vancouver.

Entrees, Luncheon Dishes

Scotch Style Pork Chops

- 4 double loin pork chops
- 1 onion
- 4 tablespoons Scotch oatmeal
- 1 teaspoon sage
- ¼ teaspoon salt
- 1 tablespoon shortening or bacon dripping

Put chops in uncovered roaster at 450°F for 15 minutes to sear. Slice the onion thinly and lay on top of the salted chops. Mix oatmeal, sage and the ¼ teaspoon of salt, shortening or bacon dripping before placing on top of the chops and onion. Add 2 tablespoons of hot water, taking care not to spill it on the dressing. Bake another 35 minutes in a moderate oven.

We suggest serving these chops with applesauce and mashed turnips. It won a prize for Mrs. T. Myles, Vancouver.

Creamed Codfish

- ½ pound salt codfish
- 2 teaspoons butter
- 4 tablespoons flour
  Few grains pepper
- 2 cups milk
- 4 hard cooked eggs, sliced
- 4 cups creamy mashed potatoes

Cover the codfish with cold water and let stand for several hours to freshen. Drain and cover with fresh water and bring to the boiling point. Again drain and flake. Melt the butter in a double boiler, add the flour and pepper and blend. Add the milk slowly and cook until thick, stirring constantly. Add the flaked fish and the hard cooked egg slices. Heat well.

Arrange the mashed potatoes around the edge of a serving or chop plate. Put the creamed mixture in the centre and serve immediately.

Serve this delicious fish dish with spinach, green peas or beans. It won a prize for Mrs. D. Malpass, Vancouver.

Oven Steak

- 1½ pounds round steak
- ½ teaspoon salt
- ¼ teaspoon pepper
- 3 tablespoons brown sugar
- 3 onions, sliced
- ½ cup catsup or 1 cup tomato juice
- 1 cup boiling water

Rub the steak on both sides with salt and pepper. Put in a heavy iron frying pan and brown quickly on both sides. When well browned cover with the sugar, onions, tomato juice or catsup and water. Cover and bake in a moderate oven of 350°F for about 1 hour, turning several times during the baking. Remove the cover the last 15 minutes to brown again. Remove to hot platter and surround with juice and onions.

This tasty steak recipe won a prize for Mrs. C. Lee, Vancouver.

Sausage Rolls

- 16 sausages (1 pound)
- 2 cups sifted flour
- 2 teaspoons baking powder
- ½ teaspoon salt
- 4 tablespoons shortening
- ¾ cup milk

Fry sausages until well browned. Sift flour once. Measure, sift again with baking powder and salt. Sift again and cut in the shortening. Add the milk gradually, stirring until soft dough is formed. Turn out on floured board and knead for 30 seconds or enough to shape. Roll to eighth of an inch and cut in 2 inch squares. Place sausage in centre of each square, folding over the dough, pinch edges together and shape into a roll, leaving the ends open. Place seam side down on ungreased baking sheet and bake at 450 deg. F. for about 15 minutes or until nicely browned.

This makes a pound of sausage meat go a long way, and it won a prize for Miss Evelyn Harris, Vancouver.

Southern Pilau

Stew a 3-pound chicken, putting salt, pepper, a little sliced onion, and a bay leaf in the pot. In a second pot put the following:

- 7 cups chicken broth
- 1 cup washed rice

Boil until tender, stirring frequently. Add more broth if necessary. Add:

- ¼ cup butter
- 1 cup blanched, toasted almonds
- 1 cup light sultanas
- 1 teaspoon salt
- ⅛ teaspoon pepper
- ½ teaspoon curry powder

Pour over chicken and serve.

This has a good flavour and is a nice change from the usual way of serving chicken. It won a prize for Mrs. Roy A. Clark.

Salmon Pot Pie

4	tablespoons butter
1	teaspoon minced onion
6	tablespoons flour
1	cup salmon juice and water
1½	cups milk
1	teaspoon salt
1	tablespoon lemon juice
	Dash of paprika
1	cup diced cooked celery
1	cup cooked new peas
2	cups canned salmon (1 pound)

Melt butter, add onion and cook for 2 minutes before stirring in the flour, salmon juice, water and milk. Cook, stirring constantly until thick and smooth. Add seasonings, celery, peas and flaked salmon. Pour into a greased casserole and top with biscuit dough rolled thin and cut in fancy shapes. Bake in a hot oven of 450°F for about 18 to 20 minutes, or until the crust is nicely browned. Buttered bread strips may replace biscuit dough if desired, in which case bake until the bread is toasted. This serves 6.

This grand luncheon dish won a prize for Miss J. Knutson, New Westminster.

Roast Veal-Spiced Rhubarb

1	veal leg roast, 4 to 5 pounds
2	pounds rhubarb
	Sugar
2	tablespoons butter
¾	teaspoon allspice
½	teaspoon cinnamon
¼	teaspoon cloves

Place veal roast in shallow roasting pan. Add 2 teaspoons salt and cover with 2 or 3 strips of bacon or salt pork. Roast in a 350 deg. F. oven for 30 minutes to the pound. Serve with watercress garnish and the following sauce:

Rhubarb Sauce

Cut the rhubarb into inch lengths. Add butter and 1 cup of sugar to each 3 cups cut rhubarb. Cook slowly until tender. Spice and serve hot.

Roast pork and applesauce is a favourite of long standing and we're sure that you'll like the combination of roast veal and spiced rhubarb sauce equally as well. It won a prize for Mrs. E.M. Olliver, New Westminster.

Grandmother's Chestnut and Onion Dressing

2	cups onion, finely sliced
¼	cup fat
3	cups milk
1	cup celery
3	cups chopped cooked chestnuts
2	loaves white bread in crumbs
1½	teaspoons salt
¼	teaspoon pepper

Fry the onion in the fat until onion is yellow, but not brown. Add the milk, and heat to the boiling point before adding the celery and chestnuts. Pour gradually over the crumbs, tossing lightly to combine. Add the seasonings. Stuff lightly in the turkey, avoid packing or the stuffing will become heavy.

The addition of a cup of walnuts is an improvement.

This popular stuffing won a prize for Mrs. F. Hart, Vancouver.

Vegetable Dishes, Salads

Stuffed Baked Potatoes (This recipe is submitted by a boy, so we will give you the recipe just as he sent it to us.)

Here's an easily prepared meal if Mother is going to be out and big brother has to get supper. At noon, put in enough well-washed, and don't skimp on the washing, potatoes in the oven to bake. By the time you get home at night they will be baked or you will be home from school in time to get them done. Split lengthwise and scoop out the insides. Mash the pulp and mix with 2 or 3 raw eggs, 1½ teaspoons salt, ¼ teaspoon pepper and ¼ cup milk. Add a little chopped onion if desired. Refill potato shells and put a strip of uncooked bacon on top of each half potato. Put back in oven until bacon is crisp.

These fluffy baked potatoes won a prize for V. Jack Tyerman, Vancouver.

Stuffed Peppers, Hungarian Style

Cut the tops off 8 green peppers. Remove the seeds and scald. Mix 1 pound of ground cooked meat with 1 cup cooked rice which has been seasoned with salt and pepper. Stuff the peppers with this mixture and cover closely in a covered casserole. Bake 15 minutes in a hot oven.

Make a sauce from 1 can tomatoes, 1 tablespoon butter, salt and pepper. Pour this sauce over the peppers and continue baking for 1 hour.

We suggest using tomato soup instead of the canned tomatoes. This recipe won a prize for Mrs. F.C. Atkinson, Vancouver.

Cranberry Salad

    1   pint cranberries
    1½ cups water
    1   cup sugar
    ½   teaspoon salt
    1½ teaspoons gelatin
    ¾   cup diced celery
    ⅓   cup chopped nuts

Cook cranberries in 1 cup of water for 20 minutes. Add the sugar and salt and stir until dissolved. Stir in the gelatin which has been soaked in the remaining water. When cool stir in the diced celery and nuts. Turn into individual moulds or a large mould that has been rinsed in cold water. Chill and when firm cut into squares or unmould. Serve on lettuce with salad dressing.

This is an ideal salad to serve with chicken or turkey. It won a prize for Mrs. T.R. Histed, Vancouver.

Frozen Date Salad

    2   cups stoned dates
    1   cup water
    2   packages cream cheese
    1   cup heavy cream
    6   tablespoons orange juice
        Red cherries

Place the dates in a saucepan with the water and simmer until all the water is absorbed. Put the cream cheese in a bowl and stir until it is fluffy and smooth. Whip the cream and add to the orange juice, dates and cheese. Freeze in a quart freezer or automatic refrigerator. Cut in slices and serve garnished with red cherries on crisp lettuce leaves.

With thin slices of bread and butter this is a most refreshing salad to serve after a bridge game. It won a prize for Mrs. Milne, Vancouver.

Hot Cross Buns

    1   cake Fleischmann's yeast
    1   cup scalded milk, cooled
    1   tablespoon sugar
    3½ cups bread flour
    ½   cup sugar
    ¼   cup butter
    ¼   cup raisins
    1   egg
    1   teaspoon salt
    1   teaspoon mace (if desired)

Dissolve the yeast in the lukewarm milk together with the sugar. Add 1½ cups of flour to make a soft sponge. Beat until smooth. Cover and let rise until light in a warm place, or until double in bulk. Cream together the ½ cup sugar and butter before adding to the sponge together with the raisins, egg well beaten, remaining flour, salt and spice. Knead lightly into a soft dough. Cover and set aside to rise until double in bulk, or about 2 hours. Shape with hands into medium-sized buns. Place in well-greased pans about 2 inches apart. Make a cross with a sharp knife. Cover and let rise again until light. Glaze with egg diluted with water. Bake in a hot oven of 400 deg. F. for 20 to 25 minutes, depending on size. Just before removing from the oven brush with sugar moistened with water. When cool fill the crosses with a plain frosting made with 1 cup confectioner's sugar, 2 tablespoons water and ½ teaspoon vanilla.

No Good Friday or Easter breakfast would be complete without Hot Cross Buns. This recipe won a prize for Mrs. H. Day, Port Alberni.

Date Bran Muffins

2	tablespoons shortening
1	cup brown sugar
2	eggs, well beaten
1½	cups sour cream
2	cups general purpose flour
½	teaspoon salt
1½	teaspoons baking powder
1	level teaspoon soda
2	cups health bran
2	cups chopped dates
1	cup chopped walnuts

Cream shortening and brown sugar before adding well beaten eggs and sour cream. Mix and sift dry ingredients and add with the bran, then dates and walnuts. Bake in greased muffin tins in a moderate oven of 375°F for 20 to 30 minutes, depending on their size.

Muffins are the perfect salad accompaniment. These won a $1 prize for Pheobe T. Prince, Prince Rupert.

Ginger Bread

½	cup shortening
½	cup sugar
1	egg
¾	cup molasses
2	cups flour
½	teaspoon salt
1	teaspoon cinnamon
1	teaspoon ginger
1	cup thick sour milk
1	teaspoon soda

Cream the shortening, add the sugar slowly and blend in the well-beaten egg and molasses. Sift the flour, salt and spices together and add to the creamed mixture alternately with the sour milk and soda. Pour into a greased and floured pan 8 inches square. Bake for 45 minutes in a moderate oven of 350 deg. F.

Remember this dessert when you are having an oven-cooked dinner. It won a prize for Mrs. Roy A. Clark, Chilliwack.

Johnny Cake

4	level tablespoons butter
¼	cup sugar
2	eggs
1	cup milk
¼	teaspoon salt
1½	cups flour
4	teaspoons baking powder
¾	cup cornmeal

Cream butter before adding the sugar. Beat eggs and add, and beat until foamy and add milk alternately with sifted dry ingredients and cornmeal. Bake in greased pan for about 20 minutes in a hot oven of 400°F.

Hot cornbread and maple syrup is enough to get the sleepiest head up for breakfast on time. This recipe won a prize for Mrs. M. Crossland, Port Alberni.

Cakes

Enchanting Raspberry Cream Cake

1	cup sifted cake flour
1	teaspoon baking powder
¼	teaspoon salt
2	eggs, separated
½	cup cold water
1	teaspoon grated lemon rind
¾	cup granulated sugar
1	teaspoon lemon juice
2	tablespoons sugar

Sift flour once, measure, add baking powder and salt, and sift together 3 times. To the egg yolks add the water and lemon rind, and beat until foamy and light. Add ¾ cup sugar gradually, beating well after each addition. Then add the flour in small amounts, beating enough to blend. To the stiffly beaten egg whites add the lemon juice and 2 tablespoons of sugar. Fold into the flour mixture and turn into 2 ungreased deep 8-inch layer cake pans. Bake in a moderate oven of 350 deg. F. for 25 minutes or until baked.

Invert on a rack to cool. When cold spread with lemon cream filling and cover top with whipped cream and crushed sweetened raspberries.

Lemon Cream Filling:

Combine 1 cup sugar and 5 tablespoons cake flour in top of a double boiler. Add 1 egg slightly beaten, ½ cup lemon juice, ½ cup water and 2 teaspoons butter, mixing thoroughly. Place over boiling water and cook for 10 minutes, stirring constantly. Remove from heat and chill before folding in 1 teaspoon grated lemon rind and ¾ cup whipped cream.

This delicious berry shortcake won a $1 prize for Mrs. George Radford, White Rock.

Peach Spice Cake

- 1 cup cooked peach pulp
- ½ cup shortening
- 1 cup sugar
- 2 eggs
- 1¾ cups sifted flour
- 2 teaspoons baking powder
- ½ teaspoon salt
- ½ teaspoon ginger
- ½ teaspoon cinnamon
- ½ teaspoon cloves
- ¼ cup milk

Mash the peaches or force them through a fine sieve. Cream the shortening and add the sugar gradually, then the beaten eggs and peach pulp. Sift together the flour, baking powder, salt, and spices. Add the dry ingredients alternately with the milk to the first mixture. Bake for 30 minutes in a greased and floured cake pan. Cover with the following icing:

- 4 tablespoons softened butter
- 2½ cups icing sugar
- Pinch of salt
- 1 egg
- 1 tablespoon milk
- ½ teaspoon vanilla

The peach flavour is not very distinct in this light spice cake that won a prize for Mrs. C.E. Wall, Vancouver.

Quick Walnut Coffee Cake

- ¼ pound butter
- ¾ cup sugar
- 2 eggs, well beaten
- 2 cups flour
- Pinch of salt
- 2 teaspoons baking powder
- ½ teaspoon soda
- 1 cup sour milk

Cream butter and sugar, add beaten eggs, then dry ingredients alternately with the milk. Grease a pan and spread half the batter in the pan, then sprinkle with half of the following mixture:

- 4 tablespoons sugar
- ½ teaspoon cinnamon
- ½ cup walnuts

Cover with the remaining batter and sprinkle with remaining sugar mixture. Bake in a moderate oven of 350 deg. F. for 35 to 40 minutes.

The topping eliminates the bother of making an icing. It won a prize for Mrs. W.J. Smith, Powell River.

Fresh Strawberry Cake

- 2 cups cake or pastry flour
- 2 teaspoons baking powder
- Pinch of salt
- 4 tablespoons butter
- 4 tablespoons shortening
- 1 cup white sugar
- 2 eggs
- 1 cup crushed strawberries and juice
- 2 teaspoons lemon juice

Sift flour 3 times with baking powder and salt. Cream together the butter, shortening and gradually add the sugar. Beat eggs well and add to the mixture. Add dry ingredients alternately with the strawberries, adding the lemon juice last. Turn into 2 greased and floured layer cake pans. Bake in a moderately hot oven of 375°F for 20 minutes. When cool ice with white frosting and garnish with sugared whole berries.

This interesting cake won a prize for Mrs. A. Armitage, Vancouver.

Sea Foam Icing

- 2 cups brown sugar
- 1 tablespoon cornstarch
- Pinch of salt
- ½ cup boiling water
- 1 egg white
- ¼ teaspoon vanilla

Make a syrup of the sugar, cornstarch, salt and boiling water. Boil until the syrup threads from the spoon, or 234 to 236 deg. F. Then beat into the stiffly beaten egg white. Add vanilla and beat with a spoon until thick and foamy and of spreading consistency. Spread on a cool cake.

This glorifies your cake. It won a prize for Mrs. Frank Matuschewski, Vancouver.

Cookies

Peanut Butter Brownies

Cream together ¼ cup butter and ¼ cup peanut butter before adding 1 cup of sugar. Cream until very fluffy, then add 2 beaten eggs, 2 squares melted chocolate and ½ cup flour which has been sifted with ½ teaspoon baking powder and ¼ teaspoon salt. Spread in a shallow pan lined with oiled paper and bake in a moderate oven for about 20 minutes. Cut into squares or strips while warm.

The peanut butter makes these brownies less expensive than when made with nuts. They won a prize for Mrs. F.W. Chrich, Vancouver.

Ginger Shortbread Cookies

- ¾ cup butter
- 1 cup brown sugar
- 1 egg
- 1 teaspoon cream of tartar
- 1 soda
- 1 teaspoon cinnamon
- ½ teaspoon ginger
- 3 cups flour
- ¼ teaspoon salt

Cream butter and sugar before adding the beaten egg. Sift all dry ingredients 4 times and add to the creamed mixture. Roll in small balls and press flat with a fork. Bake in a moderate oven of 375 deg. F. for about 15 minutes.

These cookies won a prize for Mrs. A. Ash, West Vancouver.

Chocolate Cream Puffs

Bring 1 cup of water, ½ cup butter, ¼ teaspoon salt and 1 ounce unsweetened chocolate to the boiling point. Add 1 cup bread flour and 2 tablespoons sugar, stirring until mixture leaves sides of pan. Remove from the fire and stir until smooth. Cool slightly, then add 4 eggs, one at a time, beating thoroughly after each addition. Chill the mixture and drop a heaping teaspoon of batter on a cold greased baking sheet, or shape into oblongs for eclairs. Bake 15 to 20 minutes in a hot oven of 425 deg. F., then 30 minutes in a moderate oven of 350 deg. F. This makes 13 to 16 puffs.

These are delicious filled with ice cream and served with chocolate sauce. They won a prize for Mrs. Lois Blais, Vancouver.

60 Seconds Cookie

Into an enamel mixing bowl melt ⅔ cup of shortening, butter preferred. To this add 1 cup rolled oats and ½ cup sugar and ½ teaspoon salt. Mix all together with 1 well-beaten egg and add 1 teaspoon of flavouring. Spread this in a greased 10-inch square pan and bake till quite brown in a moderate oven 350°F for about 30 minutes. Cut at once any size desired, remove from the pan as they become very brittle on standing. Part of the rolled oats may be replaced by coconut.

These cookies take about a minute or two to mix, therefore their name. They won a prize for Beatrice Drummond, North Vancouver.

Cherry Coconut Macaroons

Mix and sift together 1 cup fruit sugar and 1 tablespoon cornstarch. Gradually fold into 3 stiffly beaten egg whites. Place over rapid boiling water and cook for about 15 minutes, scraping down and folding occasionally. Remove from heat and add ¼ teaspoon salt, ½ teaspoon vanilla, ¼ cup chopped cherries, 1½ cups shredded coconut and 1 cup cornflakes. Sprinkle a cookie pan with cornstarch and drop mixture on it by teaspoon. Bake in a slow oven of 300 deg. F. for about 20 minutes.

These won a prize for Mrs. Lillian M. Baxter, Vancouver.

Swedish Cookies

- ¼ cup brown sugar
- ½ cup butter
- 1 egg yolk
- 1 cup flour

Cream sugar and butter. Add egg yolk, slightly beaten, and flour. Roll in small balls, dip in slightly beaten egg white and roll in chopped walnuts. Place on a baking sheet and press centre with finger to make small hollow. Bake in a moderate oven of 350 deg. F. for about 5 minutes. Press down centre and return to oven and bake for about 10 to 15 minutes longer. Fill centre with bright jelly or jam while still warm.

These won a prize for Mrs. J.W. Cross, Armstrong.

German Cakes

- ½ cup golden syrup
- ¼ teaspoon cinnamon
  Pinch of grated nutmeg
- ¼ teaspoon salt
- ½ teaspoon cloves
- 1 teaspoon grated orange rind
  Grated rind and juice small lemon
- 1 teaspoon melted butter
- 2¼ cups pastry flour
- 2 teaspoons baking powder

Mix together the syrup, spices, orange rind and lemon rind and juice. Leave for 24 hours. Next day put the basin over boiling water and stir in the melted butter. Mix well and remove from the hot water. Mix together the flour and baking powder and add to the syrup to make a firm dough, kneading lightly. Break off small pieces of dough and roll with the palm of the hand on a floured board until they are long thin rolls, then tie carefully into knots. Put on a greased baking sheet fairly far apart. Bake in a moderate oven of 350°F for about 10 to 12 minutes. Put on rack to cool. Store in airtight tin.

These cookies have a most unusual shape and flavour. They won a prize for Mrs. E. Ramsay, Vancouver.

Orange Coconut Cookies

- 1 cup butter
- 2 tablespoons orange rind
- 1¼ cups granulated sugar
- 2 eggs
- ¾ cup shredded coconut
- 2 cups flour
- 2 teaspoons baking powder
- ¼ teaspoon salt
- 1 teaspoon cinnamon
- 1 cup rolled oats
- 4 tablespoons milk

Cream butter with orange rind, add sugar and cream thoroughly. Add eggs, beaten well, coconut and blend. Sift together flour, baking powder, salt and cinnamon. Add rolled oats and milk. Drop from teaspoon on a greased cookie sheet about 2 inches apart. Bake in a moderate oven of 375 deg. F. for about 15 minutes.

This makes about 5 dozen small drop cookies. It won a prize for Mrs. Elsie Cairns, Vancouver.

Pies, Puddings

Lemon Chiffon Pie

- 1 teaspoon gelatin
- ¼ cup cold milk
- 1 cup sugar
- ¼ teaspoon salt
- 3 egg yolks
- 1 cup scalded milk
- ½ lemon juice
  Rind of 1 lemon
- 1 cup whipping cream

Soak gelatin in cold milk for 1 hour. Gradually add sugar and salt to beaten egg yolks. Add egg yolk mixture to scalded milk and cook till slightly thickened. Remove from fire, add gelatin and stir until dissolved. Chill and add lemon juice and rind. When mixture has thickened somewhat fold in whipped cream. Pour into cooked pastry shell and set in refrigerator to become firm. Before serving garnish with additional sweetened and flavoured whipped cream.

This delicious pie won a prize for Miss E. Williamson, Vancouver.

Coffee Chiffon Pie

- 1 tablespoon gelatin
- ¼ cup strong, cold coffee
- 4 eggs
- ¾ cup white sugar
- ½ teaspoon salt
- ½ cup hot, strong coffee
- 1 tablespoon lemon juice

Soak the gelatin in the cold coffee for 5 minutes. Beat the egg yolks slightly before adding ½ cup of sugar, salt and hot coffee. Cook over boiling water until of custard consistency. Add the softened gelatin and lemon juice to the custard and cool. When this begins to thicken, fold in the stiffly beaten egg whites to which has been added the remaining sugar. Pour into a baked pie shell. Serve with or without whipped cream.

This recipe will appeal to those particularly fond of coffee flavour. It won a prize for Mrs. J.E Turnbull, New Westminster.

Orange Cottage Pudding

Cake:

- ¼ cup shortening
- ½ cup sugar
- 1 egg
- 1½ cups flour
- 1¼ teaspoons baking powder
- ¼ teaspoon salt
- ½ cup milk
- ½ teaspoon vanilla

Cream shortening and sugar before adding the egg and sifted dry ingredients alternately with the milk and vanilla. Bake in greased muffin pans. Serve with the following:

Sauce:

- ½ cup sugar
- 2 tablespoons corn starch
- ¼ teaspoon salt
- 2 cups hot water
- 2 oranges
- 1 teaspoon lemon juice
- ½ teaspoon grated orange rind
- 1 tablespoon butter
- ½ teaspoon vanilla

Mix the dry ingredients in the top of a double boiler. Add the hot water, stirring well. Let this cook for 20 minutes. Peel the oranges with a sharp knife, and separate into segments. When the sauce is clear and thick remove from the heat and add the oranges, lemon juice, butter and vanilla.

This won a prize for Mrs. C.H. Martin, Hedley.

Banana Butterscotch Pudding

- 4 bananas
- ½ cup brown sugar
- 1 tablespoon cream or top milk
- 1½ tablespoons butter
- Allow 1 banana for each serving

Peel and scrape the bananas with a silver knife and cut into thin slices. Make a sauce of the brown sugar, milk and butter. Cook slowly, stirring constantly for about 4 minutes or until the sugar is melted and bubbling. Pour the sauce over the sliced bananas and serve with a spoonful of whipped cream on each dish. A few chopped nuts added before the sauce is poured over them is also delicious.

This dessert can be prepared on short notice. It won a prize for Hilda Hollard, Shaw Post Office.

Jam, Relishes

Grape Jam

Pulp the grapes and cook the skins and pulp separately, adding a little water to the skins to keep from burning. Put the pulp through a colander to remove the seeds. Combine the pulp with the skins and boil for 8 minutes. To each pound of fruit add 1 pound of granulated sugar and cook for about 5 to 8 minutes or until of desired consistency. Seal in sterile jars.

If the grapes are too ripe it will be impossible to get a good jelly consistency. This recipe won a prize for Mrs. Jennie Gifford, Vancouver.

Apple and Blackberry Jam

- 2 pounds blackberries
- 4½ pounds sugar
- 4 pounds apples

Put the blackberries in a small crock or jar and cover with a pound of sugar. Let stand at least 12 hours, then place in a cool oven or over low heat and heat slowly to extract all the juice. Pare the apples, core and slice. Place in a preserving pan and strain in the blackberry juice and boil till apples are soft, or for about 15 to 20 minutes. Add remaining sugar and boil 3 to 5 minutes longer. Pour into hot sterilized jars, cover with wax and seal.

This makes a delicious spread and won a prize for Mrs. P. Lapointe, Vancouver.

Plum Chutney

        3   pounds plums (weight after being stoned)
        ½   pound cooking apples (peeled, cored and sliced)
        ½   pound raisins
        ½   pound currants
            Juice of lemon
        1   ounce ginger
        2   teaspoons salt
        1   teaspoon whole cloves
        1   ounce garlic, cut very fine
        1   teaspoon red pepper
        1   teaspoon allspice
        1   pint vinegar
       1½   pounds brown sugar

Combine all ingredients and boil slowly for 2 hours. Bottle in hot sterile jars at once and seal.

This chutney is of jam-like consistency. It won a prize for Mrs. I. Secord, Kelowna.

Chili Sauce

       24   good sized ripe tomatoes
        6   onions
        6   large pears
        6   large apples
        2   large red peppers
        4   cups white sugar
        2   tablespoons salt
        4   cups vinegar
            Spice to taste

Peel and cut the tomatoes. Put onions, pears and apples through the mincer. Cut peppers fine. Tie about half a box of spice in a bag and when spicy enough for your taste, remove from sauce. Boil all ingredients for about 2 hours and seal in hot sterile jars.

This chili sauce won a prize for Mrs. R.E.T. Hunt, Kelowna.

Green Bean Pickle

        1   cup flour
        1   cup mustard
       2½   pounds brown sugar
        2   tablespoons turmeric powder
        1   teaspoon salt
        2   tablespoons celery seed
        3   pints vinegar
        5   pounds green beans (cut small and cooked for
            about 20 minutes in salted water)

Mix together the dry ingredients before adding the vinegar. Stir until smooth and boil for about 5 minutes. Add the beans and bring to the boil and bottle at once in hot sterile jars.

This popular recipe won a prize for Mrs. F. Mason, Burnaby.

Red Pepper Relish

        6   red peppers
        6   green peppers
        6   onions
        2   cups vinegar
        1   cup brown sugar
            Salt to taste
        1   tablespoon cornstarch
        1   teaspoon mustard

Mince the red and green peppers and the onion. Pour hot water over the mixture and let stand for 5 minutes. Then drain off the water and repeat the process. Add the vinegar, sugar and salt. Boil until nearly done and thicken with the cornstarch and mustard which has been moistened with some cold vinegar. Seal in hot sterile jars.

This relish won a prize for Mrs. M.A. Kenny, Nanaimo.

Rhubarb Relish

        1   quart rhubarb
        1   quart onions, chopped
        1   teaspoon cloves
        1   teaspoon cinnamon
        4   cups brown sugar
        1   pint vinegar
        1   teaspoon allspice
        ½   teaspoon red pepper
        1   tablespoon salt

Add the diced rhubarb to the chopped onions and other ingredients. Simmer until vegetables are tender and seal in hot sterile jars.

Mrs. M.G. Smith, Vancouver.

Sun Prize Winners
6th Annual Cook Book

1939

SUN
Prize Winners
6th! Annual

by
Edith Adams

COOK BOOK

COMPLIMENTS OF.
The Vancouver Sun
VANCOUVER OWNED.

CONCERNING CULINARY ART

The main object in presenting The Sixth Annual Prize Winner's Cook Book is to show you how to save money by way of the kitchen. There is usually an allotment of the family income given over to food supply. Here's where the cook gets her innings. If she saves money to the process of buying and cooking without stinting on food value the savings are hers. Whether she puts the savings on herself, in something extra for the house or even towards taxes, is her choice alone.

Cost of Meat

We have recently heard a great deal of complaining about the high cost of meat. Perhaps if we made a run on the cheaper cuts of meat the price might drop on the more expensive cuts. We have it on good authority that "the cheaper cuts of meat not only cost less but contain more food value per pound." That's all that needs to be said if there was ever any doubt on this point. It is only when these cheaper cuts are poorly prepared that the first signs of discontent appear at the table. We then blame it on the tough meat and our greatest chance of "saving up" is gone. In the section given over to meats we will show through low cost recipes and tricks in the preparation and keeping of meats how all this can be eliminated without feeling of stint in the family board.

The Test of a Good Cook

Of course the test of a good cook is the meal she serves when there apparently isn't a thing in the pantry, or it might be a day or so before pay-day when the food budget was rifled for the "grandest bargain." Well, it stands to reason the family won't be dining on the most expensive meats or out of season vegetables for a few days and besides, anyone can cook when they have an unlimited quantity of the best of everything. Here's where the real cook asserts herself without anyone knowing about that pantry. It might be the combination of a few eggs, the odd sprig of parsley and onion tops, a small end of bacon and that left-over portion of tomatoes, but the result! An omelette to go down in history. Here's where her knowledge and interesting preparation of cheap meats will help her out. And can they be delicious? Perhaps it will be a one-dish casserole meal, a stew which can only be compared to a ragout or a delicious combination in croquettes. These are only a few suggestions, but enough to fire the imagination of any cook, and what cook lacks that? If simple economy can sustain you for the odd day or two there is no reason why economy cannot become a habit and carry you through the year.

A Tip From the French

They say the average middle-class French housewife saves enough in the management of her household to retire to security in her old age! By the way, it is this middle-class French style of cookery that is held up to be the finest in the world. We're going to adapt some of these recipes and wrinkles to our own needs. But first let us examine this mysterious target we plan to aim at. First of all we meet her, so very early in the morning. Wherever can she be going? To market, of course, just as soon as they open. Anyone who gets there that early is entitled to the freshest, most tender and succulent of anything they are out to buy. Getting there is just the beginning. Then she pinches, and squeezes and nibbles, denying and arguing all the while. You can get the same results without having to go through her performance just by applying a little practical knowledge. I'll wager, though, that, barring a major accident, there isn't a thing in that market basket thrown out. Just supposing she buys a piece of boiling beef. First of all they will all sit down to a pot-au-feu, the remnants will appear in some form of hash or croquettes. If there is even one croquette over it will find its way into the soup pot. That stock pot is an institution in the French home and why shouldn't it be? A good nourishing soup with a salad or dessert is another meal. The French are the grandest people for utilizing leftovers and here's just where credit is due for thrift. A woman with a certain budget allowance for food plus a little practical knowledge in the buying and preparation of that food can actually save money.

Now for an outline of the meaning of the words vitamin, mineral and calorie content of food. It is only by applying a working knowledge of these that we can safely say we are serving a "square meal."

Those Vital Vitamins

The commonly known vitamins are "A," "B," "C," "D" and "G." These control growth and body development, increase appetite and stimulate digestion, increase resistance to infection, needed in the proper development of bones, and essential for growth and good health at all ages, respectively. Any *intelligent combination of foods will give the daily vitamin requirement to our daily diet.*

Mineral "Matter"

Mineral Matter builds and regulates body process. The list of minerals in the various foods is a long one. We will deal only with the very common. Calcium and phosphorus is needed in the formation of healthy bones, sound teeth, tissue building and cell growth. You obtain your supply from dairy produce, fruit and vegetables, whole grain products, nuts, clams, oysters. Iron is needed for healthy red blood. A good source of this mineral is to be found in lean meats, whole grains, leafy vegetables, liver, potatoes and nuts. Iodine is always associated with goitre. The iodine requirement of our body is slight but it is essential in the proper functioning of the thyroid gland. This mineral is found in milk, green vegetables, sea food and iodized salt.
Keep these body requirements in mind when making up your menus.

Counting the Calories

Now for the calories. Vitamins and minerals are to be taken seriously but calories have for so long been associated with weight reduction or weight increase they can be juggled around a bit to the individual's need. Just keep this simple explanation in mind, food is fuel which supplies energy to the body. A unit of this fuel is called a calorie. When more food is taken than can be turned over into energy it is turned into fat and usually settles where we don't want it. The calorie content of the various foods, with appropriate menus for weight increase or reduction can be yours for the asking. Cereal manufacturers and insurance companies have excellent leaflets on the subject.
Now study your recipes and begin to save.

Edith Adams

TABLE OF MEASUREMENTS
All Measurements Should Be Level

16 tablespoons equal 1 cup dry material.

12 tablespoons equal 1 cup wet material.

3 teaspoons equal 1 tablespoon.

2 cups equal 1 pint.

2 pints equal 1 quart.

4 quarts equal 1 gallon.

8 quarts equal 1 peck.

4 pecks equal 1 bushel.

16 ounces equal 1 pound.

4 cups flour equal one pound.

2 ⅔ cups powdered sugar equal one pound.

2 ¾ cups brown sugar equal one pound.

2 cups butter equal one pound.

2 tablespoons butter equal one ounce.

1 square bitter chocolate equals 1 ounce.

1 ounce chocolate equals ¼ cup cocoa.

1 pound walnuts or pecans in shells equals ¼ pound shelled.

1 cup walnuts or almonds shelled equals ¼ pound.

12½ pounds green tomatoes equal 1 peck.

1 cup uncooked rice equals 3 cups cooked rice.

1 cup cream equals 3 cups whipped cream.

the juice of one lemon equals 2 tablespoons.

Can Sizes

No. ½ holds 1 cup (enough for 2 people)

No. 1 (tall) holds 2 cups (enough for 4 people)

No. 1 (flat) holds 2 cups (enough for 4 people)

No. 2 holds 2 ½ cups.

No. 2½ holds 3½ cups.

Average Portions

1 cup soup serves 1 person.

1 pound fish serves 2 generously.

1 pound meat serves 2 generously (stew).

Soups

Did You Ever

Sieve a couple of hard-boiled eggs into clear soup?

Add chopped chives to cream soups, or a little chopped pimento? It looks nice and tastes grand.

Squeeze lemon juice into the clam chowder? Not too much but a decided improvement.

Poach an egg in consomme? Serve it in a flat soup plate. It's easier to get at the stranded egg. A dessert or salad course would give a well balanced inexpensive meal here. Have a bowl of croutons (small squares of toasted bread) on the table with a thick cream soup? Just help yourself to a handful and throw them in your soup.

Add grated cheese to almost any soup? Try it soon.

Economical Tomato Soup

1½ cups cooked tomatoes
1   teaspoon sugar
    Pinch of soda
    Pepper
¾   teaspoon salt
1   pint milk
1   slice onion
1   tablespoon flour
1   tablespoon butter
¾   cup cooked mashed potatoes and peas

Stew tomatoes and sugar and strain if desired. Add the soda and seasoning. Scald milk in double boiler with the onion. Add flour, which has been well blended with melted butter. Cook thoroughly. Remove onion from milk and combine the two mixtures, adding the tomatoes to milk slowly. Stir well, then add potatoes and peas.

Serve at once. It makes a very satisfying luncheon dish for school children.

This tempting soup won a prize for Mrs. G.R. Mawson, Abbotsford. Like all prize-winning recipes, it has been tested in the Home Service Kitchen of the B.C. Electric by Miss Mutch and her assistants.

Celery Soup

Cut several stalks of celery very fine, or 3 cups, using the tips but not the leaves. Cut 1 large potato into small pieces, or 2 cups. Put the potato and celery in 3 cups of cold water and bring slowly to the boil. Let it boil until celery is thoroughly soft. Add 2 cups milk and let simmer, but not boil, for 10 or 15 minutes. Add pepper and 1 teaspoon salt and a tablespoon of butter. Stir well and serve.

Chopped oysters are delicious added to this soup.

This inexpensive soup is most nourishing. It won a prize for Miss E. Fry, Vancouver. Like all prize winning recipes it has been tested in the Home Service Kitchen of the B.C. Electric by Miss Jean Mutch and her assistants.

Vegetable Chowder

4   tablespoons butter
1   cup cubed celery
1   cup carrots
2   tablespoons grated onion
12-oz. tin whole kernel corn
½   cup water
1   teaspoon salt
       Few grains pepper
1   teaspoon sugar
1   quart milk
1   cup cooked peas
2   tablespoons chopped parsley

Melt butter in kettle, then add celery, carrots, onion, corn, water, salt, pepper and sugar. Cover and cook slowly for an hour. Add the milk and peas. Heat thoroughly before adding the parsley.

Pour into tureen. Float split Boston crackers on top and sprinkle with grated cheese.

This colourful and nourishing dish is ideal for luncheon or winter supper. It won a prize for Miss Josephine Rowa, Vancouver, and has been tested by Miss Jean Mutch of the Home Service Department of the B.C. Electric.

Fish

Here's where the housewife of British Columbia could shine as a hostess. Specialize in some fish dish to offer your prairie visitor and your American neighbours. Granted that most of them have some variety of fish where they come from, but surely not the variety that we have! Fresh, smoked, pickled, shell and canned. Talking about visitors I've never had one from the south who didn't want to take back some bacon, marmalade or black currant jam. That's an idea for a parting gift, but how did it get stuck in with the Fish?

Fish is richest in protein and mineral in the form of iodine. Extracts from the oil of the halibut and cod are a rich source of supply in Vitamins A and D.

It seems silly to tell a person how to choose fresh fish. It's so obvious if it isn't fresh. However, if his head is on, look him square in the eye. They're supposed to be bright and full. The flesh should be firm. Perhaps you could tell this by looking at it.

To keep fish over for a day, unwrap it at once. Wipe off with a clean, damp cloth and if you intend to boil it rub it over with lemon juice and lots of salt and pepper. If it is to be fried oil it and salt and pepper it. Then put it in a covered dish in the cooler.

By the way, never take fish from a cooler or refrigerator and expect good results in frying. It should be at room temperature before it is fried, otherwise it will cool your fat off too much.

Never wash oysters. You'll take all the flavour away. Just wipe them with a damp, clean cloth.

When boiling fish, tie it in a piece of cheesecloth, set this on an old plate and put the whole thing in your boiling pot. Cover with cold water. Now throw in your seasonings. If approximately two quarts of water is used go by the following: 2 tablespoons of salt, ½ cup lemon juice or vinegar, 2 carrots, 2 onions (stick a few cloves in), 4 stalks of celery, few sprigs parsley, bay leaves and a few peppercorns.

Don't put lemon juice in if the fish is red. It will bleach it. Grand for white fish, seems to make it so much whiter.

Left-over boiled, baked or fried fish can be utilized in soups, salads or croquettes.

Time Table for Cooking Fish

Baking, thick fish	10 to 15 minutes per pound
Baking, thin fish	8 to 10 minutes per pound
Boiling, thick fish	10 to 12 minutes per pound
Boiling, thin fish	8 to 10 minutes per pound
Frying, fillets or steak	about 5 minutes
Frying, smelts or trout	about 3 minutes

A Few Simple Fish Sauces

Parsley Butter: 6 tablespoons butter, creamed. Add 6 tablespoons minced parsley, then ¾ teaspoon salt and slowly add 6 teaspoons lemon juice. Turn this on a flat surface, make a pattern with a fork on it and square it off. Put a square on each serving of fish, fried or boiled.

Lemon Butter: 4 tablespoons butter, 2 teaspoons lemon juice. Cream the butter and work in the lemon juice. Same as above.

Melted Butter: Just before serving fish melt the quantity of butter you wish, add a little lemon juice and some pepper.

Curry Butter: 4 tablespoons of butter and curry powder to taste. Same as above.

Pan Fried Fillets

2	pounds fillets
	Salt, pepper, flour
4	tablespoons butter
	Juice of 1 lemon
1	tablespoon minced parsley

Roll fillets in seasoned flour. Have pan ready with very hot oil. Fry fillets until cooked a nice brown on each side. Remove to hot platter. Melt butter, add lemon juice and parsley. When very hot pour over the fillets and serve at once.

Serves 4.

Fried Clams

	Clams
	Cornmeal or bread crumbs
1	beaten egg
	Lemon butter sauce

Drain and dry the clams. Dip each clam in cornmeal, then in beaten egg and again in cornmeal. Fry in very hot, deep fat until a golden brown. Drain on paper and serve with lemon butter sauce.

Oyster Stew

- 1 quart milk
- 1 slice onion
- 2 stalks celery
- 2 sprigs parsley
- Bit of bay leaf
- 4 tablespoons cracker crumbs
- 1 pint oysters
- 3 tablespoons butter
- ½ teaspoon salt
- Paprika

Scald milk with onion, celery, parsley and bay leaf for 20 minutes. Strain and add the cracker crumbs. Heat the oysters in their own juice until the edges curl. Combine the oysters with the milk and season with butter, salt and paprika. Serve immediately.

The savoury addition of celery, onion, parsley and bay leaf to the standard oyster stew is an improvement. This recipe won a prize for Mrs. H.W. Pollock, Vancouver. Like all prize winning recipes it has been tested in the Home Service Kitchen of the B.C. Electric by Miss Mutch and her assistants.

Salmon Bacon Pats

- 1 cup soft bread crumbs
- 1 egg
- ½ cup juice from canned salmon
- 1 tablespoon scraped onion
- 2 tablespoons chopped parsley
- Dash pepper, salt and sage
- 2 cups canned salmon
- 6 slices bacon

Combine bread crumbs with egg and salmon juice. Add onion, parsley and seasonings. Flake salmon and mix lightly with first mixture. Shape six patties and wrap slice of bacon around each and fasten with toothpick. Bake in a hot oven of 450°F for 15 minutes or until bacon is crisp and salmon mixture hot.

These can also be made from left over cooked salmon. They won a prize for Mrs. Ernest Little, Half Moon Bay. Like all prize winning recipes it has been tested in the Home Service Department of the B.C. Electric by Miss Jean Mutch and her assistants.

Bismark Herring

- Salt Alaska herring
- Allspice
- Minced onion
- Minced green pepper (optional)
- Lemon thinly sliced (optional)
- Vinegar

Either bone the herring and roll or cut crosswise, bones and all, about ½ inch thick. Put a layer of herring in a crock. Sprinkle well with allspice (this means peppercorns, bay leaf,

paprika) and the minced onion, green pepper and lemon. Continue till you have enough. Cover with vinegar. Ready in about a week.

Meats

Braised Oxtail

- 2 pounds oxtail cut in 2-inch pieces
- 2 sliced onions
- 2 sliced carrots
- 3 cups boiling water
- Seasonings

Roll oxtail in plenty of flour. Sear well in hot fat. Place in deep pan with onions and carrots. Add the water, a bay leaf, 2 cloves, peppercorns and cover pan. Simmer gently about 2½ hours. Season with salt, pepper, chopped parsley and 1 tablespoon lemon juice.

Serves 4.

Corned Beef Hash

- 2 cups cold corned beef
- 2 cups cold boiled potatoes
- 4 tablespoons minced onion
- 2 tablespoons minced parsley
- 1 cup boiling water
- Salt and pepper
- 2 tablespoons butter or bacon fat

Chop beef and potatoes until well blended. Add onion and parsley, water and seasoning. Mix well. Melt butter or fat in frying pan. Add hash mixture, spread evenly in pan and cook over a slow fire for about ½ hour. Cover hash at first so that it will be thoroughly cooked and steamed. At about the end of the cooking time when a brown crust has formed on the under side of the hash fold like an omelet.

Serves 4.

Jellied Tongue

Select a nice fresh tongue, wash and simmer until it is tender enough to skin easily (2½ to 3 hours). Add to water in which tongue is boiled 1 onion, 3 sprigs parsley, 1 bay leaf, 1 sprig mint, a little green pepper, salt and pepper to taste.

Line a mould the size required to hold the tongue with stuffed olives and sliced, hard-cooked eggs. Boil down 2 cupfuls of the liquor until reduced to 1 cupful. Add ½ teaspoon gelatine, which has previously been soaked in ¼ cup water, to the hot stock. Pour over the tongue and let stand until well set. Turn out on platter and garnish with parsley.

For a cold supper this jellied tongue would be an attractive and delicious main dish. It won a prize for Mrs. Arbo, Vancouver, after being tested in the B.C. Electric Home Service kitchen by Miss Jean Mutch and her assistants.

Roast Loin of Pork

        4 pounds (8 ribs) pork loin roast
        ½ teaspoon salt
       1½ cups cooked prunes
        2 cups thinly sliced apples
        2 cups diced celery
        ½ teaspoon nutmeg
        3 tablespoons fat

Make a pocket in roast by cutting three-quarters through meat between ribs and outer edge. Rub inside and out with salt. Cook prunes 10 minutes in water to cover. Drain, pit and cut in pieces. Combine with apples, celery, salt and nutmeg. Saute in fat 5 minutes. Fill the pocket with mixture. Sew or skewer together.

Roast 2½ to 3 hours at 350 deg. F., or about 30 minutes to the pound.

This flavourful roast won a prize for Miss M. McLaughlin, Vancouver. Like all prize-winning recipes it has been tested in the Home Service Kitchen of the B.C. Electric by Miss Mutch and her assistants.

Roast Veal, Turkey Style

        5 pounds veal from leg
        1 teaspoon sage
        1 tablespoon salt
        1 tablespoon mustard
        1 tablespoon brown sugar
        ¼ teaspoon pepper
        3 tablespoons vinegar
        1 cup hot water
        6 slices bacon

Wipe the meat and place it in an uncovered roaster in a hot oven of 400 deg. F. Brown quickly. Remove from the oven and rub the meat with the sage, salt, mustard, brown sugar and pepper mixed together.

Mix the vinegar and water and pour into the pan around the meat. Lay the fat bacon strips across the top and cover the roaster. Return to the oven, reduce the heat to 300 deg. F. and continue baking for 2½ hours longer. Baste frequently with the liquid that is in the pan.

Try this recipe if your veal is inclined to be dry because this one is juicy. It won a prize for Mrs. J.A. Popie, Vancouver, and has been tested in the Home Service Kitchen of the B.C. Electric by Miss Jean Mutch.

English Beefsteak Pudding

        ½ lb. chopped suet
        4 cups flour
        2 teaspoons salt
        4 teaspoons baking powder
        2 pounds round steak
   2 or 4 veal kidneys
           Salt and pepper to taste
        ½ cup water

Chop suet very fine then sift the flour, salt and baking powder and mix thoroughly with the suet. Add water sufficient to make a damp paste. Turn out onto floured board and roll to about half inch thickness. Butter a pudding basin and then line with paste so that it comes a little over the top, retaining sufficient paste to cover pudding.

Cut steak into small pieces with a little fat. Cut the meat from the kidneys, cut into small pieces. Sprinkle a little flour over the steak, pressing it into the meat. Place meat and kidney in bowl. Add ½ cup water and salt and pepper to meat, cover with remaining paste, rolled to half-inch thickness. Press edges of top and lining together. Cover with a cloth that is well covered with flour. Tie floured cloth on bowl and place the pudding into fast boiling water. Keep water at a continual boil for 4 hours, adding more water as necessary. To serve turn pudding out of bowl onto hot platter.

This English favourite won a prize for Mrs. Ed. Gomm, New Westminster. Like all prize-winning recipes it has been tested in the Home Service Kitchen of the B.C. Electric by Miss Jean Mutch and her assistants.

Bacon and Liver Loaf

Remove skin from 1 pound of beef liver. Cut into slices and cook in boiling salted water for 5 minutes. Drain and put through meat grinder and add:

        1 cup stale bread crumbs
        3 tablespoons tomato catsup
        ⅓ cup fresh pork, chopped
        1 tablespoon chopped onion
        1 egg, beaten
           Juice of ½ lemon
           Salt and pepper to taste

Mix well and turn into a baking pan lined with slices of bacon. Press mixture firmly into the pan and lay strips of bacon on top. Bake in a moderate oven of 350 degrees F. for 1½ hours. Serves four.

This savoury loaf won a prize for Mrs. O.B. St. John, Boston Bar. Like all prize-winning recipes, it has been tested in the Home Service Kitchen of the B.C. Electric by Miss Jean Mutch and her assistants.

On 30 September 1955 the *Vancouver Sun* reported, "A taste of Sukiyaki and a cup of tea, Japanese style, were enjoyed by Mrs. J.C. Nation, 1989 West Thirty-seventh Avenue, when she attended Marianne Linnell's first Japanese cooking progam and travelogue (with slides) in Edith Adams' *Sun* Cottage."

Bran Pancakes

1¾ cups milk
1 cup whole bran
1½ cups sifted flour
3 teaspoons baking powder
2 teaspoons sugar
1 teaspoon salt
2 eggs, well-beaten
1 tablespoon melted butter

Pour milk over whole bran. Sift flour once, measure, add baking powder, sugar and salt, sift again. Add eggs to bran mixture, add flour and blend. Add butter and bake on a hot greased griddle.

This makes 12 cakes. Serve immediately with syrup.

These pancakes have a delicious nutty flavour and would be good served with crisp bacon. They won a prize for Miss O.M. Clayton, Vancouver. Like all prize-winning recipes they have been tested in the Home Service Kitchen of the B.C. Electric by Miss Mutch and her assistants.

Red River Gems

1½ cups flour
3 teaspoons baking powder
½ teaspoon salt
1½ cups Red River cereal
½ cup brown sugar
1 cup seedless raisins
2 eggs
1 cup milk
1 teaspoon vanilla
2 tablespoons shortening

Sift together flour, baking powder and salt and mix with Red River cereal, sugar and raisins. Make a depression in the centre and pour in the eggs which have been well beaten with milk, vanilla and the melted butter. Stir gently until all ingredients are well-mixed.

Turn into well greased muffin pans and bake in a 375°F oven for 25 minutes.

Perhaps you find it difficult to get your family to eat their cereal as porridge, but we don't think you will find these unpopular because they have a delicious flavour. They won a prize for Mrs. A.R. Kung, Vancouver, and have been tested by Miss Mutch in the Home Service Department of the B.C. Electric.

Breads

Slices of fresh, thin, buttered bread, crusts off, pressed into muffin pans and browned quickly. Quick cases for creamed peas, crab and so on.

Cream grated cheese with butter. Spread on all sides of stale bread strips, have these strips pretty thick. Roll in poppy seeds and brown in moderate oven. Serve with soup or salads.

Prepare any "family favourite" sandwich, dip these in egg and milk mixture, seasoned, saute in hot fat.

Griddle Cakes

1 cup flour
2 teaspoons baking powder
2 tablespoons sugar
¼ teaspoon salt
1 cup milk
2 tablespoons melted butter
1 egg, well beaten

Sift and mix dry ingredients. Add milk and beat thoroughly, then add melted butter. Mix again and add beaten egg. Cook on hot griddle and turn only once. It is time to turn when bubbles appear through the cake.

Makes about 12 cakes, small.

Pies and Tarts

Chocolate Chiffon Pie

- 3 egg yolks
- 6 tablespoons sugar
- ¼ teaspoon salt
- 1½ squares chocolate
- 1½ teaspoons gelatin
- 3 tablespoons cold water
- 6 tablespoons boiling water
- 1 teaspoon vanilla

Meringue:
- 3 egg whites
- ¼ teaspoon cream of tartar
- 6 tablespoons sugar

- 1 cooled, baked 8-inch pie shell

Beat egg yolks slightly, blend in sugar, salt and melted chocolate. Cook over hot water, stirring constantly, until smooth and thickened. Soak gelatin in cold water, dissolve in hot water and stir into custard.

Cook until mixture begins to set, add vanilla, then beat until light and fluffy. Beat egg white with cream of tartar, add sugar gradually until meringue is stiff and glossy.

Fold into gelatin custard mixture and fill lightly into baked cool shell. Top with the following:
- ¾ cup cream (before beating)
- 1 tablespoon sugar
- 1 teaspoon vanilla

Whip cream, add sugar and vanilla, then smother the custard with this mixture and top with chocolate.

"The consistency of the filling in this delicious pie is excellent," says Miss Jean Mutch of today's recipe, which won a prize for Mrs. J.N. Short, Chilliwack. Like all prize-winning recipes it was tested in the Home Service Kitchen of the B.C. Electric by Miss Mutch and her assistants.

Tarts

- 1 cup brown sugar
- 1½ tablespoons butter
- 2 eggs
- ¼ cup chopped walnuts
- ½ teaspoon vanilla
  Pastry

Mix sugar and butter, add well-beaten eggs, nuts and vanilla. Drop into small pastry-lined tart tins. Bake in 400°F oven for 10 minutes, then reduce heat to 350°F for 3 minutes.

These butter tarts won a prize for Mrs. J. Delong, Sechelt. Like all prize-winning recipes they have been tested in the Home Service Kitchen by Miss Mutch and her assistants.

Cherry Pie

- 2½ cups canned cherries with juice
- 1 tablespoon butter
- 2 tablespoons cornstarch
- ¾ cup sugar
- 1 unbaked pie shell

Heat cherries and juice, add butter. Mix cornstarch with sugar and gradually stir into hot cherries. Pour in unbaked pie shell. Bake in a hot oven of 450°F for 15 minutes, then 20 minutes in a moderately hot oven of 400°F. Top with meringue or whipped cream.

This pie is delicious either hot or cold. It won a prize for Mrs. H.B. Gibson, Lynn Creek. Like all prize-winning recipes it has been tested in the Home Service Kitchen of the B.C. Electric by Miss Jean Mutch and her assistants.

Angel Pie

- 4 egg whites
- ⅛ teaspoon salt
- ¼ teaspoon cream of tartar
- 1 cup sugar
- 4 egg yolks
- ½ cup sugar
- 3 tablespoons lemon juice
- 2 teaspoons grated lemon rind
- ½ pint whipping cream

Beat the egg whites with ⅛ teaspoon salt until stiff but not dry. Add cream of tartar and 1 cup of sugar, gradually beating until it is shiny and stands in peaks. Spread in a well-greased 9-inch square pan and bake 1 hour in a slow oven. During the first 20 minutes bake at 275 deg. F., then increase to 300 deg. F. and bake 40 minutes longer.

Filling:

Beat the egg yolks with a pinch of salt until thick. Add ½ cup sugar, juice and rind of lemon and 3 tablespoons hot water. Beat well and cook in a double boiler until thick. When meringue is cool spread with a layer of flavoured whipped cream and cover with the cooled lemon custard. Top with more whipped cream. Chill for several hours before serving.

This delicious dessert won a prize for Mrs. G. Player, Vancouver. Like all prize-winning recipes it has been tested in the Home Service Kitchen of the B.C. Electric by Miss Jean Mutch and her assistants.

Cookies

A few dainty little cookies will brighten up any afternoon tea to say nothing of the appetizing effect they have on a packed lunch. Most cookies are easy to make and the less flour used the more pleasing the result. It is not necessary to grease a cookie pan unless the morsels contain molasses or fruits that are apt to make them stick. Remember that drop cookies have a remarkable tendency to spread further than you have made allowance for, so space them at least 2 inches apart on the baking sheet.

There are as many ways to make and decorate cookies as there are colours in a Canadian sunset and this section does not aspire to even touch on the basic methods but simply offers a few tested recipes which should prove tasty to your cookie jar.

Some true patriotic cookies can be decked up merely by placing wide strips of red, white and blue icing across the flat cooky surfaces. Make little heart-shaped cookies for Valentine's Day and touch them up with deep red icing, remembering that especially on that day, hearts are trumps. A shamrock shape tinted with green will do St. Patrick proud.

Easter glows a glorious yellow so match your cookies with the chicks by topping them with marshmallows, dipped in yellow colouring. Cook the "mellow" a little so that it will stick to the cooky foundation. Or you can make brown Easter eggs by rolling dates and other chopped fruit in shredded coconut and browning them in the oven.

Carry through the haunting air of Halloween even to your cookies by using lots of molasses and bright orange trimmings; cut them out to represent witches, brooms, pumpkins and cats. At Christmas you can add a sparkle to your table with a plate of glistening "tree cookies." Merely sprinkle sugar on tree-shaped cookies before putting them in the oven.

Walnut Chews

Mix well together 1 cup brown sugar and 3 tablespoons flour. After mixing well add 3 tablespoons melted butter into which has been broken 1 egg. Add 1 cup crushed walnuts, ⅓ cup coconut and ½ teaspoon vanilla. Mix well and drop by teaspoonfuls on baking sheet. Bake in a moderate oven. When cool store in airtight container.

These cookies spread but have a delicious chewy flavour. They won a prize for Mrs. W.H. North, Kamloops, and have been tested by Miss Jean Mutch and her assistants in the Home Service Kitchen of the B.C. Electric.

Butter Cherries

     ¼ cup butter
     ½ cup sugar
     1 egg yolk, beaten
     ½ teaspoon vanilla
     1 tablespoon orange rind
    1½ teaspoons lemon rind
     1 tablespoon lemon juice
     1 cup flour
     1 cup finely chopped walnuts or coconut
        Cherries

Cream butter, add sugar and cream well. Add egg yolk and flavouring. Add flour and chill. Shape into balls ½ inch in diameter. Roll in slightly beaten egg white then in chopped nuts or coconut. Press a ring of cherry on each. Bake for about 20 minutes in a moderate oven of 350°F.

These little cookies will be most attractive on your tea table. You won't be disappointed in the flavour either. They won a prize for Mrs. H.W. Miller, Nanaimo. Like all prize-winning recipes it has been tested in the Home Service Department of the B.C. Electric by Miss Mutch and her assistants.

Rolled Pecan Wafers

     ¼ cup butter
     ½ cup brown sugar
     1 egg
     2 tablespoons flour
     ¼ cup finely chopped pecans
        Dash of salt

Cream butter and gradually add sugar, then add well beaten egg. Stir in the flour, nuts and salt. Drop the mixture on a greased cookie sheet about 5 inches apart. Spread in a very thin layer with a knife. Bake 10 to 12 minutes in a slow oven of 300 deg. F. Remove from the oven and loosen cookies one at a time and roll while hot over the handle of a wooden spoon. Fill with sweetened whipped cream.

If the cookies become stiff return to the oven for a moment.

These make a rich dainty with the cream, but could also be served plain as a crisp afternoon tea cookie. They won a prize for Miss Catherine Patterson, Blairmore, Alberta, and have been tested by Miss Jean Mutch and her assistants in the Home Service Kitchen of the B.C. Electric.

On 5 October 1960 the *Vancouver Sun* reported, "Taking a Thanksgiving turkey from the rotisserie of her gas range, Mrs. Marianne Linnell made simple the mysteries of modern cooking for a capacity audience attending the Edith Adams Cottage Gas Cooking Show Tuesday."

Cakes

Cake making, perhaps more than any other branch of cooking, tests the ability of the cook to be accurate. Too little fat makes a porous cake that tends to dry quickly, while too much fat produces a cake heavy in texture. Not enough flour will make a cake soggy and often cause it to fall and then again too much flour might cause the top of the cake to crack and be crumbly.

For all cakes, except angel or sponge cakes, the pan should be well greased either with or without a paper lining. If a paper lining is used grease it well. In order to assure yourself of having a cake of even depth make a slight indentation in the middle of the batter and be sure that the cake batter is well out towards the edges and corners of the pan. Fill the tin ⅔ full of the batter. If you are using fruits and raisins in your cake be sure to bathe them in flour to prevent them sinking to the bottom of the cake.

It's a good idea to keep a little bread in the box with cakes for it helps them stay moist and fresh.

Cinnamon Fluff

- ½ cup butter
- ⅔ cup sugar
- 2 eggs
- 1½ cups sifted flour
- 1 teaspoon soda
- 1 teaspoon baking powder
- ¼ teaspoon salt
- 2 tablespoons cinnamon
- 1 cup sour milk

Cream butter, add sugar gradually, and cream thoroughly. Blend in well beaten eggs. Sift flour, soda, baking powder and salt together and the cinnamon. Add to the creamed mixture alternately with the sour milk. Pour into a well-greased 8-inch pan. Set aside while mixing:

- 1 tablespoon butter
- 1 tablespoon cinnamon
- ½ cup sugar

Rub together and sprinkle over the dough. Bake in a moderate oven for 40 to 45 minutes. Serve with whipped cream to

which cinnamon has been added. Hot lemon sauce or ice cold custard is also good.

The topping kind of goes through the cake, forming a syrup mixture like an upside-down cake. This won a prize for Mrs. S.E. Hunt, Vancouver. Like all prize-winning recipes, it has been tested by Miss Jean Mutch in the Home Service Kitchen of the B.C. Electric.

Lemon Sponge Cake

Beat 3 eggs till very light, then add gradually 1 cup of sugar, beating thoroughly after each addition. Add 6 tablespoons of hot milk and ½ teaspoon lemon extract and beat again. Sift together 1 cup of pastry flour, 2 teaspoons baking powder and ½ teaspoon salt, three times. Then add to first mixture and fold in thoroughly. Bake in a 325 degree F. oven in a lightly floured pan.

When serving cut in squares and put lemon filling between, dust top with icing sugar.

This may also be baked in layers in a 350 degree F. oven, and put lemon filling between layers and lemon or orange icing on top.

This fluffy cake won a prize for Mrs. Arthur Thompson, Courtenay. Like all prize-winning recipes it has been tested in the Home Service Kitchen of the B.C. Electric by Miss Mutch and her assistants.

Buttermilk Spice Cake

- ⅔ cup butter
- 1 cup brown sugar
- ½ cup molasses
- 2 eggs
- 1 cup buttermilk
- 1 teaspoon baking soda
- 2½ cups flour
- 2 teaspoons baking powder
- 1½ teaspoons cinnamon
- ½ teaspoon cloves
- 1½ cups raisins
- ½ cup walnuts

Cream butter and sugar, add molasses, beaten eggs and buttermilk in which soda has been dissolved. Sift flour, baking powder, spices and add to the raisins and nuts. Combine the dry ingredients with the first mixture. Pour into an oiled pan and bake in a moderate oven of 350 deg. F. for 40 minutes.

This popular spice cake won a prize for Mrs. Reg. Harley, Milner. Like all prize-winning recipes it has been tested by Miss Jean Mutch and her assistants in the Home Service Kitchen of the B.C. Electric.

Puddings and Desserts

Caramel Custard

   3   eggs
   ½   cup brown sugar
   2¼ cups milk
   1   teaspoon vanilla or rum flavour

Beat the eggs, add sugar and beat again. Add the hot milk and flavouring. In the bottom of each custard cup put a tablespoon of brown sugar. Fill cup with custard and bake in a 350°F oven in a pan of water.

Turn out of cups, upside down, to serve as the sugar in the bottoms makes a sauce that runs down over the custard.

Good custard is always a welcome dessert. It won a prize for Mrs. Ed. Harries, Vancouver, and has been tested in the Home Service Kitchen of the B.C. Electric by Miss Jean Mutch.

Ice Box Roll

   1   tin Christie's chocolate wafers
   ½   pint whipping cream

Pile up wafers with whipped cream between each wafer. When it gets too high lay the roll lengthwise. Cover roll with whipped cream. Let set in refrigerator for two or three hours. Slice sideways to make a black and white combination.

This is a simple dessert to prepare for a busy day because it can be prepared and forgotten for several hours, as it improves on standing. It won a prize for Mrs. S. Loughran, Vancouver. Like all prize-winning recipes it has been tested in the Home Service Kitchen of the B.C. Electric by Miss Jean Mutch and her assistants.

Creamy Rice Pudding

   4   tablespoons rice
   1   quart rich milk, or 3 cups fresh and 1 cup
        evaporated
   2   tablespoons butter
   ½   cup sugar
   2   teaspoons vanilla
   ½   teaspoon salt
   ⅛   teaspoon cinnamon

Put washed rice in baking dish with barely enough water to cover, and set over low flame until the water is absorbed. Add milk and other ingredients, stirring till it begins to boil, then place in moderate oven of 325 deg. F. for about 1¾ hours. Stir 3 times, breaking up crust first time; after that, slip spoon carefully under it from the edge, and stir rice thoroughly from the bottom. There should be lots of creamy liquid left which thickens as it cools. Chill a few hours before serving.

Sometimes garnish with preserved figs, crushed canned pineapple or peaches.

Miss Dorothy D'Ersby, Vancouver, says her grandmother served this recipe regularly once a week. Her prize-winning recipe has been tested in the Home Service Kitchen of the B.C. Electric by Miss Jean Mutch and her assistants.

Raspberry Meringues

   ¼   teaspoon salt
   4   egg whites
   1   teaspoon vinegar
   1   cup fine fruit sugar

Add salt to egg whites and beat until stiff. Add vinegar and the sugar, a little at a time, and continue beating until mixture can be cut with a knife. Turn into 8 well-greased muffin pans, or drop by spoonfuls on a greased wax paper. Bake in a slow oven of 300°F for 40 to 50 minutes.

When ready to serve, lift off the tops, fill cavity with a spoonful of vanilla ice cream, replace caps and cover with sweetened fresh raspberries and top with whipped cream.

If you find it difficult to remove the top just put the ice cream on top; however, the ice cream will hold the broken top together, too. This won a prize for Miss Beela Paterson, Pioneer. All prize-winning recipes are tested in the Home Service Kitchen of the B.C. Electric.

"*I think it's the most Interesting paper!*"

THAT'S why The Vancouver Sun has been coming to our house every day for years . . . It is the most INTERESTING newspaper ● There are more things in The Sun to keep me and the rest of my family in step with life, to keep our minds lively and in tune with the feelings, thoughts and actions of people like ourselves ● The Sun's editors and reporters put more life, more VITALITY and humanity into their stories of the things that happen ● The Sun's editorials are always in the best interests of most of the people, and my husband and myself feel that The Sun's viewpoint is fair and honest . . . and NEVER dull ● I can rely on the Social news to be accurate and smartly written, the Sports pages to be entertaining and all the other departments to be up-to-the-minute and well done ● Without The Sun's store news I would be simply lost, for the fine advertisements by reliable firms not only tell me what's new and good; they save me MANY times what we pay for the paper ● And there would be excitement, I can tell you, around our house if The Sun failed to bring the children their favorite features   In short, I suppose I could have said at the beginning: The Sun is the BEST paper!"

The Vancouver Sun
• A VANCOUVER OWNED NEWSPAPER •

VANCOUVER SUN SUBSCRIPTION RATES

Delivered by Carrier, wherever Carrier service is maintained. 75c a month.

BY MAIL

In British Columbia and Yukon Territory:
Single month	$ .75
Three months	2.00
Per year	8.00

Balance of Canada, Great Britain and Postal Union:
Per month	$ .75
Per year	9.00

United States and Mexico:
Per month	$ 1.00
Per year	12.00

Foreign:
Per month	$ 1.75
Per year	21.00

SUNDAY SUN, by Mail:
Canada and Great Britain, $3.00 per year; U.S.A., $3.50 per year; other countries, $5.00 per year.

Pickles and Relishes

Mint Relish

 2 pounds green apples
 ¾ cup seeded raisins
 6 small onions
 1 large red pepper
 1 green pepper
 1 cup mint, chopped
 1 cup vinegar
 1 pound brown sugar
   Salt to taste
 2 ounces mustard seed

Put apples, raisins, onions and peppers through food chopper, add chopped mint. Add one cup water to vinegar and boil for three minutes with the sugar, salt and mustard seed. Then remove from the fire, add vegetables and mix well. Pour into hot sterile glasses and seal.

This very seasonable recipe won a prize for Mrs. J.C.B. Williamson of White Rock. Like all prize-winning recipes it was tested in the Home Service Department of the B.C. Electric.

Tomato Ketchup

 5 quarts tomato juice
 5 onions
 3 teaspoons pickling spice
 3 teaspoons salt
 1½ cups white sugar
 3 cups vinegar

Cut tomatoes in pieces, slice onions and add pickling spices. Cook well, then strain through strainer. Add salt, sugar and vinegar and let boil until thickens. Cap in sterilized bottles while hot.

This truly seasonal recipe won a prize for Mrs. J.C. Hawse, Penticton. It was tested in the Home Service Kitchen of the B.C. Electric by Miss F. Hay and her assistants.

Sweet Pickled Crab Apples

 1 peck crab apples
 1 quart vinegar
 3 pounds brown sugar
 1 stick cinnamon
 1 teaspoon whole cloves

Wash the crab apples, and remove blossom ends. Steam until tender. Make a syrup of vinegar, sugar and spices. Cook apples in this syrup 10 minutes and put them into jars. Boil down the syrup and pour it over the fruit. Seal.

Many are the requests for crab apple recipes, so this prize-winning method should be a welcome one. It won a prize for Miss Josephine Rowa, Vancouver, and like all prize-winning recipes it was tested in the Home Service Kitchen of the B.C. Electric by Miss Jean Mutch and her assistants.

Bengal Chutney

 5 pounds sour juicy apples
 1 pound raisins
 ¼ pound garlic
 ½ pound mustard seed
 ½ pound onions
 2 quarts vinegar
 1 ounce cayenne pepper
 1 pound brown sugar
 ½ pound of salt
 ¼ pound powdered ginger

Apples should be pared and cored; raisins stoned and chopped fine and the garlic cut up very thin. Boil the apples, raisins, garlic and chopped-up onions together with the mustard seed in 1 quart of vinegar until they are soft. Then mix the cayenne pepper, sugar, salt and ginger with the remainder of the vinegar and add to the first boiled mixture. Stir the two mixtures together and boil for a few minutes. Set the chutney aside to cool and then seal tightly in glasses. The longer this chutney is kept the more pleasing the flavour becomes.

Mrs. L. Beach, of Clinton, who won a prize for this recipe writes: "This recipe was given to my brother over 50 years ago by a retired English officer who was connected with an Indian Royal household and is exactly as it was used there." Miss Jean Mutch of the B.C. Electric, where this chutney was tested, recommends it only for those who like a very hot relish.

IMPORTANT PERSONAGE

THE whole family revolves around this lad. He is king of a realm that extends to the farthest and most doting uncle. His slightest wishes can cause vast upheavals among his subjects . . . but they seldom do. For he is a benevolent monarch, good-natured and benign and passes his time calmly in the pleasant diversions of eating, sleeping, growing and taking notice of things in a marvellous world. In short, he is a MODERN baby, cared for in the modern manner by an intelligent and modern mother who has at her finger-tips the wisdom of the world on the subject of babies. Not for her the well-meant experiments by which the young mother of the past learned, aided by the loving advice of practically everyone, how to bring up her first-born and inflicted much punishment on her child and herself in the process. THIS baby's mother merely follows the advice of Myrtle Meyer Eldred, which appears in the Vancouver Sun every day. For special matters she writes to Mrs. Eldred and receives the answer. THIS baby will grow up with strong body, steady nerves . . . a healthy and balanced citizen well able to cope with whatever life brings.

•

MYRTLE MEYER ELDRED

A mother herself, Mrs. Eldred is recognized as one of the foremost authorities on the care of infants. In her daily column in the Vancouver Sun she presents practical advice based on a full acquaintance with all modern knowledge on the rearing of children, from pre-natal care onward. The Vancouver Sun is proud to offer its women readers her invaluable help in the most important task of womankind.

"Your Baby and Mine"
By MYRTLE MEYER ELDRED
Daily in Vancouver Sun

•

Edith Adams 7th Annual Cook Book

1940

THE VOICE OF A CITY

A CITY has a mind and a character as well as a throbbing physical life. Despite all their diversities its people have feelings, thoughts, aims in common. They move in a direction together, as all the rushing currents of a river are together its course.

Every city expresses its life and thoughts. Sometimes a man or woman; sometimes an institution deeply rooted in its history will be the voice that declares for all the citizens the things they think and do together.

In Vancouver the people have a voice in their Vancouver-owned newspaper. A look back through the years in which the city and The Sun have grown together . . . back to the days when Vancouver was a forest hamlet on the edge of the sea . . . shows how true this is.

The things Vancouver has done, the things that her people have willed to be, these things have been foreshadowed and have taken shape in the columns of The Sun—times without number many years before their achievement.

The obstacles that have lain in the path of Vancouver—obstacles which have one by one been overcome and passed—have first been recognized by The Sun, have been fought and defeated by The Sun and the people working in purposeful teamwork.

In the building of the city's cultural life as well as in its material achievements The Sun has often led: it has ALWAYS been a loyal working member of the community's effort in the things the people have thought it best to do.

Now, when new vistas of achievement open out before Vancouver, The Vancouver Sun is embedded in the life of the city. The management and every employee are Vancouver people who live here and have no other interest in the future of Vancouver except that it be fine and worthy.

Vancouver will do great things, and in the doing there will always be the united effort without which a city cannot be great. In the building that will make it nobler both materially and spiritually The Sun will play the part of a good citizen.

And when, as always, the thoughts of Vancouver are given voice, the voice will be The Vancouver Sun.

Vancouver Owned
The Vancouver Sun

Meal Planning in Wartime

How best to utilize our own food resources and substitute for imported foods, during time of war, will prove no problem to the older housewife with past experience to rely on, but to the younger generation of homemakers this will need a bit of explaining.

Food conservation begins in the kitchen. More and more women will do home canning and buy to better advantage in all food commodities, and more thought will be given to food marketing with a view to "the next meal," and serious consideration will be given to food values. This knowledge is so necessary when it comes to using food substitutes in the diet of a healthy and growing family. There is certainly no saving at the expense of an inadequate and poorly balanced diet. The foods necessary for this balanced diet should be chosen from the following groups. These are classed as "protective foods."

Dairy Products: Milk, butter and cheese.

Growing children should have 1 quart of milk a day and adults 1 pint, but where this is not possible allow 1 pint for each member of the family daily. Milk can be added to the diet in the form of soups, puddings and cream sauces. Dried and evaporated milk have the same food value as fresh milk and, in some places, cost less. When sweetened condensed milk is used reduce the amount of sugar in the recipe. When substituting for fresh milk use the following proportions:

½ cup evaporated milk, plus ½ cup water
½ cup condensed milk, plus ½ cup water
4 tablespoons powdered milk, plus 1 cup water

Butter: Butter should be used freely, if possible, but it can easily be substituted in cookery by using vegetable fats, peanut butter, dripping and lard. With an adequate milk allowance in the food budget butter-substitutes may be used.

Cheese: Cheese made from whole milk has, of course, the same food value as milk and can be used alone or combined with other foods.

Cereals and Breads: Whole grain cereals and breads are one of your best sources of food values. Cereals should form a part of every active person's breakfast and some form of bread should be served at every meal. When a farinaceous dish is part of the meal, serve a whole wheat bread.

Vegetables: The old rule of 2 vegetables daily, plus potatoes, is still the best to follow. The additional vegetables should be leafy—either raw or cooked—and a root vegetable, such as carrots, turnips, parsnips, etc.

Fruits: Fruits should be served, raw or stewed, every day. Use them often as the basis of a dessert or fruit salad. It is an advantage, of course, to have the extra benefits of some fruit juice. Prunes, dates, raisins and figs can often be substituted for out of season fresh fruit.

Meat, Fish, Eggs: A meat or fish food should be served daily. Meat can be substantially conserved by using cheaper cuts and using the meat extras such as kidney, liver, etc. Substitutions, such as cheese, dried beans, lentils, etc., are old standbys and high in food values. Our own abundance of British Columbia fish, fresh, canned or smoked—shellfish, too—will get full honours as a meat substitute and when variety must be considered in meal planning.

Eggs: Eggs are another of the "musts" for a balanced diet and should only be substituted in cooking where a number of eggs are called for in a recipe. In custards, custard puddings and pies, for instance, use 2 tablespoons of cornstarch or arrowroot for one of the eggs. During the season when eggs are cheap they can be preserved in water-glass for future cooking use.

Sweets: Sugar consumption can easily be reduced by using honey, syrup, molasses and brown or raw sugar in cooking. We may mention here, however, that honey and sugar are practically the same in sweetness, but honey, having a water content, calls for a reduction in liquid when it is used in cooking. Reduce the liquid ¼ cup for each cup of honey used. Use low top range heat or moderate oven temperature when cooking honey-flavoured dishes as they tend to burn easily. This rule also applies when using syrup and molasses.

Substitutions

How to Make 1 Pound of Butter Into 2

Take the top cream from a bottle of milk and add enough milk to make 2 cups. Soak 1 tablespoon gelatin in 2 tablespoons milk for 5 minutes. Place over hot water until gelatin dissolves. Cut 1 pound butter into small pieces and when soft gradually whip milk and dissolved gelatin mixture into butter with dover beater. After milk is all thoroughly beaten in add 1 teaspoon salt. Place on ice to harden.

1 tablespoon baking powder	¼ teaspoon soda and ½ teaspoon cream of tartar.
1 cup butter	⅘ cup bacon fat, clarified.**
1 cup butter	⅞ cup cottonseed, corn or nut oil.
1 cup butter	⅞ cup lard, with addition of salt.
1 cup butter	½ cup suet, with addition of salt.**
1 square chocolate	2⅔ tablespoons cocoa, plus ½ tablespoon shortening.
1 tablespoon cornstarch	2 tablespoons flour (for thickening purposes).
Milk substitutes	Page 102, left column.
1 cup molasses	1 cup honey
1 cup pastry flour	1 cup bread flour less 2 tablespoons.
1 cup sugar	¾ to 1 cup molasses, plus ¼ to ½ teaspoon soda.*
1 cup sugar	1 cup honey, plus ¼ to ½ teaspoon soda.*
1 cup sugar	1 cup maple syrup plus ¼ teaspoon soda.*

(*) Reduce liquid ¼ cup.
(**) Increase liquid ¼ cup or more.

Fish

Our British Columbia waters are lavish in their variety of fish, both fresh and salt, and every taste is taken into consideration in marketing them. The various fish are frozen, smoked, filleted and cured, pickled and canned—and still we have the delectable shellfish family, fresh and canned. With such a selection, no housewife should ever complain of "menu monotony."

In choosing fresh fish, see that the eyes are clear and bright and the flesh firm and springy, and scales are easy to remove.

FISH HINTS: To keep fish over a day, unwrap at once. Wipe off with a clean, damp cloth and sprinkle with salt and pepper. If the fish is to be fried, rub with oil, salt and pepper. Place fish in a covered dish in cooler.

When boiling red fish do not add lemon juice to the water, as it has a tendency to bleach, but it's grand with white, boiled fish.

Thaw out frozen fish by placing in cold water before preparing.

Let all fish stand at room temperature before cooking. If the fish is to be fried, chilled fish will cool the fat off too much.

Never wash oysters, just wipe with a clean, damp cloth. Left-over boiled, fried or baked fish can be utilized in casserole dishes, soups, salads and croquettes.

Court Bouillon

- 2 qts. water
- 2 tbsp. salt
- ½ cup vinegar or lemon juice
- 2 carrots
- 2 onions (spiked with a few cloves)
- 4 stalks celery
  Few sprigs parsley
- 1 small bay leaf
  Few peppercorns

Place all the ingredients in a saucepan, bring to the boil and add the fish, which has been placed on a plate and tied in a cheesecloth. This seasoned boiling water is always used when boiling or steaming fish.

Deviled Fish

- 6 strips of bacon
- 4 tablespoons minced green pepper
- 2 tablespoons minced onions
- 2 cups tomato pulp and juice
- ¼ teaspoon cloves
- 1 pound flaked fish
- 6 minced olives
- 1 cup crumbs

Cook the bacon crisp. Remove from pan and mince; cook pepper and onion for just 2 minutes in bacon fat. Add tomato and seasoning and boil for 5 minutes. Add flakes, minced bacon, olives and more seasoning as desired. Place in a greased ramekin, cover with crumbs, dot with butter and bake 20 minutes at 400°F.

Mrs. James A. Butler, Atlanta, Georgia, wins a $1 prize for this tasty supper dish.

Salmon Schooners

Bake 5 potatoes; split them in half lengthwise and mash the centres with the following:

- ½ cup milk
- 1 beaten egg
- 2 teaspoons browned chopped onion in 2 tablespoons butter or dripping
- 1 medium size tin salmon

Restuff the potatoes and bake until they are golden brown on top in an oven of 325° to 350°F.

If you have run out of ideas for serving potatoes then try this one. The recipe won a prize for Mrs. P. Molberg, Vancouver.

Meats

Many people think that dinner is just "not dinner" if it doesn't include a meat course. While that is not entirely correct we do associate meat with dinner more than any other meal. Of course meat can take its bow at breakfast in the form of sausages or bacon and most certainly at luncheon in a variety of forms.

It is rather impossible to attempt to discuss meat in general terms when it rightly falls into many very different sections. The average housewife is well schooled in the purchasing and cooking of the more expensive cuts of meat, but it is also well for her to have a usable knowledge of the cheaper and equally versatile cuts. Government inspection and grading of meat is now highly specialized and thus the homemaker can be assured as to the quality of even the cheaper bargains.

For those who rely on the cheaper cuts of meat there is endless variety in their preparation. Tasty stews, pot roasts, braised meats and ground meats are yours to choose from. Added nourishment at low cost is to be had in the "inside meats," such as liver, heart, tripe, oxtail, tongue, etc.

Stews and fricassees are still tops in popularity—someone usually ends the argument with . . . "well-browned chunks of meat, then add a little water or soup stock, a clove of garlic, an onion or two, celery, green pepper, a few peppercorns, a bit of bay leaf; then about 40 minutes before it's ready, add the carrots and potatoes." Someone with a bit more imagination goes systematically through the pantry and rinses out that remnant of ketchup, adds a bit of relish and a drop or two out of this and that condiment bottle. The result is way out of the stew class—it's a dream!

When your budget and taste agree on some fancy cut, choose something thick and tender, whether steak or chop, and broil or pan-fry to a rich brown with a hint of "scorch" and rare and juicy within.

Ragout of Beef

    3   pounds stewing beef, or half beef and half kidney
    2   medium size onions, minced
    1   green pepper, minced
    1   teaspoon sugar
    1   tablespoon vinegar
    4   tablespoons tomato ketchup
        Salt and pepper to taste
        Water, tomato juice diluted with water or stock, to cover the meat and vegetables
    4   medium size carrots, sliced
    2   large stalks celery, cut into small lengths

Dredge the meat in flour and sear until well browned in a little smoking fat. Place pan over low heat and add remaining ingredients, except the carrots and celery. Cover with the liquid. Cover stewing pot tightly and bring to a low simmer, using either top range or oven heat. The ragout should simmer slowly about 2½ to 3 hours in all.

About 1 hour before serving put in the carrots and celery, adding more liquid if required. Small whole potatoes, cubes or thick slices, may be added at this time. Dust the top lightly with paprika. When these additional vegetables are tender the ragout is ready for serving. Serves 6.

Roast Leg of Lamb

Select a leg of lamb with or without part of the loin; do not remove fell or thin skin which protects the meat and shortens roasting time. Wipe meat with a damp cloth, sprinkle with salt and pepper, and rub well with flour. Lay the roast skin side down on rack in roaster or open pan; if meat is very lean, lay several strips of bacon on top. Place the roast in a very hot oven (450 deg. F.) and sear for ½ hour, or until browned. Reduce heat rapidly to around 300 deg. (slow) and continue roasting until of the desired rareness. Allow 25 to 30 minutes per pound for medium-done meat and 30 to 35 minutes per pound for well-done meat. If meat is dry, baste occasionally with drippings in the pan. A five-pound leg of lamb will require from 2½ to 3 hours and a seven-pound leg will require from 3½ to 4 hours.

The following chart gives good timing idea for the various cuts:
BEEF

Beef Cut	Method	Temperature	Approximate Time
Roasts Rare Medium Well-done	Roasting	500 deg. for 15 min. and 350 deg. for remainder of time	 18–20 min. per pound 22–25 min. per pound 27–30 min. per pound
Boned Roasts	Roasting	500 deg. for 15 min. and 350 deg. for remainder of time	Add 10–15 min. per pound
Pot Roasts	Braising	Very low	3–4 hours
Steaks 1-inch 2 inches	Broiling	500 deg.	 About 10 mins. (medium) About 20 mins. (medium)
Swiss Steak	Braising	Very low	2 to 3 hours
Round Steak	Braising	Very low	About 1 hour
Stews	Stewing	Below boiling	2 to 2½ hours
Corned Beef	Simmering	Below boiling	3 to 4 hours
Beef Loaf	Baking	300 deg. to 350 deg. (moderate)	1½ to 2 hours
Tongue (fresh)	Simmering	Below boiling	2½ to 3 hours
Heart	Braising	Very low	3 to 4 hours
Liver	Braising Broiling	300 deg. (moderate)	About 1½ hours About 10 minutes
Kidney	Broiling Stewing	425 deg. (very hot)	About 10 minutes About 1½ hours

Lancashire Hot Pot

2 pounds neck of mutton
3 sheep kidneys
12 large oysters
1 tablespoon butter
2 pounds potatoes
1 large onion
½ pint gravy
Seasonings to taste

Divide the meat into pieces, trim off skin and greater part of fat. Grease a casserole and put in a layer of sliced potato, arrange the pieces of meat on top of potatoes letting them slightly overlap each other. On each place one or two slices of kidney and oysters; season well. Put in the remainder of potatoes and brush over with the butter. Take the onion and lean trimmings and odd bones from meat and beards of oyster and boil down for gravy. Then pour down side of dish. Cover with a butter paper and cook for 1½ to 2 hours in a moderate 350 deg. F. oven. Towards the end of the cooking remove the paper to allow for browning. Serves 6.

This Old Country recipe won a prize for W. Compton, Vancouver.

Smothered Chicken

One fryer chicken (2 lbs.). Split the chicken down the back and wipe dry. Season with salt and pepper and rub inside and out with softened butter. Dredge well with flour and place breast down on a low rack in a deep pan. Cover with bacon slices, tomato slices, shredded green pepper and a few very finely cut onion slices. Dot all over with butter. Pour hot water in the pan up to the rack, or cover the pan tightly if no rack is used. Bake in a moderate oven (350 deg. F.) for one hour. Uncover and thin the gravy with hot water and bake until tender and brown. Serves two.

Fried Chicken, Southern Style

2 small chickens
Salt and pepper
Flour
¼ cup fat

Clean and wipe chicken with a damp cloth and cut each chicken into four pieces. Sprinkle with salt and pepper and roll in plenty of flour. Saute the chicken in the hot fat, turning frequently to brown both sides, until tender. Drain the pieces well and arrange on a warm platter and keep hot until gravy is made. Serves four.

Creamy Gravy: Pour off all except three tablespoons of the fat. To the remaining fat add three tablespoons flour and stir until smooth. Then stir in two cups of milk, or one cup milk and one cup cream. Cook until thickened, stirring constantly. Season well with salt and pepper and serve with or over the chicken.

Game

We offer the following simple recipes for the preparation of game. Game meat is usually served rare, but this, of course, is entirely up to the individual. You must keep in mind, though, that many of the game meats are lean and have a tendency to dry out during a long cooking period.

Roast Wild Duck

Prepare the duck for roasting and stuff with an apple or onion. Truss. Dust lightly with flour, salt and pepper. Cover the breast with a few slices of very fat bacon and place in a baking pan with one-half cup of water and 1 tablespoon fat. Bake in a hot oven (450 deg. F.) for 15 minutes. Pour off some of the liquid, cover the roasting pan and return to moderate heat (350 deg. F.). Bake 15 minutes longer, or according to taste. Remove the apple or onion before serving.

For goose, roast at 400 deg. for at least 2 hours.

Roast Grouse

Prepare the grouse for roasting. Dust lightly with flour, salt and pepper and place over each breast slices of fat bacon. Roast in a moderate oven about 45 minutes, basting frequently.

Roast Pheasant

Prepare as for grouse or duck. Roast the bird in a moderate oven 45 to 60 minutes, according to size and age. Baste frequently.

Rabbit Stew

Clean and cut rabbit into serving pieces. Season with salt and pepper and dredge with flour. Saute the rabbit in melted fat (about 4 tablespoons) until it is nicely browned. Add boiling water or soup stock to a depth of about ½ inch. Add 1 medium onion, sliced; 1 or 2 stalks celery, chopped; a few small carrots, sliced; ½ bay leaf and a few peppercorns. Cover closely and simmer gently until the meat is tender. Remove meat and add flour to dripping (about 4 tablespoons); mix until smooth and add milk or stock to the desired consistency.

Leg or Saddle of Venison

Wipe the meat with a damp cloth. Insert one or two small buds of garlic by means of a small, sharp knife incision, right down to the bone. If the meat is lean, rub some fat into it. Sprinkle with salt and pepper and, if you wish, lay some bacon strips across it. Place in a roaster and bake in a very hot oven for about 10 minutes. Reduce the heat to moderate and finish roasting at 12 to 15 minutes per pound, basting about every 15 minutes. Venison is another of the game meats usually served rare and if this is the way you wish it allow about 1½ hours for a 10-lb. roast.

Game Sauce

A simple, tasty "game gravy" is to pour off excess fat from the dripping and add some currant jelly, a little extra seasoning and, if you wish, a little lemon juice. Bring this slowly to the boil and serve with game.

Vegetables

Glazed Squash

    3   cups squash, cut in 1-inch cubes
    4   tablespoons melted butter
    ½   teaspoon salt
    1½ tablespoons brown sugar
    2   tablespoons lemon juice

Combine squash, butter, salt, brown sugar and lemon juice. Bake in a covered casserole in a hot oven (400 deg. F.) for 30 minutes. Remove the cover and cook 15 minutes longer, or until squash is tender and glossy in appearance. Serves 4.

Parsnips Parisienne

    4   parsnips
    4   tablespoons melted butter
        Salt and pepper to taste
        Dash of nutmeg

Peel and slice parsnips ½ inch thick. Cook in boiling, salted water about 20 minutes. Drain and place in a casserole. Combine butter, salt and pepper and pour over the parsnips. Sprinkle with nutmeg and cook, covered, in a hot oven (400 deg. F.) for about 30 minutes. Serves 4.

Glazed Onions

    1½ pounds small white onions (or mild onion slices)
    2   tablespoons butter
    ½   cup water
    1½ tablespoons sugar
        Salt and pepper
    1   tablespoon flour

Peel onions. Melt butter, add onions and the water and sugar mixture. Season to taste and simmer gently until tender (about 15 minutes). Add a paste made from the flour and 2 extra tablespoons water, mixing well. Place in a covered casserole and bake in a moderately hot oven (375 deg. F.) for about 20 minutes. Serves 6.

Candied Sweet Potatoes

    6   medium sweet potatoes
    ⅓   cup melted butter or Crisco
    1   cup brown sugar
    ¼   cup water
    ½   teaspoon salt

Cook potatoes until tender. Drain, peel, cut in halves lengthwise and arrange in a shallow, greased pan. Cover with the fat and a syrup made by cooking the brown sugar and water together for 5 minutes. Sprinkle with salt and bake in a slow oven of 350°F. for 1 hour. Baste frequently. Serves 6.

The potatoes should be quite transparent when candied in this manner. The recipe won a prize for Mrs. H. Kingswood, New Westminster.

Carrots Fried in Parsley Butter

Wash and scrape spring carrots. Cut enough into slivers to fill two cups. Cook for 20 minutes or until tender in 4 cups boiling water with 1½ teaspoons salt.

Beat 1 egg and add ½ cup evaporated milk, ¼ teaspoon baking powder and ¾ cup pastry flour. Finally add 1 tablespoon chopped parsley and ½ teaspoon salt and mix well. Dip carrots into batter and fry until brown (about 2 minutes) in deep hot fat. Drain on soft paper.

You will find these French fried carrots equally as tasty as French fried potatoes. The recipe won a prize for Mrs. H.M. Summers, Nanaimo.

New Potatoes Baked with Lemon Butter

Scrape small new potatoes, parboil 10 minutes, drain and bake at 450 deg. F. until soft, basting three times with four tablespoons melted butter mixed with the juice of ½ lemon. Sprinkle with parsley before serving.

New potatoes are always a treat and especially if served with lemon butter. This recipe won a prize for Mrs. H.M. Summers, Nanaimo.

Salads

Of all the health-giving contributions to a meal little else can beat a good salad. During the last few years salads have become such a seemingly necessary part of our menus that we seldom think of a complete dinner without some kind of a refreshing salad to go with it.

Salad-making should be a comparatively simple thing for British Columbians since fruit and vegetables abound in this province. Don't try to mix too many of either fruits or vegetables in one salad. A simple but attractive salad is undoubtedly the best.

The basis of many of the most appealing salads is nothing more than some crisp leafy greens and a really good dressing. The dressing is almost as important as the choice of ingredients in a salad. There should be something tangy about a salad dressing that will give zest to even a slightly flat salad.

Sour Cream Mayonnaise

- ½ cup sour cream, whipped
- 2½ tablespoons confectioner's sugar
- 1 tablespoon lemon juice
- ½ cup mayonnaise

Fold sour cream, lemon juice and sugar into mayonnaise. Makes 1½ cups dressing.

Hearty Toss Salad

- 1 cup cooked green beans
- 1 cup cooked carrot strips
- 1 cup celery strips
- ½ cup French dressing
- 1 head lettuce
- 1 cup cooked ham cut in slivers
- 2 hard-cooked eggs, sliced

Marinate green beans, carrot and celery in French dressing for 2 hours. Break lettuce in pieces in salad bowl. Arrange marinated vegetables and ham, spoke-fashion, with egg slices in centre. Serve with nippy mayonnaise dressing. Serves 6 to 8.

Cottage Cheese Salad

Take 10¢ worth of cottage cheese and mix it with:

- Salt and pepper to taste
- 2 finely chopped hard-cooked eggs
- 3 large grated radishes
- 3 finely chopped spring green onions

For individual salads, place a large spoonful of mixture on shredded lettuce leaves, top with more grated radish and garnish with sections of tomatoes. Serves 6.

For large centre salad, cover platter with shredded lettuce, then put spoonfuls of the mixture around the edge for a border, and place sections of tomato between each spoonful of cheese mixture. Centre can be filled with circle of overlapping slices of cucumber. A large spoonful of salad dressing in the very centre topped with dash of paprika is the finishing touch.

The centre of the salad may be filled with any left-over vegetables such as green peas, beans, asparagus, slivered carrots, etc. These additions make it suitable for a main course luncheon dish.

This recipe won a prize for Mrs. H.W. Bucke, Vancouver.

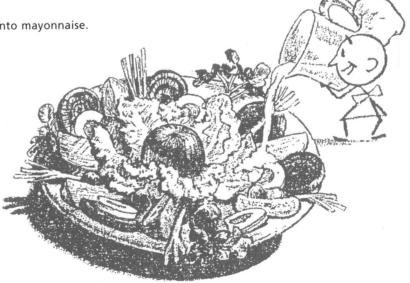

Breads

Breads are classified as yeast breads and quick breads. The lady of the home usually masters the art of making the quick breads which include such things as popovers, waffles, muffins and baking powder biscuits before she attempts the more complicated task of making yeast bread. However many Canadian housewives are experts at making their own bread. There's something about the aroma of warm, fresh, home-made bread that is very hard to surpass for sheer delicacy of fragrance.

Oven Temperatures for Baking

Slow oven	250 to 350 degrees Fahrenheit
Moderate oven	350 to 400 degrees Fahrenheit
Quick or hot oven	400 to 450 degrees Fahrenheit
Very hot oven	450 to 500 degrees Fahrenheit

Baking Powder Biscuits

- 2 cups flour
- 4 teaspoons baking powder
- ½ teaspoon salt
- 4 tablespoons shortening
- ¾ cup milk, about

Mix and sift dry ingredients. Cut in the shortening. Add enough milk to make a soft dough that is not sticky. Turn out on a lightly floured board and roll gently for one-half inch thickness. Cut with floured cutter and place on ungreased baking sheet. Space the biscuits if you wish a crusty biscuit, or place them close together if you wish a higher, soft biscuit. Bake in a hot oven (375°F) for 15 to 20 minutes. Makes about 16 two-inch biscuits.

For cheese biscuits add about ½ cup grated cheese to the sifted dry ingredients.

Parker House Rolls

- 2 cups milk
- 2 tablespoons sugar
- 6 cups sifted flour
- 2 teaspoons salt
- 1 cake compressed yeast
- ¼ cup lukewarm water
- 2 tablespoons butter

Scald the milk, then add the sugar and cool the mixture to lukewarm. Sift the flour and add the salt. Dissolve the yeast in lukewarm water and add it to the milk and sugar and then sift half the flour into this mixture and beat well. Add the melted butter and then the remainder of the flour and beat well. Knead on a lightly floured board until smooth and elastic.

Place in a greased bowl and brush the surface with melted butter, cover and leave in a warm place until it doubles in bulk. Knead down again and let rise again until double in bulk.

Roll the dough about ⅓ inch thick and cut with a round cutter. Crease deeply through the centre with the back of the knife. Spread half the roll lightly with butter. Fold over and press the edges together. Place about one inch apart on greased baking sheet and bake in a 375°F oven for 15 to 20 minutes.

Holiday Rolls

- 2 cups thick sour cream
- 1 cake compressed yeast
- ¼ teaspoon soda
- 2 teaspoons salt
- ¼ cup white sugar
- 4 cups flour
- Melted butter
- Brown sugar
- Red and green cherries

Scald cream and cool to luke warm. Crumble yeast cake and stir into ⅓ cup luke warm cream. Add soda, salt and white sugar to the remaining cream and mix well. Combine the two mixtures and add flour gradually, stirring constantly until smooth. Brush with melted butter, cover and put in warm place and let rise to about 2½ times the original size. Knead lightly for about one minute and cut dough into two parts.

Roll out, one part at a time in rectangular shape about ⅛ inch thick. Brush with melted butter, sprinkle with brown sugar and spread with chopped cherries. Roll up like jelly roll and cut into one-inch pieces. Place the pieces in buttered small muffin tins with cut edges up. Let rise in warm place until double in size. Bake in a hot oven (425°F) for 10 to 15 minutes, or until golden brown. Brush with butter, if desired.

This recipe makes 24 small rolls and it won a prize for Louise Woodean, New Westminster.

Pastry

Pie making is an old-fashioned art but there are many modern twists that you can give it. The fact that even good King Arthur and his Knights of the Round Table are supposed to have eaten pie is no reason why you should let it appear on the table always in the same style. After you've mastered the art of making good plain pastry try your hand at puff pastry, flaky pastry, hot water pastry and then, too, try some of the newer commercial product pastries.

The secrets of a perfect crust are fine ingredients, proper proportions of flour, fat and liquid, skill in handling and correct baking. Handle the dough as little as possible, just rubbing in the shortening quickly and lightly until all the particles of fat are coated with flour, then adding the liquid a drop or two at a time. Mix the dough until it can be shaped into a ball. A pie blender is a fine utensil, but there's something about using your fingers for the mixing that enables you to tell "by the feel" just how soon the ingredients are blended sufficiently.

When baking a pie shell without the filling, prick the crust with a fork many times before baking, and that will keep the shell from blistering.

Plain Pastry

    2½ cups sifted cake flour
    ½   teaspoon salt
    ⅔   cup cold shortening
    ⅓   cup cold water (about)

Sift flour once, measure, add salt, and sift again. Cut in shortening until pieces are about size of small peas. Add water, sprinkling small amount over the flour mixture and mixing only enough to make flour hold together. Continue until all flour has been mixed in separate portions. Wrap in waxed paper. Chill thoroughly. Roll out on a lightly-floured board using a light, springy touch. Bake in a hot oven (450 deg. F.) for about 15 minutes.

Flaky Pastry

    3   cups flour
    ½   teaspoon salt
    ½   cup shortening
    ½   cup butter

Sift and measure flour and then sift again with salt. Add cold shortening and blend it in well. Add about one-half of the butter. Cut into the flour mixture until butter is in tiny pieces. Mix with ice-cold water until the dough is dry and soft. Roll out dough into a rectangular shape on floured board and spread with half of the remaining butter. Roll up like a jelly roll and roll out once again, then spread with the remaining butter and roll up again. Wrap in waxed paper and place in refrigerator to cool for several hours.

Roll out to ¼ inch thickness and cover outside of inverted pans. Prick with fork and bake in a hot oven (400 deg. F.) until a delicate brown.

Puff Pastry

    3½ cups sifted flour
    1½ teaspoons salt
    2   cups butter (1 pound)
    1   cup ice water (about)

Mix and sift flour and salt, and cut in ¼ cup butter until evenly mixed in quite coarse particles; add ice water in small amounts to dry ingredients, stirring with fork and tossing aside pieces of dough as soon as they are formed. Turn out on a lightly-floured board and knead about 5 minutes; chill thoroughly.

Cream remaining butter until soft and smooth, and chill; divide dough in half and roll, each into rectangular sheet ⅛ inch thickness. Roll butter on lightly-floured board into rectangular shape and place between two sheets of dough; press edges together. Fold opposite sides to make three folds, one over and the other under, and press edges together; fold other sides in same manner and chill about 1 hour. Pat dough straight with fold, then make quarter turn and pat again; roll as directed; roll again in thin sheet, lifting paste to make sure that it doesn't stick to the board; then fold and chill thoroughly.

Repeat rolling, folding and chilling of dough three more times. If you are not going to use the paste at once roll it in waxed paper and store in refrigerator; when ready to use, roll ¼ to ⅓ inch thick, cut as desired and place on baking sheet rinsed with cold water and thoroughly drained. Prick shapes and chill. Bake in a very hot oven (450 deg. F. to 500 deg. F.) for about 7 minutes, or until paste has risen its full height; then reduce heat to about 350 deg. F. and continue baking for 10 to 20 minutes or until the pastry is delicately browned. Turn it frequently. Makes about 3½ dozen fancy pastries.

Magic Maple Frosting

- 1⅓ cups sweetened condensed milk
- ⅓ cup maple syrup
- 2 cups confectioner's sugar
- Nut meats

Blend sweetened condensed milk and maple syrup thoroughly in the top part of a double boiler. Cook over boiling water for 10 minutes, stirring occasionally until mixture thickens. Cool. Add sifted sugar. Beat until smooth. Spread on cake. Garnish with chopped nut meats. Makes enough to cover top and sides of 2 nine-inch layers or about 24 cup cakes.

Seven Minute Frosting

- 2 egg whites, unbeaten
- 1½ cups sugar
- 5 tablespoons water
- 1½ teaspoons corn syrup
- 1 teaspoon vanilla
- Whole nuts

Put unbeaten egg whites, sugar and water and corn syrup into the top part of a double boiler. Beat with a rotary egg beater until the sugar is dissolved. Place over boiling water, beating constantly with egg beater and cook seven minutes or until the frosting will stand in peaks. Remove from heat. Add flavouring and beat until thick enough to spread. Decorate the top layer of the cake with nuts.

Peach Ginger Shortcake

- ¼ cup butter
- ½ cup brown sugar
- 1 egg
- ½ cup molasses
- ½ cup sour milk
- ½ teaspoon soda
- 1¼ cups flour
- 1 teaspoon baking powder
- ⅛ teaspoon cinnamon
- ⅛ teaspoon ground ginger
- ¼ teaspoon salt

Cream butter and sugar; add egg, well beaten. Add molasses, then sour milk to which soda has been added. Mix well, then add flour and baking powder and spices sifted together.

Bake in greased pan for 25 minutes in a slow oven (325°F). Split while hot and pile fresh, sliced, sugared peaches generously between layers and on top.

A little whipped cream will completely deck out this cake which won a $1 prize for Mrs. A.J. McLeod, Vancouver.

Cakes

A good cake seems to be just the thing to have on hand when you plan to mark some special occasion. The wide variety of cakes makes it possible for them to lend themselves to every event, whether it be a wedding, an anniversary, a birthday, a graduation or just one of your particular days. Then too, when a friend drops in for an afternoon or evening tete-a-tete it's always just a little more friendly if you have a piece of nice cake to serve with a cup of tea.

Be particularly accurate with your ingredients when you make a cake—the best advice would be to get a good tested recipe and follow it carefully. If you use too little shortening you will have a porous cake that will dry quickly, and if you use too much fat ingredient the cake will be heavy of texture. Insufficient flour will make your cake soggy and often cause it to fall, but too much flour might cause the top of the cake to crack.

Fill the cake pan, which is always greased except for sponge or angel cakes, ⅔ full of the batter. Be sure that the batter is spread well out towards the edges of the cake pan if you would have a cake of even depth.

In baking fruit cake be sure to dredge fruits well in flour to prevent them from sinking to the bottom of the cake.

Frosting is important on many cakes because it finishes them off besides giving extra flavour. The cake should be cold and free from all loose crumbs before you attempt to ice it. Be sure that the surface of the cake is level and then start by frosting the sides first, spreading the icing lightly from the top edges. Then ice the top centre and work out towards the edges, making swirls and folds with a spatula.

Daffodil Cake

White Part:

- ½ cup cake flour
- 1¼ cup egg whites
- ¼ teaspoon salt
- 1 teaspoon cream of tartar
- 1 cup plus 2 tablespoons fruit sugar
- ½ teaspoon vanilla

Yellow Part:

- 5 egg yolks
- ⅔ cup cake flour
- ¼ teaspoon salt
- 1 teaspoon orange juice

Sift flour 4 times. Beat egg whites with ¼ teaspoon salt until foamy, add cream of tartar, and continue beating until stiff but not dry. Add sugar gradually, using a folding motion with slotted spoon.

Divide this mixture into 2 parts, leaving a little more than half for the white part.

Into white part fold ½ cup flour and vanilla. Into other part fold egg yolks which have been beaten until thick and lemon coloured. Add flour, salt and orange juice. Mix each part just enough to blend ingredients. Put by teaspoons into an ungreased angel cake tin, alternating white and yellow mixture. Bake in a slow oven (300°F to 310°F) for 1 hour to 1 hour and 10 minutes.

When done invert pan, allow to stand 1 hour to cool. Ice with seven minute icing to which has been added a few drops of yellow colouring, and a few drops of almond essence for flavouring. Swirl icing to make more attractive, decorate with tiny silver balls.

The recipe for this attractive spring cake won a prize for Miss Dora Williamson, Victoria.

Cookies

Chocolate Cookies

- 1⅛ cups flour
- ¼ teaspoon salt
- ½ teaspoon baking soda
- ½ cup butter
- ¾ cup brown and white sugar mixed
- 1 egg
- ½ teaspoon vanilla
- ½ cup walnuts
- ¼ pound sweetened chocolate (cut in small pieces)

Measure and sift dry ingredients. Cream butter and sugar together; add beaten egg and vanilla. Then add dry ingredients, nuts and the chocolate last. Fold these in well.

Drop by teaspoonfuls on greased cookie sheet, and bake in a hot oven for 15 minutes.

The recipe for these dainty little cookies won a prize for Mrs. Ray A. Weaver of Cranberry Lake, Powell River.

"My Ideal" Cookies

- 1½ cups white sugar
- ½ cup butter
- ⅓ teaspoon salt
- 1 teaspoon cinnamon
- 1 teaspoon nutmeg
- 2 egg yolks
- ½ cup sweet milk
- 2 teaspoons baking powder
- 2½ cups pastry flour

Cream sugar, butter, salt and spices and then add egg yolks. Pour in milk and add flour and baking powder to make a soft dough. Roll pieces of dough (size of large marbles) into a ball, and roll balls in granulated sugar, coating all sides.

Place on greased cookie sheet one inch apart and bake in a 375 degrees F. oven to a pale brown colour. This recipe makes 60 cookies.

These little delights can be varied by cutting up a little candied ginger or chopped cherries and adding to dough; or the cookies spread on the pan can be made to look like macaroons by adding another ½ cup of flour to the recipe.

"Fold in sweetened apple sauce to the stiffly beaten egg whites which are left over from this cookie recipe and you will have a dessert with which to serve the cookies," says Mrs. Ernest Robinson, Kamloops, who won a prize for this recipe.

Oatmeal Date Cookies

  2 cups oatmeal or rolled oats
  2 cups flour
  1 cup butter (melted)
  1 cup brown sugar
  ½ teaspoon baking powder
  1 teaspoon cream of tartar
     Pinch of salt

Mix ingredients as usual, and use just enough milk to make a stiff dough. Roll out thin and bake at 375 deg. F. for 7 to 8 minutes and then place together with date filling.

Date Filling:

  2½ cups chopped dates
  2   tablespoons sugar
  ½   cup water

Cook these three ingredients for about five minutes.

Mrs. Violet L. Hills of Alberni wins $1 for her favourite cookie recipe.

Dream Bars

  ½ cup butter
  ½ cup brown sugar
  1½ cups flour

Mix together to a crumbly mass like pie crust. Put into a buttered 9-inch pan. Bake in a moderate oven (350°F) until slightly browned. Then mix together:

  1 cup brown sugar
  2 eggs
  1 teaspoon vanilla
  ½ teaspoon baking powder
  ¼ teaspoon salt
  1 or 1½ cups coconut
  ½ or 1½ cups nut meats, chopped

Pour this over baked mixture; bake again at 350°F until browned (20 to 25 minutes). When cool, cut in bars.

The recipe for these cookies won a prize for Mrs. Joe Labinsky, New Westminster.

Coconut Macaroons

  1 cup white sugar
  3 tablespoons cold water
  1 tablespoon Lily White syrup
  2 egg whites stiffly beaten with a pinch of salt
  2 tablespoons cornstarch
  3 cups coconut

Put sugar, water and syrup into a saucepan. Stir until dissolved, then boil without stirring until syrup spins a fine thread (250 deg. F.).

To stiffly beaten egg whites add the cornstarch. Beat again until mixture peaks. Pour hot syrup over egg whites, beating constantly until very fluffy. Add coconut; blend. Drop by teaspoonfuls on cookie sheet well oiled. Bake in slow oven (325 deg. F.) for 15 to 20 minutes. Makes 36 macaroons.

Mrs. James Hargraves of Williams Lake, won a $1 prize for this cookie recipe.

Puddings

While a pudding is certainly not the most important part of a meal still there is something about a good pudding that sends the family from the table with a satisfied feeling.

Most people will agree that even the best meal tastes just so much better if it is topped off with just the right dessert. And a dessert must be just the "right" one to even hope for general approval. If the meal tends to be on the heavy side then indeed the accompanying pudding must be light but if the meal is something simple the dessert may take a more substantial form.

For the warmer days in summer a light and fluffy cottage pudding with a tasty lemon sauce is far more suitable than a steamed fruit pudding and caramel sauce. However, in winter, when the colder breezes blow, a slice of hot, steamed pudding is often a welcome finale to dinner.

Many a wise young woman makes desserts that can be served twice. Lots of delicious puddings are good both hot and cold—one way today, the other tomorrow. Of course, souffles must be served very hot because they start to fall as soon as they are taken from the oven, and a good many steamed puddings will become soggy if they are left standing until cold.

Fruit puddings are always popular and in a province like British Columbia where fruit is so plentiful it shouldn't be any trick to prepare appetizing and nutritious desserts in this form.

To make a delicious sauce for puddings, whip bits of left-over jelly until light, and combine with chopped nut meats and a little whipped cream.

Peach Snow

        1   can (No. 2) peaches or 2 cups stewed fresh
            peaches, sweetened
        1   teaspoon lemon juice
     2½   tablespoons cornstarch
        2   egg whites
       ½   cup whipped cream

Drain the peaches, force through a sieve and add lemon juice. Combine juice and pulp; this should make up about 2½ cups. Heat and stir in cornstarch which has been mixed to a smooth paste, with ¼ cup cold water. Cook, stirring constantly till thick and clear and there is no taste of raw starch. Fold in the stiffly-beaten egg whites then the cream which has been whipped until stiff. Turn into a cold damp mould and chill until firm. Serve unmoulded, garnished with a few peach slices. This makes six servings.

The recipe for this light and delightful dessert won a prize for Evelyn Harris, Vancouver.

Apple Raspberry Topsy Turvy

In an 8-inch square pan melt 2 to 3 tablespoons butter. Sprinkle with ½ cup brown sugar. In the pan arrange thick cored apple slices or rings; heat in oven while preparing batter and cover with ¾ cup well-drained canned raspberries before turning in the batter.

Batter:

     1¾   cups sifted flour
        3   teaspoons baking powder
       ½   teaspoon salt
     5⅓   tablespoons butter or butter and shortening
            mixed
       ⅔   cup fine granulated sugar
        1   egg
       ½   cup milk

Measure flour, add baking powder and salt. Cream butter and gradually blend in sugar. Beat and add egg. Add dry ingredients, alternately with milk. Spread over apples and raspberries in pan and bake in moderate oven, about 350°F for about 50 minutes.

Turn upside-down in hot serving dish, cut in squares and serve with cream. This recipe makes 9 to 12 servings.

Miss Vera Anderson of Fraser Arm suggests several fruit variations for the recipe which won her a $1 prize. These include inch thick banana slices with chopped candied ginger and broken walnuts; canned pineapple slices with maraschino cherries, drained; or drained unsweetened apricots and prunes alternately placed in prepared pan.

Maple Tapioca

        2   cups milk
       ⅓   cup quick cooking tapioca
            Pinch of salt
        1   cup maple syrup
        1   egg

Cook the milk, tapioca, salt and maple syrup together for 15 minutes in double boiler, stirring frequently. Add beaten egg yolks and cook for two minutes longer. Let cool slightly then stir in well-beaten egg white. Place in cool place until serving time. Serve with whipped cream, flavoured with vanilla. Serves four.

This nutritious dessert won a prize for Mrs. Knowles, Vancouver.

Sherbet

        1   tablespoon gelatine
       ½   cup water
     2½   cups scalded milk
     1¼   cups sugar
       ¼   cup lemon juice
        1   cup fruit pulp or juice
        2   egg whites

Dissolve the gelatine in water and add to the milk and sugar. Chill. Add lemon juice, fruit pulp and egg. Whites should be beaten stiff. Put in the refrigerator and stir two or three times while freezing to make it more creamy.

This delicious sherbet recipe won a prize for Helen Bevington of Hammond.

Plum Marmalade

  4 pounds plums
  4 oranges
  1 lemon
  4 pounds sugar

Stone plums and put through mincer. Slice oranges and lemon very thin, removing seeds. Mix fruits and sugar and let stand overnight and cook until thick, stirring frequently. Pour into hot, sterilized jars and seal with parawax when cold.

A little marmalade will pep up many a winter breakfast. This recipe won a prize for Miss Josephine Rowa, Vancouver.

Pear Marmalade

  4 lemons
 12 pounds pears
  ½ pound crystallized ginger or 1 small piece for flavouring
  8 pounds sugar

Boil lemons in clear water until peel is soft. Remove and take out seeds, then chop fine. Peel and core pears; cut into narrow strips. Chop ginger fine. Put all ingredients into preserving kettle and simmer gently for two hours. Bottle and seal.

This recipe for a seasonal marmalade won a prize for Mrs. C.C. Wilcox, Vancouver.

Jams and Jellies

Spiced Blueberry and Peach Jam

  4 pounds ripe peaches
  1 quart blueberries
  ½ cup water
 5½ cups sugar (2½ lbs.)
  ½ teaspoon salt
  2 sticks cinnamon (4 ins.)
  1 teaspoon whole cloves
  ½ teaspoon whole allspice

Wash, peel and pit peaches and put through food chopper, using coarse cutter. Measure 4 cups of peaches. Pick over and wash blueberries and measure 4 cups of the prepared fruit. Combine fruits and water and bring to a boil in covered saucepan. Cook 10 minutes, stirring occasionally. Add sugar, salt and the spices in a cheesecloth bag. Cook slowly until sugar dissolves and mixture boils. Boil hard 10 minutes or until fruit is clear and of the desired consistency. Stir often, remove spices and skim. Fill hot, sterilized jars and seal. Yields 7½ pints or 9 6-oz. glasses.

Here is a jam with a "different" and delicious flavour. The recipe won a prize for Mrs. B.M. Clarke, Vancouver.

Raspberry Jam

  4 cups raspberries
  4 cups sugar
     Juice of 1 lemon

Boil the raspberries and sugar together until slightly thickened. Add the lemon juice and cook one minute more. Pour immediately into hot glasses and seal.

Pickles and Relishes

Pickled Onions

    2 quarts tiny silver skinned onions
    1 cup salt
    4 tablespoons allspice
    3 tablespoons peppercorns
    2 tablespoons white mustard seed
    1 quart vinegar
    1 cup sugar
    ¼ cup silver horseradish root

Peel onions, cover with cold water, and let stand overnight. In the morning drain and cover with brine made by dissolved salt in four cups boiling water. Let stand for three days. Drain and cover with clear boiling water. Let stand 30 minutes. Drain and let stand in alum water for two hours. Rinse in clear water. Tie spices in a small cheesecloth bag and add to vinegar and sugar in preserving kettle. Add horseradish root and bring to the boiling point. Add onions and bring again to boiling point. Pack onions in hot, sterilized jars and pour over vinegar to cover. Seal and store in a cool, dark place.

Mushroom Ketchup

Use 4 quarts mushrooms, peeled and sliced; add 1 cup water and 1 bay leaf and cook until soft; then press through a sieve. Add 1 cup vinegar, 1 tablespoon salt, ¼ teaspoon each ground cayenne, cloves and mace, and ½ tablespoon ground cinnamon. Cook about one-half hour. Pour into clean hot jars and seal. Approximate yield is 2 quarts.

Pickled Peaches

    6 pounds peaches
    3 pounds sugar
    1 pint cider vinegar
    1 cup water
    2 tablespoons cloves, heads removed
    2 sticks cinnamon

Pare large peaches and weigh. Boil sugar, vinegar, water and spices tied in a bag about 12 minutes until clear. Add peaches, enough for one jar at a time, and cook until thoroughly heated.

Lift out and place in jars and cover to keep hot. Continue same way until all peaches are cooked. Cook syrup down a little and pour hot over peaches, and then seal immediately.

Green Gooseberry Chutney

    1 quart green gooseberries
    1 pint vinegar
    2 cups brown sugar
    3 teaspoons salt
    ½ teaspoon turmeric powder
    2 teaspoons ginger
    ½ teaspoon cayenne
    1 teaspoon mustard
    1 pound onions
    1 pound raisins

Simmer these ingredients slowly for one hour and then bottle and seal.

This simple chutney recipe won a prize for Mrs. O. Hughes, Langley Prairie.

SERVE DELICIOUS MEALS Without Spending a Lot

Edith Adam's Prize Winners' 8th Annual Cook Book

1942

PREFACE

This Eighth Annual Edition of The Vancouver Sun Cook Book appears in a world that is vastly different in outlook from that of previous editions. This is a world where liberty-loving peoples are forced to defend the rights of their inheritance with every ounce of human endurance.

We are proud in the realization that Canadians are among those who carry the torch of democracy far beyond the reach of all who dare to challenge its right of illumination.

Each and every one of us has a part in this national scheme of war time efficiency. Canadian men and some Canadian women have found their places on the front lines of "active service," but fortunately the majority of the women of Canada can serve with equal thoroughness on the "home front." The strength of a nation is deep-rooted in its homes, and so it is that men of strong arms and stout hearts go out from Canadian hearths.

The Canadian woman, armed with a knowledge of home nutrition and domestic economy, wields a powerful weapon in the defense of her country and democracy. She has been quick to recognize her sacred responsibility. For this reason the preserving season of 1941 took on a new and deeper significance. The idea of preservation of food became something of a patriotic act as well as an intelligent practice of home economy. Waste has no part in our national scene.

"Vitamins for Victory" might well be the motto adapted by every homemaker in our Dominion, as with a nutrition yardstick she measures the health and ultimate strength of these free peoples.

This little cook book is the direct creation of the capable British Columbia homemakers by their contribution of seasonal and economical recipes. If it serves to assist other homemakers in their task of preparing food for the "home front" then it will have fulfilled its mission.

Edith Adams

Cookery Editor

Fish

Finnan Haddie in Milk

    1   finnan haddie (about 2 pounds)
    1   cup water
    1   cup milk (warmed)
    2   tablespoons butter

Cover the fish with water and simmer until thoroughly heated. Drain and add 1 cup warm milk and two tablespoons of butter. Place in the oven to keep warm but do not leave long enough for the milk to curdle. Serve with a garnish of bacon curls if desired. Serves 6.

Herring, Nova Scotia Style

Scale and clean herring; add spice, bay leaves, celery seed, cloves, salt and pepper. Barely cover with water and boil a short time until the fish are tender. Drain off one-half the liquid; add an equal amount of vinegar and let stand a few hours before serving cold.

Herring recipes are apparently hard to get so we welcome this one from Mrs. V.G. Copp, New Westminster.

Light Fluffy Fish Batter

    1   cup flour
    2   teaspoons baking powder
    ½   teaspoon salt
    1   egg, separated
    1   tablespoon butter
    ½   cup lukewarm water

Put flour, baking powder and salt sifted into basin. Break egg yolk in centre and mix thoroughly. Add butter which has been melted in the water. Beat egg white stiff and fold it in. Dip fish in batter and fry in deep fat. Serves 5.

Mrs. Moriez, Nanaimo, won a prize with this recipe.

Fish Sauces

Caper Sauce

    ⅓   cup butter
    4   tablespoons flour
    1½   cups water
    1   teaspoon salt
    2   teaspoons lemon juice
    2   tablespoons capers
    ⅓   cup cream
    2   eggs, slightly beaten

Melt butter, add flour and blend thoroughly. Add water and cook, stirring constantly, until the mixture thickens. Add salt, lemon juice and capers. Then add cream mixed with the slightly-beaten eggs. Continue cooking over low heat two minutes longer. Serve hot with baked or boiled fish.

Drawn Butter Sauce

    ⅓   cup butter
    4   tablespoons flour
    2   cups boiling water or fish stock
    ¼   teaspoon salt

Melt 4 tablespoons butter, add flour and blend thoroughly. Add water gradually and cook 5 minutes, or until thick and smooth, stirring constantly. When ready to serve, add salt and remaining butter, beating well. Serve with fried or broiled fish.

Norwegian Sauce

Mayonnaise with finely grated horseradish added. Good with cold, boiled fish or fish salad.

Cucumber Sauce

Mayonnaise with grated cucumber and seasonings. Good with cold fish or fish salads.

Meats

The main meal of the day for most people includes some form of meat, and the fact that we spend more money for this item in our diet than any other food should prompt us to buy to the very best advantage.

Once the home-maker acknowledges "his" or "their" preference in the meat line it is a simple matter to plan menus—the various kinds and cuts give such choice. And still we haven't mentioned the "inside," smoked and pickled meats! It must be admitted, though, that the different cuts of meat should coincide with their appropriate cooking method. We doubt if anyone has become famous for grilling a flank steak to substitute for a tenderloin; but given a flank steak, a little flour, seasoning, etc., and our own unhurried time, you can give that tenderloin an awful run for his money!

The following guides will prove a help in meat buying and its preparation.

One pound of boneless meat, such as ground meat or liver, serves 4.

One pound of meat with little bone, round steak or round bone pot roasts, serves 3.

One pound of meat with moderate amount of bone, short ribs, shoulder cuts, rump, brisket or plate, serves 2.

The tender cuts are best cooked by dry heat:

1. Broiling: Cooking by direct heat at a temperature of 475 deg. F.–500 deg. F.
2. Pan-broiling: Cooking in a very hot frying pan with no fat.
3. Pan-frying: Cooking in a hot frying pan with a small amount of fat.
4. Roasting: Cooking in an open roasting pan in a moderate oven (300 deg. F.–350 deg. F.) without water.

The less tender cuts are best cooked by moist heat:

1. Braising: The meat is browned on both sides in a small amount of fat either on top of the stove or in a hot oven (425 deg. F.). Water or stock is then added and the meat is covered tightly and cooked either on top of the stove at a low temperature or in the oven (300 deg. F.) for several hours.

2. Stewing: The meat is usually cut into small pieces and cooked in a small amount of hot water at a low temperature for a long period of time.
3. Cooking in Water: Although we speak of "boiled meat" this is incorrect. The meat is immersed in hot water and cooked slowly at a low temperature until tender. Meat used for soup stock is placed in cold water, brought to a simmer and cooked at this temperature.

Pot Roast

Brown 3½ pounds boneless beef in a little bacon fat. Add 2 teaspoons salt, pepper and 1 cup chopped carrots. Also add 1 cup chopped turnips, 1 tablespoon sugar, 1 large tin canned tomatoes, 1 large onion, chopped and 1 tablespoon celery seed.

Cover and simmer over low heat for 3 hours. Thicken the liquid and serve with hot biscuits. Serves 6.

Mrs. E.J. Vandal of Allison Harbor won a prize for this economical recipe.

Smothered Spareribs

        4   pounds spareribs, quite lean
        2   teaspoons salt
        ½   teaspoon pepper
        1   onion, chopped or 2 teaspoons onion salt
        1   tablespoon bacon dripping
        1   tablespoon flour
        ¼   teaspoon chili powder
        3   cups boiling water
        1   cup tomatoes

Cut spareribs into serving pieces; sprinkle with salt, pepper and onion salt. Place the bacon fat in pan and heat. Sear the spareribs to a golden brown; add flour and chili powder to the hot fat until well blended. Stir in boiling water; then stir in tomatoes. Cover and simmer for 1 hour.

Thicken the gravy with a little flour mixed with cold water. Serves 6.

This recipe won a prize for Mrs. C. Stalman, North Vancouver.

Ham Steak Casserole

Cut slices of ham one-quarter of an inch thick. Spread the desired number of servings with stuffing; roll up and fasten with toothpicks. Put in a baking dish and cover with canned apple juice. Bake at 350°F for 40 to 45 minutes.

For stuffing use equal portions of cooked sweet potato and bread crumbs and season with a little onion, salt and pepper and a small piece of butter.

These stuffed ham slices are delicious served with spiced baked pineapple slices. The recipe won a prize for Mrs. C. Keeley, Vancouver.

Stuffed Breast of Veal

    4 pounds breast of veal
    1 cup bread crumbs
    2 slices fat salt pork
    ½ teaspoon pepper
    1 teaspoon thyme
    1 teaspoon salt
    1 teaspoon sweet marjoram

If requested the butcher will prepare the veal for stuffing. If this is not done, make an incision between the ribs and the meat. Fill this cavity with stuffing made from bread crumbs, pork and seasonings. Roast in a very hot oven (500 deg. F.) for 15 minutes, then reduce the heat to 350 deg. F. and allow 20 to 30 minutes per pound of meat. Unless cooked in double roaster, baste every 20 minutes, using the liquid in the bottom of the pan as soon as there is sufficient for basting. Make a gravy from the drippings, using one tablespoon flour and one cup of water to one tablespoon of drippings. Serves 6.

Vegetables

Scalloped Potatoes

    6 medium-sized potatoes
       Salt and pepper
    2 tablespoons flour
    4 tablespoons butter
       Milk

Pare raw potatoes and cut them into thin slices. Place in a baking dish a layer of the potato one-inch deep. Season with salt and pepper and sprinkle a portion of the flour over each layer, adding a part of the butter in bits. Add another layer of the potato and seasoning, as before, and continue until the required amount is used. Add milk until it can be seen between the slices of potato, cover and bake (350 to 400 deg. F.) until potatoes are tender when pierced with a fork (about 1½ hours). Remove cover during the last 15 minutes to brown on top. Serves 6.

Candied Parsnips

Parboil parsnips. Place in baking dish, with 1 or 2 tablespoons butter. Be sure that the vegetables are well coated with melted butter—sprinkle with brown sugar and salt. Bake until tender and golden. This method transforms a somewhat colourless vegetable into an epicurean tidbit.

   Mrs. E.M. Guthro, of Nootka, B.C., won a prize for this unusual recipe.

Sweet Potato Puff

    2 cups mashed sweet potato
    2 tablespoons butter or shortening
       Salt and pepper
    ¼ cup milk or cream
    1 egg

To the mashed potatoes add the melted butter, seasonings and milk. Beat the egg yolk and white separately, add the yolk to the potato mixture and then fold in the white. Put the mixture into a baking dish or individual moulds, set in a pan containing hot water and bake in a 375 deg. F. oven until puffy and brown. Serves 6.

Scalloped Cauliflower

    1   medium cauliflower
    2   hard boiled eggs or 4 tablespoons grated cheese
    1½ cups medium white sauce
        Bread crumbs

Break the cauliflower into flowerets before boiling. Drain. Place a layer of the cooked cauliflower in a greased baking dish, then a layer of egg slices or grated cheese, then a layer of white sauce. Repeat until all the cauliflower is used. Put a layer of crumbs over the top and bake in a moderate oven (350 to 400 deg. F.) for 15 to 30 minutes. Serves 6.

Corn Custard

    2   cups corn (about 6 ears)
    ½   cup water
    1½ cups milk
    1   teaspoon salt
    2   teaspoons sugar
        Few grains pepper
    ¼   cup butter
    2   tablespoons green pepper
    2   eggs, beaten
    6   slices ripe tomato
    1   tablespoon butter

Husk and silk corn and with a sharp knife cut off tops of kernels; with back of knife scrape cobs (in one direction only) until all pulp and milk has been pressed out. Combine corn with water, milk and seasoning; add ¼ cup butter and simmer for 5 minutes. Remove from heat, add green pepper and mixture slowly to beaten eggs. Pour into buttered custard cups; place in a shallow pan of hot water and bake

20 minutes in a 350°F. oven. Saute tomato slices in 1 tablespoon butter until browned and place on top of custards just before serving. Serves six.

This is a tasty way to serve corn. The recipe won a $1 prize for Mrs. Alfred Wood, Nelson.

Casserole and Luncheon Dishes

Cheese Dreams

½ pound Canadian cheese
1 pkg. cream cheese
½ teaspoon baking powder
2 tablespoons butter
1 egg, beaten
Bread, cut into rounds

Mix grated cheese and cream cheese with baking powder, butter and egg. Beat until a very creamy mass. Toast rounds of bread. Spread with cheese mixture. Place under broiler until slightly browned and puffed.

These tasty cheese snacks won a prize for L.R. Stocks, Atlanta, Georgia.

Hot Lobster in Potato Jackets

6 large potatoes
Salt and pepper
2 tablespoons butter
2 tablespoons flour
1 cup milk
¼ teaspoon pepper
½ teaspoon salt
1 cup lobster (6-ounce tin)

Scrub potatoes, rub with melted fat and bake in a hot oven (425 to 450 deg. F.) until done. Cut a slice from top, scoop out the inside and mash; season with salt and pepper and butter.

Melt the 2 tablespoons butter in saucepan, add flour

and blend. Add milk gradually and stir until thickened.

Season with salt and pepper.

Dice lobster, saving claws for garnish and add with mashed potato to sauce.

Pile this mixture back into potato shells and serve while hot. Garnish with lobster claws, sliced cucumber, radishes and parsley. Serves 6.

Mrs. V. Wessels, R.R. No. 3, Cloverdale, won a prize for this recipe.

Seven Layer Dinner

Into a baking dish put one-inch layer of raw potatoes, sliced thin. Then add a fine layer of sliced onion and a one-inch layer of carrots. Next add a layer of uncooked rice (about ¼ cup) and then a can of peas and a one-inch layer of pork sausage (1½ pounds for a nine-inch casserole). Cover all with one can of tomato soup.

Bake in a moderate oven for 1½ hours in a covered dish and then for another half hour uncovered. Serves 6.

This supper recipe won a prize for Mrs. Wesley T. Williamson, Vancouver.

Nut Roast

2 cups ground dried bread crumbs
1 cup ground walnuts
1 teaspoon salt
1 teaspoon sage or savory
Pepper to taste
2 medium onions, chopped fine
1 egg, beaten
1 cup milk
1 heaping tablespoon butter, melted

Mix the dry ingredients first and add the egg, milk and butter. Have the oven of a medium temperature before putting in the roast and cook slowly at 325 deg. F. for 25 minutes. Chopped parsley may be added, if desired. Serves 5.

This nut roast is nice served with tomato sauce or apple sauce, and sandwiches made with it are very tasty.

The recipe won a prize for Miss Alice Potter, North Vancouver.

Macaroni, Cheese and Mushrooms

2 cups macaroni (measured before cooking)
½ teaspoon salt
½ pound mushrooms
½ cup water
2 tablespoons butter
1 pimento, chopped (¼ cup)
1¾ cups white sauce
½ cup grated cheese
6 strips lean bacon

Cook macaroni in boiling salted water until tender. Simmer mushroom skins and peelings in water to make a stock.

Drain. Slice mushroom caps and saute in butter for 5 minutes, reserving 4 or 5. Drain macaroni, add mushrooms, pimento, white sauce in which cheese has been melted. Add ½ cup mushroom stock.

Turn into baking dish. Place bacon strips over top and remaining mushrooms. Bake in hot oven (400°F) 30 to 40 minutes, or until nicely browned. Serves 7 to 8.

White Sauce:
    2 tablespoons butter
    2 tablespoons flour
    ½ teaspoon salt
       Pepper and paprika
    2 cups milk, or 1 cup milk
       and 1 cup vegetable water

Melt butter, blend in flour and seasoning, and when smooth and bubbling add liquids gradually, stirring constantly to prevent lumping. Cook 15 to 20 minutes.

Make in double boiler. Makes 1¾ cups sauce.

This is a tasty Lenten dish that may be used in place of meat. The recipe won a prize for N.L. McDonald, New Westminster.

Salads

"Any cold dish of meat, shellfish, fruit or vegetables, served singly or in a combination and covered with French dressing, mayonnaise or the like." That is the dictionary definition of a salad. You can write your own definition in much more enthusiastic terms when you've had experience in making and eating some delicious salad combinations.

A salad can suit most any occasion or season. It can act merely as a colourful and dainty side-plate at a meal or, with equal ease, assume the main role of a hearty and nutritious dish.

In summer when fruits and vegetables are abundant in British Columbia and the temperature climbs cool, crisp salads are worth twice their weight in gold in reviving wilted appetites. The salads must never have a trace of wilting about them or they lose their coveted role of refreshers. On the other hand, when cool breezes blow and the mercury seeks shelter in the bottom of the thermometer, the wholesome meat and fish salads are ushered to the limelight to balance what might otherwise prove "heavy, unhealthy meals."

Hard-Cooked Egg Dressing
    1   teaspoon mustard
    1   teaspoon salt
    ¼   teaspoon paprika
    ½   teaspoon sugar
    1   egg yolk
    3   hard-cooked eggs
    4   tablespoons oil
    2½ tablespoons vinegar

Mix mustard, salt, paprika, sugar with uncooked egg yolk. Mash yolks of hard-cooked eggs with a fork working them into the mixture. Add oil and vinegar slowly, beating constantly and alternating them. When all is well blended add the chopped whites of the eggs.

This dressing is particularly suitable for mixing with plain greens in a salad bowl. The recipe won a prize for Mrs. Ella Haywood, Vancouver.

Lemon French Dressing
    ½   cup lemon juice
    ½   cup salad oil
    1   teaspoon each salt and paprika
    2   tablespoons sugar or honey

Shake well before serving.

Leaf Lettuce, Country Style
    1   large head garden lettuce
    4 or 5 slices bacon
    ½   cup vinegar
    2   teaspoons sugar
    1   teaspoon salt
            Pepper

Wash and dry the lettuce and tear it into pieces. Dice the bacon and cook it in a frying pan until it is crisp and brown. Add the vinegar and seasonings and bring to the boiling point. Add the lettuce and toss in the hot vinegar until it has wilted. Serve immediately. Serves 4 to 6.

Salmon Salad
    ½   tablespoon salt
    ½   tablespoon dry mustard
    1   tablespoon sugar
    2   eggs
    ¾   cup sweet milk
    ¼   cup white vinegar
    1½ tablespoons gelatine
    ¼   cup cold water
    1   one-pound can salmon

Make a salad dressing of the salt, mustard, sugar, eggs, milk and vinegar. Then soften gelatine in cold water and dissolve it in the hot dressing. Stir constantly to prevent lumping; strain.

Add flaked salmon and turn into moistened mould; chill and then unmould on crisp lettuce bed. Garnish with stuffed olives and celery, diced, and serve with mayonnaise. Serves 6.

Breads

Blueberry Muffins

    ¼ cup shortening
    ⅓ cup sugar
    2 eggs
    2 cups flour
    3 teaspoons baking powder
    1 teaspoon salt
    ⅔ cup milk
    ½ cup blueberries

Cream shortening and sugar together; add beaten eggs and mix well. Sift 1½ cups flour, baking powder and salt, and add alternately with milk to first mixture. Dredge blueberries with ½ cup of flour and stir in lightly.

Bake in greased muffin pans in hot oven (400 deg. F.) for 25 to 30 minutes. This recipe makes 12 large muffins or 24 afternoon tea muffins.

With blueberries in season you should be able to put this recipe to good use. It won a prize for Miss Lillian Burke, Vancouver.

Spice Fig Loaf

    1½ cups brown sugar
    ¾   cup shortening
    2   eggs
    2   cups bread flour
    1   teaspoon soda
    2   teaspoons baking powder
    ¼   teaspoon salt
    2   teaspoons cinnamon
    1   teaspoon nutmeg
    ¾   cup sour milk
    ½   cup chopped cooking figs
    ½   cup chopped walnuts

Sift brown sugar, add creamed shortening, then the beaten eggs. Sift three times the flour, soda, baking powder, salt, cinnamon and nutmeg. Add to the mixture alternately with the sour milk. The figs should be soaked in warm water for 15 minutes, then chopped. Add the nuts and figs last. Bake in a 350 deg. F. oven in a loaf pan for 45 to 60 minutes.

Mrs. Katherine A. Graham, Vancouver, won a prize for this recipe.

Pancakes

Mix 2 cups flour, 2 tablespoons sugar, ¾ teaspoon salt, and 3 teaspoons baking powder. Beat 2 eggs and add 1 cup milk. Add to dry ingredients. Add 3 tablespoons molasses and 4 tablespoons melted shortening. Beat well. Bake on hot griddle. Serves 4.

For a breakfast treat try these pancakes. The recipe won a prize for Mrs. E. Markle, Vancouver.

Butter Horns

Put 2 cups milk in saucepan and add ½ cup sugar, 1 teaspoon salt, ¾ cup butter and ¾ cup shortening. Bring to the boil, then take off stove and cool. While this mixture is cooling break up 1 yeast cake in ½ cup lukewarm water; to it add 1 teaspoon sugar. Let it rise in cup until milk mixture has cooled to lukewarm, then add 2 beaten eggs and yeast to milk.

Sift 7½ cups flour into saucepan and add to it the milk-egg-yeast mixture. Let rise double in bulk, knead down and let rise again. Then roll out on floured board and brush with melted butter. Cut in ¾ inch strips and roll up like jelly roll and put into pans about 3½ inches apart. Let rise again until light. Bake at 400 deg. F. for 10 to 15 minutes. Then when cool spread with butter icing and dip in crushed walnuts. Makes 3 dozen butter horns.

This original recipe won a prize for Mrs. A. Lingnau, Vancouver.

Pastry

"Never-Fail" Pastry

Pour one-half cup boiling water over one-half pound shortening and mix into paste. Then add 3 cups sifted flour into which 1 teaspoon baking powder and 1 teaspoon salt have been added. Allow to stand 24 hours; then use as required.

This reliable and simple recipe for pastry won a prize for Mrs. A.H. Harwood, Lower Capilano.

Gingersnap Crust

- ½ cup butter
- ¼ cup powdered sugar
- 1½ cups gingersnaps, crushed
- ½ cup browned chopped almonds

Cream butter and sugar together and blend in crumbs. Pack firmly into pie plate. Sprinkle chopped almonds on top of crumbs and pour in filling. Chill and spread with whipped cream. Serves 6.

Pumpkin Chiffon Pie with Gingersnap Crust

- 1 tablespoon gelatin
- ¼ cup cold water
- 3 eggs
- 1 cup sugar
- 1½ cups cooked and drained pumpkin
- ½ cup milk
- ½ teaspoon salt
- ½ teaspoon ginger
- ½ teaspoon nutmeg
- 1 teaspoon cinnamon
- 1 cup whipping cream

Soak gelatin in cold water; beat egg yolks, then add ½ cup sugar, pumpkin, milk, salt and spices. Cook in double boiler until of custard consistency, stirring constantly. Add gelatin to hot custard, stir well until dissolved, then cool. When mixture begins to thicken fold in stiffly beaten egg whites to which remaining sugar has been added. Pour into pie shell. Chill. Spread with whipped cream.

Plum Tarts

Cook 10 or 12 plums in ¼ cup water until soft and tender. Drain. To the juice add ⅜ cup sugar and 2 tablespoons of cornstarch. When mixed well add plum pulp and cook over double boiler for 10 minutes or until no taste of raw cornstarch remains. When thick add 1 tablespoon butter, and ½ teaspoon cinnamon. Fill prebaked tart shells and top with whipped cream. Makes six tarts.

The recipe for these seasonal tarts won a prize for Mrs. L. Hibberd, Hollyburn.

Mock Cherry Pie

Cook 1 cup cranberries, ¾ cup raisins and ⅔ cup water together until soft; add ¾ cup white sugar and stir until dissolved.

Stir 1 tablespoon cornstarch and ⅓ cup cold water and add to mixture with ¼ teaspoon (scant) almond flavouring and a pinch of salt. Let cool before putting between crusts. Bake at 450 deg. F. for 15 minutes and at 425 deg. F. for 10 minutes longer. Makes sufficient filling for one small pie.

This recipe is an excellent substitute for cherry pie. It won a prize for Mrs. T.M. Lyall, Vancouver.

Cakes

Chocolate Mint Roll

6 tablespoons cake flour, sifted
½ teaspoon baking powder
¼ teaspoon salt
¾ cup sifted sugar
4 egg whites, stiffly beaten
4 egg yolks, beaten until thick and lemon-coloured
1 teaspoon vanilla
2 squares unsweetened chocolate, melted

Sift flour once, measure, add baking powder and salt and sift together three times. Fold sugar gradually into egg whites. Fold in egg yolks and vanilla. Fold in flour gradually. Then beat in chocolate, gently but thoroughly. Turn into pan which has been greased (a 15 by 10-inch pan), lined with paper to within one-half inch of edge and again greased.

Bake in hot oven (400 deg. F.) for 15 minutes or until done. Quickly cut off crisp edges of cake and turn out on cloth covered with powdered sugar. Remove paper.

Spread half of mint frosting over cake and roll as for jelly roll. Wrap in cloth and cool for 5 minutes. Cover with remaining frosting. When frosting is set cover with bitter-sweet coating made by melting 2 additional squares of unsweetened chocolate with 2 teaspoons butter.

Mint Frosting:

2 egg whites, unbeaten
1½ cups sugar
5 tablespoons water
1½ teaspoons light corn syrup
Green colouring
⅛ teaspoon peppermint extract

Mix egg whites, sugar, water and corn syrup in top part of double boiler, beating with rotary beater until thoroughly mixed. Place over rapidly boiling water and beat for 7 minutes or until frosting will stand in peaks. Add colouring gradually to hot frosting to give a delicate tint. Remove from boiling water; add flavouring and beat until thick enough to spread. Use as filling for jelly roll. Serves 8.

Mrs. Margaret Bunch, Vancouver, won a prize for this recipe.

Blueberry Cake Dessert

¼ cup shortening
¼ cup sugar
1 egg
1 cup flour
¼ teaspoon salt
1½ teaspoons baking powder
¼ cup milk
¼ teaspoon vanilla
1½ cups fresh blueberries

Follow the usual cake method and pour into an 8-inch square pan. Cover with the blueberries and then the following topping:

Topping:

⅓ cup flour
⅛ teaspoon salt
2 tablespoons butter
½ cup sugar

Mix flour and salt; cut in butter and add sugar. Bake the cake in a 375°F oven for about 30 minutes. Serve with blueberry sauce.

Blueberry Sauce:

1½ tablespoons flour
⅓ cup sugar
¼ teaspoon salt
¾ cup water
1 cup blueberries
2 tablespoons butter
1 tablespoon lemon juice

Mix flour, sugar and salt in a saucepan. Add water and blueberries. Cook over a low heat until thickened, stirring constantly; add butter and lemon juice.

This tasty way of using the seasonal blueberries won a prize for Miss L. Gracey, Vancouver.

Nutty Cake

1 cup brown sugar
⅓ cup butter
1 egg
Rind and juice of orange
1½ cups flour
¼ teaspoon salt
1½ teaspoons baking powder
1 cup chopped walnuts
½ cup milk

Mix in the usual way and after spreading the batter in a greased pan cover with the following topping:

½ cup brown sugar
½ cup rolled walnuts
½ teaspoon cinnamon

Bake in a moderate (350°F) oven for half an hour.

Mrs. Harold V. Cook, Vancouver, won a prize for this cake recipe.

Cookies

Chocolate Nut Wafers

  1 cup sugar
  2 squares unsweetened chocolate, melted
  ½ cup melted butter
  2 eggs, beaten
  ½ cup flour, sifted
  ½ teaspoon vanilla
     Chopped nuts

Mix the ingredients and blend them together. Spread thinly on greased cookie sheet, then cover with chopped nuts. Bake slowly in a 325°F oven for 25 minutes. When cold cut in squares.

This simple cookie recipe won a prize for Mrs. A.E. Kennedy, Vancouver.

Ribbon Cookies

  2½ cups flour
  1½ teaspoons baking powder
  ½ teaspoon salt
  1½ cups sugar
  1 cup butter or shortening
  1 teaspoon vanilla
  1 egg, beaten
  ¼ cup each of candied cherries and broken pecan nuts
  1 ounce milk chocolate, melted
  2 tablespoons grated orange rind

Sift flour, measure and sift twice with baking powder and salt. Cream sugar and shortening until light, add vanilla and egg and beat until smooth and fluffy. Add flour mixture a little at a time and mix thoroughly. Divide dough into three portions, add chopped cherries to one part, nut and chocolate to the second part and the orange rind to the third part.

Line a small bread pan with heavy waxed paper, pack the chocolate and nut mixture in the bottom as evenly as possible; over this pack the cherry dough and top it with the orange rind mixture, cover with waxed paper and chill in the refrigerator or ice box overnight.

When ready to bake, turn out of pan and slice very thin, place on lightly greased cookie sheet and bake in a hot oven (375°F) about 10 minutes or until lightly browned. Cool a little before taking off the sheet as they break very easily. Makes 8 dozen cookies.

This dough may be stored in the refrigerator or ice box for a few days and baked as desired.

The recipe won a prize for Mrs. W. Leigh Waring, Vancouver.

Grandma's Sour Milk Cookies

  2 cups sugar
  1 cup butter
  2 eggs
  1 cup sour milk
  1 teaspoon soda
  6 cups bread flour
  ¼ teaspoon salt

Mix all together and roll out. Sprinkle with sugar and cut with a large cookie cutter. Bake in a 400°F oven. Makes about 4 dozen cookies.

This cookie has good keeping qualities and since it is not rich or sweet it is particularly suitable for small children. The recipe won a prize for Peggy Richter, New Westminster.

Butterscotch Squares

  ¼ cup butter
  1 cup brown sugar
  1 egg
  ¼ cup flour
  1 teaspoon baking powder
  ¼ teaspoon salt
  1½ teaspoons vanilla
  ½ cup chopped walnuts or 1 cup of walnuts, if desired

Cook butter and sugar until well blended. Cool to lukewarm; add egg, unbeaten and beat well. Add flour sifted with baking powder and salt. Beat and add vanilla and nut meats. Blend and spread like fudge in shallow pan. Bake for 25 minutes in a moderate oven (350°F). Cut in about 36 squares.

The recipe for these little tea-time snacks won a prize for Mrs. H. Gordon Findlay, Prince Rupert.

Puddings and Sauces

Steamed Preserved Ginger Pudding

8 tablespoons butter
½ cup sugar
2 eggs
2 cups general purpose flour
3 teaspoons baking powder
1 teaspoon salt
½ cup water
3 ounces preserved ginger
3 tablespoons ginger juice

Cream butter and sugar. Add eggs, well beaten, then flour and baking powder, salt, sifted together, alternately with the water.

Cut the ginger into small pieces and add, then add the ginger juice. Put into a pudding mould and steam for about 1¼ hours. Serves 8 to 10 people.

The preserved ginger gives this pudding a nice flavour. The recipe won a prize for Mrs. H.W. Stones, Burton.

Gooseberry Delight

2 pounds gooseberries
1 cup brown sugar
1 teaspoon butter
1¼ cups pastry flour, well sifted
1¼ teaspoons baking powder
2 tablespoons shortening
¼ teaspoon salt
½ cup sugar
2 eggs, separated and beaten
1 teaspoon vanilla
½ cup milk

Place the gooseberries, brown sugar and butter in a large round dish. Mix together the remaining ingredients and put on the top of the gooseberries; bake for 50 to 60 minutes in a 350°F oven. Turn out upside down on a plate and spread with sweetened and flavoured whipped cream. Serves 12.

If this pudding is served with plain cream use a little more sugar over the gooseberries. The recipe won a prize for Mrs. Clarence Newby, Sardis.

Fresh Strawberry Mousse

¼ cup orange juice
½ cup sugar
1 cup thoroughly crushed strawberries
1 cup whipping cream
1 egg white
   Pinch of salt

Add the orange juice and sugar to the strawberries. Heat until the sugar is dissolved. Cool.

Whip the cream. Fold in the stiffly-beaten egg white, to which salt has been added. Add the crushed strawberries. Stir well. Turn into freezing tray and freeze without stirring. Or turn into mould, pack in ice and salt and let stand three hours. Serves six.

This dessert recipe won a prize for Mrs. R.S. Sears, Kamloops.

Blackberry Buckle

Cream ½ cup shortening and ½ cup sugar. Add 1 beaten egg and mix well. Sift 2 cups flour, ¼ teaspoon salt and 2 teaspoons baking powder. Add this to the creamed mixture alternately with ½ cup milk. Pour into greased 8-inch layer cake pan and sprinkle 2 cups fresh blackberries over the batter. Mix ½ cup sugar, ½ cup flour, ½ teaspoon cinnamon and ¼ cup butter until crumbly. Sprinkle over blackberries. Bake in a moderate oven (350 deg. F.) for about 50 minutes. Cut in wedges and serve hot.

This seasonal recipe won a prize for H.M. Summers, Nanaimo.

Jams and Jellies

Gooseberry Bar-Le Duc

Select one quart of gooseberries that are not quite ripe. Wash, drain and remove the tails. Put 3 cups of sugar in a saucepan with an inch wide strip of fresh orange and lemon peel. Add one cup boiling water, stir over fire until boiling, then boil for 8 minutes without stirring. Add the gooseberries and boil slowly for about 15 minutes or until the juice is thick enough to coat the spoon. The berries should remain whole. Skim out the fruit peel. Put into jars.

Miss Agnes Spence, Courtenay, won a prize for this recipe.

Red or Black Currant Jam

    4   cups (two pounds) crushed fruit
    ½   cup water
    7½ cups (3¼ lbs.) sugar
    ½   bottle fruit pectin

To prepare fruit: Crush thoroughly or grind about 2 pounds of fully ripe fruit; measure into large kettle. With red currants add ½ cup water; stir until mixture boils (with black currants use ¾ cup water). Simmer, covered, for 15 minutes. Add sugar, mix well and bring to a full rolling boil over hottest fire. Stir constantly before and while boiling. Boil hard 1 minute. Remove from fire and stir in fruit pectin. Skim; pour quickly. Paraffin and cover at once. Makes about 11 glasses (6 fluid ounces each).

Rhubarb and Strawberry Jam

    1   quart rhubarb, cut into pieces
    1   quart strawberries, cut into pieces
    4   cups sugar

Mix the fruit and sugar and let stand for an hour. Bring to the boiling point and cook rapidly for about 30 minutes or until thick. Stir frequently to prevent burning. Turn into clean hot fruit jars and seal, or put in jelly glasses and cover with melted paraffin or transparent seals.

Loganberry Jam

Partially crush 4 quarts loganberries in a large kettle. Heat slowly until the juice flows and then rapidly boil the juice down to one-half the original quantity. Measure precooked fruit; add ⅔ cup sugar to each cup fruit. Boil rapidly until thick and clear, stirring to prevent burning. When the jam is sufficiently cooked it will sheet from a spoon. Pour into hot, sterilized jars and seal. Makes 14 (6 ounce) glasses.

Pickles

Mixed Sweet Pickles

2 quarts cucumbers, cut in about 1-inch pieces
3 pounds small onions (pickling)
2 heads cauliflower

Place in layers and sprinkle with salt, not too liberally (use 1 scant cup of salt) and leave overnight. In the morning drain thoroughly and rinse if too salty. Pour 1 cup of vinegar over them.

In another kettle boil the following:

3 pints vinegar
4 cups sugar or slightly less
2 tablespoons celery seed
2 tablespoons mustard seed
2 tablespoons turmeric seed
1 tablespoon ground cinnamon
2 tablespoons mixed pickling spice tied in a cloth bag and remove after boiling all for 15 minutes.

Pour the boiling hot dressing over the pickles and bring to boiling point and let simmer 3 minutes. Bottle and seal in hot, sterilized jars.

If you desire ¾ cup flour and ⅓ cup mustard may be mixed with 1 cup cooked dressing and added.

This recipe won a prize for Mrs. M.A. Clarke, Burnaby.

Pickled Beets

48 tiny beets (12 to a jar)
1 quart cider vinegar
1 cup water
1 cup sugar
2 tablespoons salt
1 pint pickling onions

Wash beets and boil about 45 minutes; drain, cover with cold water and rub off skins. Simmer remaining ingredients until onions are tender and then pour over the beets packed into hot, sterilized jars. Seal. Yields about four pints.

Red Cabbage Pickle

Wash 1 head of cabbage. Remove outside leaves and shred the others fine. Put a layer in a crock and sprinkle with a layer of salt. Repeat until the crock is full. Let stand for 2 days, turning over several times to drain it well.

Boil 2 cups vinegar, 1 blade of mace, 6 cloves, ½ teaspoon whole pepper and ¼ cup sugar. Pour boiling hot over the pickle and seal in hot glass jars.

Icicle Pickles

4 medium cucumbers (10 to 12 inches)
3 cups vinegar
1 cup water
¼ cup salt
1 teaspoon powdered alum
1 cup sugar
1 teaspoon celery seed
1 teaspoon white mustard seed

Quarter the cucumbers lengthwise and soak for four hours in water with ice. Drain well. Pack in hot, sterilized jars with one small onion in each jar.

Mix ingredients listed above, and make into syrup. Pour syrup while boiling hot over the cucumbers. Seal immediately.

This recipe makes 2½ quarts of pickles, and was submitted by Mrs. W. Madaski, Salmo.

Cooking for a Crowd

Because of popular request this section, which was published in *The Vancouver Sun*, is reprinted here with the hope that it will help others who cook for a crowd.

Far be it from us to advise any well-established club group on the correct procedure to serve a meal for say 100 persons. Long association and co-operating upsets many rules, successfully! We do think, though, that a brief outline would prove helpful to younger groups and members who have in mind some program dealing with quantity cooking and serving.

First, choose a general chairman—she will have to be experienced, tactful and with lots of time to devote to details and management. Then, of course, a sub-chairman and committees are appointed for each of the various duties. Your organization would be something like this:

(a) A marketing committee.

(b) A food preparation committee.

(c) A dining room service committee.

(d) A cleaning up committee.

When this has been agreed upon each helper should be made familiar with her duties.

Now we'll see how each committee lines up for success.

(a) The marketing committee compares values and prices of the supplies required and buys to the best advantage. A checker is appointed to check all supplies.

(b) The food preparation committee—here's where real efficient home-makers shine and money is saved. Yes, and most of the work is done here, regardless of what the dishwashers say! Helpers should be appointed to prepare and cook all the hot foods, and others to prepare and keep chilled the cold and frozen dishes. A competent carver should be delegated for any meat carving. Others should be appointed to dish up, with all necessary plates and equipment conveniently at hand. Have serving tables and dishing-up stands as near to the dining room as possible. Arrange for the heating or chilling of all serving dishes and plates. Arrange for buttering bread or biscuits; and for keeping rolls or biscuits hot. Appoint a competent tea or coffee maker and arrange for service. Food to be served hot should be kept in large double boilers or some steam table arrangement and food to be served chilled or frozen should be stored in refrigerator or packed in ice.

(c) The dining room service: This starts off with cooking utensils. Try and have all meat loaves, puddings, jellies or salad moulds a uniform size. The same applies to pies, cakes, etc. They cut to better advantage and look neater. Then, of course, a grand way to serve bulk food such as creamed foods, mashed vegetables,

salads, etc., is to use an ice cream scoop. Try to borrow or rent one—a size 8 is a ½ cup serving and a size 12 a ⅓ cup size. Another handy article is a butter cutter which makes a pound of pats in one operation. Keep the butter pats in a bowl of water and ice cubes. The actual serving of a plate dinner, for instance, can be accomplished with a bit of practice—by the time it passes through a few hands and is quickly checked there should be no omission. If the kitchen is small and quite a distance from the dining hall, do try to have a half-way service table where plates and replenished dishes may be passed to the waitresses, and soiled dishes picked up—it saves unnecessary crowding in the kitchen. Just because the waitress volunteers her services is no excuse for inefficiency—and this applies to social as well as money-raising ventures. It is a good idea to have a dining room supervisor, one who speeds up service with tact, and is able to meet any emergency. Another thing, avoid all unnecessary clutter and, yes, we might as well say it—chatter! Have full dining hall equipment lined up, chairs, tables, linen, glass, china, etc., etc. See that soiled dishes are kept cleared and supplies replenished as needed. Each waitress should easily handle two or three tables, each seating four; or 10 to 12 people at a long banquet table. She should be responsible for full salts and peppers, creams and sugars, condiments, water glasses or water pitchers and, something very important, the neat and clean appearance of her table or table section. The simplest service for amateurs to remember is to place, remove and pass all food from the left—beverages, of course, are served from the right. If food is passed, hold the serving dish low to enable easy handling.

(d) Cleaning up: And now we'll give the dishwashers and wipers a break! Have an abundance of hot water, clean dish towels, soaps and cleaners. There should be someone to check over linen, cutlery, etc., and be responsible for the return of any borrowed article. See that all refuse is disposed of and the kitchen left clean and tidy. Some tentative arrangement should be made ahead of time for any left-over food or supplies.

Christmas

A great part of your Christmas dinner can be leisurely made in advance—in fact weeks ahead of time. This will include all the baking of cake and cookies and the steaming of the plum pudding.

Inexpensive Plum Pudding

- 1½   cups soft bread crumbs
- 1½   cups brown sugar
- 1½   cups seedless raisins
- 1½   cups currants
- ¼   cup shredded citron
- ½   cup nut meats
- ¾   cup sifted flour
- ¾   teaspoon baking soda
- 1½   teaspoons salt
- 1½   teaspoons cinnamon
- ⅓   teaspoon each of grated nutmeg, cloves, allspice and ginger
- 1   cup finely chopped suet
- 1   cup each of grated raw carrot, potato and apple
- ¼   cup sour milk or cream

Mix together bread crumbs, sugar, fruits and nuts. Sift and mix in remaining dry ingredients. Add the suet, then the carrot, potato and apple. Add the liquid and mix thoroughly. Turn into greased mould to ¾ full. Tie down with greased paper. Steam about 4 hours. Keep in cool dry place. Re-steam 1 hour before serving.

Hard Sauce

- ⅓   cup butter
- 1   cup confectioner's sugar
- 2   tablespoons vanilla

Cream the butter thoroughly. Add sugar gradually and beat until light. Add the flavouring and set in a cool place until needed. Brandy, grated lemon or orange rind, nutmeg or cinnamon may be substituted for the vanilla.

Mincemeat

- 3   pounds lean beef
- 3   cups suet
- 2   quarts tart apples, chopped
- 4   cups currants
- 4   cups seeded raisins
- 1   cup citron peel
- 1   cup candied orange peel
- 5   cups brown sugar
- 4   teaspoons salt
- 2   cups meat stock
- 2   cups sweet apple cider
- 2   teaspoons ground cloves
- 2   tablespoons cinnamon
- 2   tablespoons nutmeg
- 2   tablespoons ground mace

Cook the beef until it is tender and allow it to cool in its own stock, then put meat and suet through food chopper. Core and chop finely enough tart apples to make eight cupfuls. Clean and wash currants, chop seeded raisins, citron and candied orange peel. Combine the meat, suet, fruits, sugar and salt. Add beef stock and apple cider and simmer slowly for one hour. Stir in spices and pack in hot, sterilized jars and seal. Makes 5 quarts.

Christmas Cake

- 1½   cups melted butter
- 2   cups sugar
- 2   cups molasses
- 4   cups flour
- 1   teaspoon cinnamon
- 1   teaspoon cloves
- 1   teaspoon allspice
- 1   teaspoon nutmeg
- 1   teaspoon baking soda
- 5   eggs
- 1   cup milk
- 1½   pounds raisins
- 1   pound currants
- ½   pound chopped nuts
- ½   pound peel

Cream together the butter, sugar and molasses. Mix and sift flour, spices and soda. Beat until light and fluffy. Mix in the eggs and milk and then add the fruit and nuts which have been dredged in flour. Pour into cake pan and bake in a slow oven for about 3 hours.

Almond Paste

- 1   pound sieved icing sugar
- 1   pound ground blanched almonds
    Juice of 1 lemon
- 2   eggs—yolks and whites or either

Mix together and knead thoroughly. Rose water may be used in place of lemon juice in this recipe.

Ornamental Frosting

    4   egg whites
    4   cups sifted confectioner's sugar
    ¼   teaspoon salt
    1   teaspoon vanilla

Beat the egg whites until very stiff. Then slowly add the sugar and beat constantly until the icing will hold its shape and will be of spreading consistency. Add salt and flavouring and spread on the cooled cake with a light swirling motion. Your cake can be given the real festive touch by arranging chopped cherries in shapes of stars, wreaths or a Christmas tree.

Weddings

The nature of a wedding reception depends on the time of the wedding ceremony and the number of invited guests. If the wedding takes place early in the day then a wedding breakfast is usually served. This may be either a buffet or a sit-down meal at which the entire bridal party is seated with the guests at one table. However, if the guest list is long, then buffet service is found to be more convenient.

For the afternoon or evening wedding the meal takes the form of a buffet reception with the food being passed by friends or relatives of the principals.

The wedding cake, glistening white, is always the centre of attraction on the wedding table. There seems to be more sentimentality attached to a wedding cake which has been made at home, and for that reason we offer you a recipe for a wedding cake which will serve 100 guests and do justice as a centre to a beautifully-appointed bridal table.

Wedding Cake (14 pounds)

    1   pound almonds
    3   pounds currants
    3   pounds raisins
    1   pound mixed sliced peel
    2   cups cognac brandy
    4   cups sifted cake flour
    2   teaspoons baking soda
    3   teaspoons cinnamon
    1   teaspoon cloves
    ½   nutmeg, grated
    1   pound shortening
    1½   cups firmly packed brown sugar
   16   eggs
    3   drops wintergreen
    1   cup molasses
    1   cup sour cream

Blanch and shred almonds; mix with fruits, peel and brandy, and let stand in closely covered jar two days.

Mix and sift flour, soda and spices. Cream shortening until soft and smooth. Gradually add sugar, creaming until fluffy. Beat in thoroughly 1 egg at a time, then wintergreen and molasses. Add flour mixture alternately with sour cream, mixing well after each addition. Stir in brandied fruits and nuts.

Turn into greased loaf pans, lined with paper and again greased, filling them about ¾ full. Cover tightly with waxed or greased paper and steam 2 hours. Then bake in very slow oven (250 deg. F.) for about 2 hours, removing paper the last ½ hour to dry surface.

Decorating

For a decorative two-layer cake use frosted sticks of cardboard to support the upper layers. Tie little bells on the sticks, which look like marble columns, and on each corner of the lower layer stick small bows of "wedding" veil.

The frosted rosettes and scroll work which are so definite a part of a wedding cake can be bought in the five and ten stores and applied to your own glistening white frosting.

But if you are not quite sure of your skill as a cake decorator you can pay your local baker to decorate it for you in his best professional manner.

Ornamental Frosting

Sift confectioner's sugar and measure 5 cups. Cream 4 tablespoons of butter well and add part of the sugar gradually, blending well after each addition. Add the remaining sugar alternately with 2 unbeaten egg whites and 2 tablespoons cream until the frosting is the right consistency to spread. Beat after each addition, until smooth and creamy. Add 1 teaspoon vanilla and ¼ teaspoon salt. Spread the frosting smoothly on the outside of the cake and use the remainder of it with a pastry tube to make the decorations.

"The Sun's Cookery Pages save me money and effort---and benefit my family!"

THOUSANDS of Vancouver Sun reader-families have more and better prepared food by reason of the Vancouver Sun's daily recipes and famous cookery pages edited by Edith Adams. Housewives add to their skill and enjoyment in cooking, cut their household budgets and make their work vastly easier and more interesting when they buy food, prepare and serve it to grateful families with the aid of the Sun's cookery features. Join them in the march to more nourishing and tastier meals for everyone!

Send in Recipes and win cash prizes!

★

And if YOU have some recipes you're specially proud of, send them in to Edith Adams! If they're as good as you think they are you'll win cash prizes . . . and OTHER housewives will praise and bless you!

Edith Adam's Wartime 9th Annual Cook Book

1943

THE SUN
PRIZE WINNING
WARTIME RECIPES
SUBSTITUTIONS
LUNCH BOXES
BUDGET STRETCHING
WARTIME CANNING
THE VANCOUVER SUN 9th ANNUAL
Edith Adam's
Wartime
COOK BOOK

PREFACE

The Ninth Annual Cookbook goes forth into a world of homemakers facing more stringent food shortages than they have ever known before. To elaborate on the subject of rationing and lack of variety on the markets would be gross selfishness. We are thankful our food situation is as happy as it is. Nevertheless, "what to serve the family" is a problem.

The recipes in this book were chosen because they call for only materials available on our markets. A section is devoted to the current problem of packing lunch buckets and parcels for men in service, both overseas and in Canada. A large section is devoted to home canning, a chore which has become of greater importance since we cannot depend on the buying of commercially canned foods.

EDITH ADAMS

Substitutions

Sugar Substitution

1 cup sugar—½ cup honey, ½ cup sugar, with ¼ less liquid.

1 cup sugar—¾ cup honey, with ¼ less liquid.

1 cup sugar—¾ cup molasses, with ¼ less liquid plus 1 teaspoon baking soda.

1 cup sugar—1 cup corn syrup, with ⅓ less liquid.

1 cup sugar— ¼ cup corn syrup and ¾ cup sugar with ⅓ less liquid.

1 cup sugar—1⅓ cups maple syrup.

1 cup molasses—1 cup honey.

Very often syrup, molasses and honey are substituted 1 cup for each cup of sugar required. But when absolute accuracy is the feature of a recipe, rules should be followed for sugar substitution.

Shortening Substitution

1 cup butter—¾ cup smoked or fresh pork fat clarified.

1 cup butter—⅔ cup chicken fat clarified (double salt in recipe).

1 cup butter—⅞ cup beef fat clarified.

1 cup butter—½ cup suet (double amount of salt and add ¼ cup liquid).

1 cup butter—⅞ cup cottonseed, corn or nut oil.

1 cup butter—⅞ cup lard (add some salt).

Table of Substitution

1 square unsweetened chocolate—3 tablespoons cocoa (in cake or cookie batter which calls for chocolate, also add 1 tablespoon shortening).

1 tablespoon cornstarch—2 tablespoons flour (for thickening).

1 tablespoon cornstarch—2 teaspoons arrowroot.

1 teaspoon baking powder— ¼ teaspoon baking soda plus ½ teaspoon cream of tartar.

1 cup sweet milk—1 cup sour milk plus ½ teaspoon baking soda, and minus 2 teaspoons baking powder in the recipe.

1 cup sour milk—1 cup sweet milk into which 1 tablespoon of vinegar or lemon juice has been stirred; or 1 cup buttermilk.

Mock Whipped Cream

2 marshmallows

1 cup of cream or top milk

Vanilla

Cut the marshmallows in small pieces and soak in milk all day or overnight. Chill and whip. Add vanilla to taste.

This looks very much like whipped cream, writes M.E. Colman, Vancouver.

Wartime Whipped Cream

½ teaspoon gelatine

2 teaspoons cold water

1 cup table cream

Soak gelatine in cold water and dissolve in top of double boiler. Add one cup of cream and stir until completely dissolved. Chill for 20 minutes or until slightly thickened. Whip until stiff. Sweeten and flavour to taste.

Coffee Substitute

6 cups cooking bran

3 tablespoons molasses

½ teaspoon salt

½ cup whole wheat (optional)

1 cup coffee

Put bran and molasses into a roasting pan, mix thoroughly with a fork, add salt and put into oven. Roast until good and brown. When it is cold roll with a rolling pin. Roast the whole wheat till it is brown, grind together with the coffee and mix with first mixture. Brew as for ordinary coffee, using 3 tablespoons in a 6-cup percolator. Let it percolate or boil for 5 minutes. It may be kept any length of time.

Mrs. J.H. Lyne, North Vancouver.

Substitute Almond Paste

1 cup bread crumbs rubbed very fine

1 cup icing sugar

1 egg

Bitter almond flavouring

Mix bread crumbs and icing sugar thoroughly. Bind with well-beaten egg and flavouring. Sufficient for one cake.

Mrs. L.E. Sanders.

Bee-Nut Butter (A substitute for peanut butter)

Soak 1 cup small white beans overnight with a pinch of soda. Cook until soft and strain well. Put through mincer and add 2 tablespoons of Bovril for flavour. Spread chili sauce on bread with the bee-nut butter. Makes a tasty sandwich.

Mrs. E.H. Cooke, Vancouver.

Make One Pound of Butter Into Two

Take the top cream from a bottle of milk and add enough milk to make 2 cups. Soak 1 tablespoon gelatin in 2 tablespoons milk for 5 minutes. Place over hot water until gelatin dissolves. Cut 1 pound butter into small pieces and when soft gradually whip milk and dissolved gelatin mixture into butter with a dover beater. After milk is all thoroughly beaten in add 1 teaspoon salt. Place on ice to harden.

Whipped Butter

Cream butter to the "whipped" stage, as you would for a cake. If you do it by hand add a little hot milk to make the beating easier. This increases the volume and the mixture will be easier to spread, and goes farther. One pound of whipped butter (without added ingredients) will spread 3 one-pound loaves of bread.

Sugar Saving Cakes

Molasses Layer Cake

- 1 egg (or 2 yolks)
- 1 cup molasses or golden syrup
- 1 tablespoon melted butter
- 2 cups flour
- 1 teaspoon soda
- ½ teaspoon salt
- 1 teaspoon cinnamon
- ½ teaspoon cloves
- ½ cup boiling water

Beat egg; add molasses and beat thoroughly. Add melted butter and beat again. Sift flour, soda, salt and spices together. Add to syrup mixture. Lastly add boiling water. Bake in two layers in a 375 degrees F. oven for 25 minutes. Put together with jam or jelly and frost top as desired.

   Mrs. Alex Fisher, Ladner.

Honey Cake

- ½ cup shortening
- ⅓ cup brown sugar
- ½ cup honey
- 1 egg
- 1¾ cups sifted bread flour
- ½ teaspoon soda
- 1 teaspoon salt
- 1 teaspoon baking powder
- ½ teaspoon each cinnamon, ginger, nutmeg and cloves
- ⅞ cup milk
- 1 cup raisins

Cream shortening and brown sugar, add honey and egg, unbeaten; sift flour, soda, salt, baking powder and spices and add alternately with milk. Add raisins which have been dredged in a little of the flour. Bake at 350°F oven for 1 hour.

   Mrs. E. Colarch, Revelstoke.

Victory Cake Frosting

- 1 egg white
- ½ cup dark corn syrup
- 2 tablespoons white sugar
  Pinch of salt
- ¼ teaspoon cream of tartar
- 1½ teaspoons vanilla

Put all ingredients except the flavouring in double boiler and cook until the icing stands in peaks, about 7 minutes. Beat constantly. Finally add vanilla.

   Mrs. C.W. Hales, Nanaimo.

Sugar Saving Cookies

War Cookies

- 1 cup sifted flour
- 1 teaspoon baking powder
- ½ teaspoon salt
- 1½ cups oatmeal
- ½ cup seeded raisins
- ¼ cup firmly packed brown sugar
- 1 egg, beaten
- ¼ cup molasses
- ¼ cup jam or marmalade
- ½ cup melted shortening

Sift and measure flour and sift again with baking powder and salt. Stir in the oatmeal and raisins. Beat brown sugar into egg, add molasses, jam and melted shortening. Gradually stir in the flour-oatmeal-raisin mixture. Drop from a teaspoon onto a lightly greased baking sheet and bake at 375°F for about 12 minutes. Store in a closely covered tin box and they will keep. Leave out the raisins, if desired.

Makes about 2½ to 3 dozen.

Mrs. Robert Heath.

Crunchies

- ½ cup dark corn syrup
- ¼ cup molasses
- ⅛ teaspoon salt
- 2 tablespoons butter
- 1 tablespoon vinegar
- 4 cups puffed cereal

Mix syrup, molasses and salt and cook to 240 deg. (when small drop forms medium hard ball in cold water). Add butter and vinegar and quickly stir in cereal. Pack in well-greased eight by eight inch pan. Cut into two-inch squares with sharp knife.

Miss Josephine Rowa, Vancouver.

On 17 March 1950, Edith Adams Cottage staff celebrate the third anniversary of the opening of the Cottage at 510 Beatty Street; left to right: Marion McGill, Eileen Norman, Marianne Linnell, Mary Hult, Shirley Pinchin, Myrtle Gregory, Gail Macpherson, Lillooet Davidson, Olga Jurisin, Tom Barber (the Garden Man).

Sugar Saving Pies

Wartime Lemon Pie

- ½ cup golden syrup
- ½ teaspoon salt
- 1 cup (half milk, half water)
- ¼ cup sugar
- 3 tablespoons cornstarch
- 2 egg yolks (slightly beaten)
  Rind and juice of 1 lemon

Mix all the ingredients except the lemon together and bring to a boil. Allow them to cook over a double boiler for 12 minutes to cook the starch. Cool and add lemon juice and rind. Pour into an eight-inch baked pie shell. Cover with meringue made with two beaten egg whites and 5 teaspoons of sugar and ⅛ teaspoon of salt. Brown in a 300 deg. F. oven for 20 minutes. If a stiffer mixture is wanted add one more tablespoon of cornstarch.

Mrs. Judith P. Briggs.

Honey Raisin Pie

- 1 cup orange juice
- 1 tablespoon lemon juice
- ⅔ cup cold water
- ½ cup honey
- ½ teaspoon salt
  Grated rind ½ orange
- 3 tablespoons cornstarch
- 1⅔ cups seedless raisins
- 1 tablespoon butter
  Pastry for double 9-inch crust

Combine juices, water, honey, salt and rind and heat to boiling. Moisten cornstarch with a little cold water, add to hot mixture. Rinse raisins and stir into hot mixture and remove from stove. Line pie plate with pastry, add filling and dot with butter. Cover with top crust and bake at 450°F for 10 minutes and 400°F for 25 minutes. Cut when nearly cool.

Mrs. F. MacLeod, New Westminster.

Maple Syrup Tarts

- 1 cup maple syrup
- 1 tablespoon cornstarch
- ¼ cup cold water
- 1 egg
- 2 tablespoons butter
- ½ teaspoon vanilla

Heat maple syrup to which has been added cornstarch mixed with cold water, then well beaten egg. Cook until clear. Mix in butter and vanilla. Beat well and cool slightly. Fill baked tart shells with mixture.

Mrs. S.F. MacLeod, New Westminister.

Sugarless Raspberry Pie

- 1 quart raspberries, firmly packed
- ⅔ cup syrup
- 4 level teaspoons minute tapioca
  Dash of salt

Line nine-inch pie plate with pastry and add above. Cover with remaining pastry and bake at 450°F for 10 minutes and then reduce the heat to 400°F for 20 minutes.

Mrs. Frank Schmidt, Abbotsford.

Butterscotch Pie

- 4 tablespoons cornstarch
- ⅛ teaspoon salt
- ¼ cup cold milk
- 1¾ cups scalded milk
- ¼ cup butter
- ½ cup brown sugar
- ¼ cup corn syrup
- 2 egg yolks
- 1 teaspoon vanilla

Mix cornstarch and salt to a paste with cold milk. Add slowly to hot milk, stirring constantly until thick. Cover and continue cooking for 10 minutes, stirring occasionally. Melt butter in an iron frying pan, add sugar and stir until brown and bubbly. Add corn syrup and blend well. Add caramel mixture to hot cornstarch mixture and continue cooking until well blended. Pour hot mixture over slightly beaten egg yolks. Return to heat and again cook for 3 minutes. Cool slightly; add vanilla and pour in a 9-inch baked pastry shell. Cover with meringue and brown in a slow oven.

Meringue:

- 3 tablespoons icing sugar
- 2 egg whites
- 1 tablespoon cornstarch

Edith M. Adams, Matsqui.

Breads

War Bread

- 1 cup bread flour
- 1 teaspoon baking powder
- ¾ teaspoon salt
- 1 cup whole wheat flour
- ½ cup bran
- 1 cup raisins
- ¼ cup honey
- 1⅓ cups sour milk
- 1 teaspoon baking soda
- 2 tablespoons melted dripping

Sift flour with baking powder and salt. Add the whole wheat flour and bran. Add the raisins.

Combine honey and sour milk and stir in the soda. Add to the dry ingredients; add melted shortening and mix only enough to wet the dry ingredients. Bake 1 to 1¼ hours in a loaf pan in a 350°F oven.

For a sweeter loaf increase honey to ½ cup and decrease amount of sour milk used.

Mrs. R. Garden, Eburne.

Custard Corn Cake

- 1 cup white flour
- 3 teaspoons baking powder
- ½ teaspoon salt
- ½ cup white sugar
- 1 cup cornmeal
- 1 cup sweet milk
- 2 eggs, beaten
- ½ cup melted shortening
- 1 extra cup sweet milk

Sift the first three ingredients into a bowl, add sugar and cornmeal. Mix thoroughly. Into a hollow shaped in the mixture pour 1 cup milk and the egg. Beat well, add melted shortening and beat again.

Pour the batter into a warm, greased heavy iron frying pan. Now pour the extra 1 cup of milk very, very slowly into the centre of the cake, drawing it gently into the batter by inserting a knife in the middle and drawing it toward the outside (in the manner of cutting a pie).

Lift carefully into a moderately hot oven and bake a rich golden brown. Serve hot, cut into pie shapes. Split, and butter before eating.

Mrs. R.L. Connell, Vancouver.

Steamed Nut Bread

- ½ cup soft bread crumbs
- ¾ cup milk
- ¼ cup molasses, corn syrup or honey
- ½ teaspoon salt
- ⅓ cup hot water
- ½ cup graham or whole wheat flour
- ½ cup cornmeal
- ½ cup rolled oats
- 1 teaspoon soda
- ½ cup chopped nuts, raisins or dates

Soak bread crumbs in milk for 10 minutes. Beat til smooth, add molasses (or corn syrup or honey). Add remaining ingredients and blend thoroughly. Oil baking powder can and fill half full. Adjust oiled lids and steam in covered steamer for 2½ hours. Remove lid and dry in a moderate oven for 15 minutes.

Miss Josephine Rowa, Vancouver.

Cornflake Muffins (Sour Milk)

- 1 cup cornflakes, crushed fine
- 1 cup flour
- ½ teaspoon baking soda
- 2 tablespoons sugar
- ¼ cup butter
- Salt
- ½ cup sour milk

Mix cornflakes, sifted flour, baking soda and sugar and cut in butter. Add salt and mix in sour milk. Bake at 375°F for 15 to 20 minutes. Serve hot.

Mrs. L.W. Berry, Ocean Park.

Lunchboxes

Sandwich Filling Suggestions

Slices of ham loaf with dressing.

Meat loaf with chili sauce.

Corned beef with sweet mustard relish.

Tongue with mustard or horseradish.

Hard cooked egg minced with dressing and a little mustard.

Salmon salad.

Cold cooked sausages sprinkled with a little dry mustard and rolled in slices of bread.

Cheese, chili sauce and chopped celery.

Double decker sandwich of cream cheese and jelly.

Thinly sliced roast lamb or veal with chutney.

Mashed baked beans and pickle on brown bread.

Liverwurst mixed with minced hardboiled egg.

Bologna with pickles and mayonnaise.

Minced liver with minced cold bacon and a little dressing.

Raw carrot and cabbage with mayonnaise.

Jam or jelly on fruit bread.

Chopped nuts and jelly.

Minced liver and olives.

Mashed avocado butter and thin ham slices.

Sprinkle a little curry powder in butter for a ham sandwich.

"Cornish" Pastries (for the Lunch Box)

Ingredients for **short pastry**:

- 3 cups flour
- 1½ teaspoons baking powder
- 1 teaspoon salt
- ½ cup fat

Sift flour, baking powder and salt. Rub in the fat. Add cold water gradually and mix to a stiff paste. Roll out as required.

Filling:

- 3 or 4 ounces of chopped raw steak or minced raw ham
- ½ cup finely chopped raw potatoes
  Salt and pepper
- 2 minced carrots (if desired)
  Small piece of onion, minced
  Few drops of water

Cut rolled out pastry in 6-inch rounds. Put small heap of filling in each round. Moisten edges and draw the opposite side of pastry together in half-moon shape and press edges together firmly. Chill for half an hour. Brush with a little milk and bake at 350 deg. F. for ¾ hour.

Mrs. L. Hermans, Vancouver.

Liver Paste

- ½ pound calves liver
- 1¾ teaspoons salt
- 2 cups boiling water
- 8 slices cooked bacon
- ½ cup light sour cream
- 2 tablespoons prepared mustard
- 2 tablespoons minced onion
- ⅛ teaspoon pepper

Simmer liver with one teaspoon of salt in boiling water until tender (about 45 minutes). Cool and put through medium blade of food chopper with bacon. Add remaining ingredients and mix thoroughly. Put into jars and chill in refrigerator. Makes 1½ cups.

Miss M. Lovatt, Vancouver.

Tasty Ham Spread

- 1 12-ounce can spiced ham
- 1 seeded green pepper
- 1 small onion
- 2 hard boiled eggs
- 1 teaspoon dry mustard (to taste)
  Mayonnaise

Put ham, green pepper, onion and eggs through food chopper, using fine blade. Season with mustard and salt if desired. Add mayonnaise to moisten. Makes 2½ cups of spread.

Ice Box Scotties

- 3 cups quick oats
- 1 cup brown sugar
- 1 cup white flour
- ½ teaspoon salt
- 1 cup butter
- 1 teaspoon (scant) soda
- ¼ cup boiling water

Mix thoroughly the oats, sugar, flour and salt, and make a hole in the centre. Melt the butter; dissolve the soda in the boiling water and pour in the whole of the dry ingredients. Mix well and shape into a roll on wax paper. Chill overnight in ice box. Slice thin and cook in hot oven (375 deg. F.) for 6 to 8 minutes. Makes about 40 cookies.

These cookies are suitable for packing in lunches. Mrs. John Clifford, Vancouver.

Packing for Soldiers

Rationed foods and those difficult to obtain in the Old Country are always a welcome gift to friends and relatives overseas. All who have undertaken to send regular food packages, no matter how small, are advised to follow strictly the rules governing the sending of food packages to civilians and the armed forces.

Limited weight includes the packing material, as well as the food. If your parcel is even an ounce over-weight it may never reach the recipient. Every article must be carefully described on the customs declaration, otherwise the parcel may be confiscated. Unless you give an alternative address on the customs declaration your box is returned to you at your own expense, if the addressee cannot be located. We suggest, when sending to a member of the armed forces, that you cross out the word "abandon" and give instructions on the declaration form that it be delivered to the Officer Commanding his unit.

Mark the word "gift" clearly on packages sent to civilians. They cannot accept anything but unsolicited gifts.

Wrap food carefully and pack each item separately. Use a strong, light-weight container. Spaces between the different articles may be filled in with any number of small items—a simple way of adding tiny "surprise packages." Wrap and tie all parcels securely, or seal with gummed paper. A good idea is to sew the package up in unbleached cotton or burlap, and then address it in indelible ink.

Cookies packed for shipping should be of a kind that keeps fresh in flavour and appearance for quite a few days. Square or oblong shapes are the easiest to pack, in a size that doesn't crumble easily. If a batch of cookies is sent separately try to pack them in a square or oblong tin box with a tight fitting cover. An important part of packing cookies is to use lots of waxed paper. It is a good idea to shred some of the paper and use it as a cushion in the bottom of the box. And don't forget when you line the box with waxed paper to cut it long enough to fold over the top—and add several sheets between layers and a good fold between rows.

The following list will give some idea of acceptable food items:

Butter, packed in a sealed tin and a carton, sugar cubes, evaporated milk, chocolate drink powder, meat spreads, canned meats, canned fish, dehydrated onion flakes, dehydrated vegetables or fruit, cheese, jams, jellies and pickles, honey, maple sugar, fruit cakes, plum puddings, fruit and nut loaves, shortbread, small packages of dried fruit, milk powder, fruit juice concentrate, egg powder, 1 or 2-pound tins of bacon and tinned nuts.

If you must send a glass jar or bottle seal the top with wax, then wrap the article in gauze squares or handkerchief tissues, and pack it in a tin can with a tightly fitting lid.

Oranges and lemons will keep well if coated with liquid paraffin wax and then allowed to dry before packing. Brush the wax on with a small-size paint brush.

To prevent a cake from breaking, try packing it in lots of popcorn. Get a strong, light-weight cardboard box, cover the bottom with popcorn, put in the cake, cover with a few thicknesses of waxed paper and then completely cover the top and fill up any side spaces with popcorn.

When the ink has dried on your parcel it can be made waterproof by brushing the writing over with colourless nail polish, a slightly warmed candle or a transparent piece of gummed tape.

Fill up all corners with useful and much needed articles, such as shoelaces, chocolate bars, nuts, dried fruit, gum, handkerchiefs and "smokes."

Wet the string when tying a package. It is easier to make a good knot, and when the string dries it shrinks, and the package is more securely tied.

When sending home-made fudge, or a similar type of candy, first line a cardboard or tin container with waxed paper—the bottom, sides and corners—pour the mixture directly into the box and send it in one solid block.

Five Ways to Cook Sausages

Sausages and Yorkshire Pudding

Cook sausages until they are done and brown on all sides. Have fat very hot and pour Yorkshire Pudding batter over them in the pan and bake them at 400°F. for 30 minutes.

Yorkshire Pudding
- ½ cup flour
- ½ teaspoon salt
- 1 cup milk
- 2 eggs

Mix flour and salt, add milk and egg, well beaten. Beat mixture vigorously for several minutes with a rotary egg beater.

Mrs. James Hargraves, Vancouver.

Sausage Surprise

- 2 cups ready-cut macaroni, uncooked
- 1 lb. small pork sausages (browned)
- 1 teaspoon dry mustard
   Salt and pepper
- 1 small tin of tomato juice

Cook macaroni in rapidly-boiling salted water for 20 minutes or until tender; drain. Grease casserole with butter and put in layer of macaroni. Then put in a layer of sausages which have been brushed with dry mustard. Repeat until all used up. Season with salt and pepper and cover with tomato juice. Dot with butter and cook for one hour in a 350 deg. F. oven.

This interesting new way to serve sausages won the $1.00 Readers' prize for Mrs. Angus Lougheed, Vancouver.

Sausage Dinner

- 1 pound sausages
- 1 onion, chopped
- 1 large can tomatoes

Cook sausages with chopped onion. Pour off any excess grease. Pour one can of tomatoes over sausages and then cover tomatoes with a batter and cook in moderate oven until brown. Serves 6.

Batter:
- 1½ cups flour
- 2 teaspoons baking powder
   Pinch of salt
- 1 egg

Combine sifted flour, baking powder and salt with beaten egg. Add enough water or milk to make a stiff dough.

Mrs. J. Smith, Vancouver.

Stuffed Sausage Roll

- 2 lbs. sausage meat
- 2 cups raw apples, minced
- 2 small onions, minced
- 2 cups bread crumbs

Pat the sausage meat into a rectangular shape about a half an inch thick on a piece of wax paper. Mix apples, onions and bread crumbs and spread over the meat. Roll like a jelly roll tucking the edges in. Place in a baking dish and bake in a moderate oven (350 deg. F.) for 45 minutes. Serves 6 to 8.

Mrs. P.W. Allen, Vancouver.

Mock Goose

- 1 pound sausage meat
- 2 pounds mashed potatoes
- 1 chopped onion
- 1 teaspoon sage
- 1 teaspoon salt
   Dash of pepper

Place a layer of sausage meat in a dish, sprinkle over it a little salt, pepper, sage and onion. Cover with a layer of mashed potatoes then another layer of meat and seasoning. Continue until the dish is full, finishing with a layer of potatoes. Bake until browned in a 350°F oven. Serves four.

Mrs. James Lefleur, Vancouver.

Three Pot Roasts

Prune Roast

- 4 pounds rump roast
- 1 teaspoon salt
- Pepper to taste
- ¼ cup cider vinegar
- 2 cups boiling water
- 2 cups dried prunes
- ¼ cup water
- ¼ teaspoon cloves
- 2 tablespoons flour
- ¼ cup brown sugar
- ¼ teaspoon cinnamon

Heat heavy, deep pan on top of stove and brown roast in it, on all sides. Season with salt and pepper, add vinegar and boiling water, cover and simmer about 2½ hours. Add prunes and simmer about 1 hour longer or until meat is tender. Remove meat. Stir in remaining ingredients which have been mixed together and cook rapidly until thick sauce is formed. Pour over meat and serve immediately. Serves 8 to 10.

Carrots may be steamed on top of the meat and it tastes even more delicious with buttered noodles.

Mrs. F. McLeod, New Westminster.

Cranberry Pot Roast

- 3 or 4 pounds of rolled chuck pot roast
- 4 tablespoons of flour
- 2 tablespoons of lard
- Salt
- Pepper
- Cranberry sauce

Dredge the pot roast with flour, and brown in hot lard. Season with salt and pepper and pour over it the cranberry sauce, together with one cup of hot water. Cover closely and simmer slowly, adding extra water if necessary. Cook for about 3 hours. When done, remove roast to a hot platter, and thicken the remaining liquid for gravy. This serves six. To make the tart cranberry sauce use one-third pound of cranberries, two-thirds cup of water and 3 tablespoons sugar. Boil the cranberries and water for 5 minutes. Add sugar and boil 5 to 10 minutes.

Mrs. Wakely, Vancouver.

Pickled Pot Roast

Put 4 lbs. cross rib into earthenware dish; cover with half vinegar and half water; cut one sliced onion, one garlic, some celery, parsley, one sliced carrot, one bay leaf, thyme, and a few whole black peppers. Cover, let stand for about three days; turn the meat daily; take meat out of brine; brown on all sides and cook as you would any pot roast, adding some of the above juice and all the vegetables, and salt to taste. For gravy, brown together one tablespoon butter, one tablespoon sugar, one tablespoon flour, and use above liquid to thin it.

Cook approximately 3 hours and 20 minutes, or allow 50 minutes to pound. Add vegetables last hour of cooking.

Miss Shirley McDonald, New Westminster.

Meat

Upside Down Orange Ham Loaf

1½ lbs. lean fresh pork shoulder (ground)
1½ lbs. smoked ham (ground)
1½ cups soft bread crumbs or 1 cup cracker crumbs
1½ cups milk
¼ teaspoon salt
⅛ teaspoon pepper

Combine all ingredients in order given.

Orange Glaze:

½ cup brown sugar
¼ cup butter
Slices of orange

Spread sugar and butter evenly in shallow baking pan. Cover with orange slices. Place ham mixture over fruit and press down evenly into a thin loaf. Bake in a moderate oven (350°F) about an hour. Turn upside down on platter, cut in squares. Serves 12. Half the recipe is enough for an average family.

Mrs. W. Lamont, Vancouver.

Lamb Loaf or Patties

2 pounds lean, ground lamb
1 cup fine bread crumbs
2 tablespoons minced onions parboiled for five minutes
½ cup chili sauce
1½ teaspoons salt
½ teaspoon pepper
½ cup milk
1 egg, slightly beaten

Combine lamb with bread crumbs, onion, chili sauce, salt and pepper. Moisten with milk and slightly beaten egg. Pack into a loaf pan or ring mould. Bake in a moderate oven (350 deg. F.) for one hour. This recipe may be made into delicious individual patties for frying or broiling by the addition of an extra ½ cup of milk. Serves 8.

Mrs. Jas. Hargraves, Vancouver.

Double Duty Chicken Dinner

5 pounds boiling fowl
¼ cup rice
Small onion, minced
3 strips bacon

Clean and wash chicken. Place in pot and half cover with water. Simmer for about two hours. Remove from liquid and cool. Add salt and pepper to taste, to chicken broth, with the rice and onion. Simmer slowly for an hour. When the chicken is quite cool stuff with your favourite dressing. Cover breast with strip of bacon and brown in a moderate oven for about an hour.

Mrs. M.E. Sostad, West Vancouver.

Sparerib Roll with Apple Dressing

2 lb. sections of spareribs
2 slices of salt pork (diced)
¼ cup chopped celery
¼ cup chopped onions
3 tablespoons butter
5 tart apples
¼ cup sugar
1 cup stale bread crumbs
¼ cup chopped parsley
Salt and pepper

Wash and wipe spareribs, either sew or skewer three sides together, leaving one open for the dressing. Cook salt pork in pan until crisp and tender. Brown celery and onion in butter for five minutes. Add peeled and diced apples, sprinkle sugar over top. Cover and cook apples until tender.

Put salt pork, onions, celery and apples in mixing bowl. Add bread crumbs, parsley and salt and pepper to taste. Mix well. Fill spareribs (pocket) with dressing and close opening. Cook uncovered at 350 degrees F. for 1¾ hours.

Fluffy mashed potatoes and brussel sprouts or mashed turnips goes well with this tasty dish which serves 4 persons.

Mrs. James Boyd, Vancouver.

Scotch Poultry Dressing

1 cup fine oatmeal
1 cup chopped suet
½ teaspoon thyme
1 hardboiled egg, minced
1 cup breadcrumbs
Salt and pepper to taste
½ teaspoon parsley
Minced onion (if desired)

Mix all ingredients and stuff bird. Equally good with chicken, duck, turkey or goose.

Mrs. Rosalind Brand, West Vancouver.

Fish

Herring in Oatmeal with Mustard Sauce

 6 herrings
 2 tablespoons flour
 1 teaspoon salt
 4 tablespoons oatmeal
   Milk
   Fat for frying
   Mustard sauce

Wipe the herring and remove heads, tails and fins. Slit down centre and remove the bone. Wipe out inside with a damp cloth. Mix together flour, salt, oatmeal and spread on a plate. Brush herrings with a little milk and dip into oatmeal. Coat the herrings on both sides, fry in hot fat until golden brown.

Serve with thin slices of lemon and mustard sauce.

Mustard Sauce:

 2 tablespoons butter
 1 tablespoon flour
 ½ pint water or stock
 1 teaspoon mustard
 1 teaspoon vinegar
 1 teaspoon Worcestershire sauce

Melt butter and add flour and cook with stock, stirring constantly. Cook three minutes. Blend mustard, vinegar and Worcestershire sauce, beating well. Add salt to taste and serve with herrings. Serves six.

Mrs. George Clement, Vancouver.

Baked Skate

Use only the wings of the fish. Cut them in three-inch squares, dip in salted canned milk (about ½ teaspoon salt to 1 cup), roll in fine breadcrumbs, sprinkle with a little salad oil and put in a greased baking dish. Bake in a very hot oven (450 deg. F.) for 15 minutes.

Fried Oolicans

These are treated like smelts. Remove heads, clean and wash. Roll them in flour and brown on a hot griddle.

Baked Cream Fish Fillets

 2 pounds fish fillets (cod, sole, haddock or halibut)
 ¼ teaspoon salt
   Pepper
   Juice of one lemon
 ¼ teaspoon paprika
 2 tablespoons flour
 2 tablespoons butter
 1 tablespoon dry mustard
 1 cup top milk
 ½ cup bread crumbs
 1 tablespoon minced parsley

Cut fillets in serving pieces. Place in shallow dish. Sprinkle with salt, pepper and lemon juice.

Make a white sauce of other ingredients and pour over fish. Sprinkle with crumbs and minced parsley.

Bake in a moderate oven (350°F) for 35 minutes. Serves five or six.

Mrs. J. Nelson, Vancouver.

Kipper Toast

 2 kippers
 1 tablespoon butter
   Cayenne pepper
 2 tablespoons tomato sauce
 2 teaspoons chopped parsley
 2 cups baked beans

Pour boiling water over kippers and leave to stand a few minutes, then remove bones and skin. Melt the butter in a pan and in it heat the flesh of the kippers with the cayenne and parsley. Also add two tablespoons of tomato sauce. Heat beans separately. Heap the kipper mixture onto rounds of hot buttered toast. Serve the beans heaped around the toast. Serves four.

Mrs. Florence Ludlow, Vancouver.

Vegetables

Garden Loaf

Blend in a large bowl:

- ½   cup grated beets
- ½   cup chopped onions
- 1   cup diced cheese
- 2   cups lukewarm milk
- 1   teaspoon chopped parsley
- 1   clove garlic, minced
- ⅛   teaspoon thyme
- 1   teaspoon salt
- 1   cup carrots
- 1   cup chopped celery
- 2   cups whole wheat bread crumbs
- 1   egg
- 1   teaspoon paprika
- ⅛   teaspoon sage
- ¼   teaspoon pepper

Press into buttered baking dish and bake in a moderate oven 45 minutes to one hour. Serve plain or with mushroom sauce made with a can of mushroom soup. Garlic may be omitted.

Poached Tomatoes on Toast

- 1   slice of hot buttered toast per person
- 3   cups tomatoes, stewed
- 6   eggs

Heat tomatoes and break in eggs. Poach and serve with part of tomatoes on a slice of toast.

Miss Shirley-Grace Bryson, Lasqueti Island.

Red Cabbage Dutch Style

- 1   medium head of red cabbage
- 1   teaspoon salt
- 3 or 4   tart apples
  Butter
- 1   teaspoon sugar
  Dash nutmeg

Cut up cabbage very fine. Add salt and enough water to keep it from scorching while it cooks slowly. Peel, core and cut up apples. Mix with cabbage. When done there should be no water left. Add butter, sugar and nutmeg and leave on back of stove for a few minutes. Serve with pork chops, roast or chicken.

Mrs. H. Houtman, Vancouver.

Parsnip Souffle

- 2   cups mashed cold parsnips (cooked)
  Butter size of a walnut
  Salt and pepper to taste
- 2   eggs, well beaten
- ½   cup top milk

Mix all ingredients well together. Put in a buttered baking dish and bake about half an hour. This is a very inexpensive vegetable dish and can be served with stew.

Jackie Lee, West Vancouver.

Marianne Linnell (left) supervises pumpkin-carving at the Edith Adams Cottage.

The Girl She Left Behind Her

NEW tasks, new purposes . . . all thoughtful women in these times of great events have left behind them many of the interests of the past, live fully and with vivid awareness in the present. To these women, with its three great news services, its intelligent, clearly-written editorials and sharply analytical columnists and commentators, the Vancouver Sun is the newspaper that appeals most positively.

A complete, interesting, reliable newspaper, preferred by intelligent women.

THE VANCOUVER SUN

Vancouver's Home-owned Newspaper

The Vancouver Sun's 10th Annual Cook Book

1945

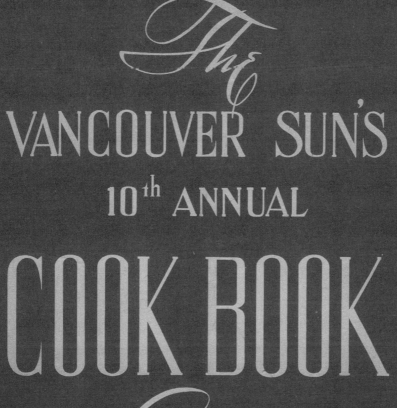

The VANCOUVER SUN'S
10th ANNUAL
COOK BOOK
Edited by
EDITH ADAMS

Including: PRIZE WINNING RECIPES
CANNING, CALORIE CHART, ENTERTAINING

Starred in this Tenth Annual Cook Book of The Vancouver Sun are the prize-winning recipes of The Sun's own readers. Women from all parts of British Columbia—as the names and addresses under the recipes will testify—have sent to The Sun their most treasured recipes, with the hope that they would win one of the daily dollar prizes and so have their recipe published for the benefit of all readers who like to cook.

Because of the war-time newsprint shortage, this Tenth Annual Cook Book has had to be confined to 32 pages. When supplies are back to normal, The Vancouver Sun will publish still another Cook Book, larger than ever before, and featured again will be the most interesting of thousands of recipes received every year from some of the best cooks in the world—the women of British Columbia.

EDITH ADAMS,
Cookery Editor

Teen-Age and Junior Cooks

Eats for the Gang!
Hamburgers in Buns:
2 tablespoons butter or bacon drippings, 1 pound ground round steak, salt and pepper, 6 buns. Shape the meat into 6 balls, handling as little as possible. Lightly flatten the balls with the palms of the hands, and salt and pepper both sides. Brown in 1 tablespoon of the butter or drippings. Add remaining 1 tablespoon of drippings, turn meat patties and brown on the other side. Place in a bun that has been split and toasted in the oven, then buttered. Serves 6.

Slapjack Sandwiches:
1 egg for each eater, 1 slice of bread for each egg, butter or bacon fat. Heat the fat in the frying pan. Drop the eggs, not more than four at a time, into the fat and then immediately slap a slice of bread right down on top of each egg. When the egg is cooked, use the egg lifter to turn the sandwich over and brown the bread side. The finished product is served, egg side up, with tomato, pickles and potato chips.

Cheeseburgers:
Place a slice of cheese on the lower half of a hot toasted hamburger bun; top with a sizzling hot 'burger pattie, then relish and lettuce and the other half of bun.

Root Beer Float:
Place a generous spoonful of vanilla ice cream into an ice-tea glass and fill with ice-cold root beer.

Toasted Frankfurter Rolls:
Simmer frankfurters for 5 minutes; drain; wrap each in a slice of bread (crusts removed) which has been spread with butter and prepared mustard; fasten with toothpicks. Bake in a hot oven (450 deg. F.) for 12 to 15 minutes.

Salad-Stuffed Rolls:
Split oblong soft rolls lengthwise through the middle without cutting clear through. Spread open and fill with salad mixture. Hot-dog rolls are best. To make the fish salad mixture, drain canned fish, flake (removing skin and bones) and mix with a quarter as much finely chopped celery and, if desired, a little grated onion. Season with salt and pepper and moisten with salad dressing; carefully fill the rolls.

Mabs' Cinnamon Toast
  1 tablespoon golden syrup
  1 tablespoon butter
  ½ teaspoon cinnamon

Mix well and spread this amount on two slices of hot toast. Cut toast into 1-inch fingers and serve immediately.

"My cinnamon toast is very good with hot cocoa."
Mabs Bradley, Vancouver.

Laurie's Prize Cookies
  1 cup brown sugar
  ½ cup shortening
  1 egg
  1 teaspoon vanilla
  2 cups sifted flour
    Pinch of salt
  2 teaspoons baking powder

Cream sugar and shortening and mix in well-beaten egg. Add vanilla. Stir in sifted flour, salt and baking powder. Roll out, and bake in hot oven.

"My cookies are so simple to make and I won first prize for them at the South Burnaby Exhibition."
Laurie Sanders, Jubilee, New Westminster.

Butterless, Nutless Fudge
  2 cups dark brown sugar
  ¾ cup milk
    Few grains of salt
  4 tablespoons peanut butter
  1 teaspoon vanilla

Cook in the usual way until a spoonful, dropped in cold water, forms a soft ball. Let cool somewhat and then beat until creamy. Pour into buttered dish.

"This is by far the nicest candy recipe I know. I have used it for years and can highly recommend it."
C. Connor, New Westminster.

Cooking for a Crowd

For 50 persons served, the following quantities of food should be purchased:

Clams for chowder–4 quarts clams; crabmeat for salad, 4 pounds; fish fillets, for frying or creaming, 14 pounds; oysters for stew, 4 quarts; salmon or tuna, 8 No. 1 tall cans.

Beef, chopped, for hamburgers, 12½ pounds; beef, rib roast, 25 pounds; cold sliced meat, 12½ pounds; chicken, roasted, 10 5-pound birds; chicken, diced, for salad, 20–25 pounds; chops (3 to pound), 17 pounds; lamb, roast leg, boned, 20 pounds; meat loaves, 5 2½-pound cooked loaves; pork, mutton, veal, same as lamb; roasts, not boned, 25 pounds; turkey, 40 pounds.

Vegetables, canned, 10 No. 2 cans (5 servings each); green beans, 8½ pounds; beets, 15 pounds; cabbage, cooked, 20 pounds; cabbage, for cole slaw, 10 pounds; carrots, 12 pounds; cauliflower, 12 pounds; celery, diced, about 10 medium heads; corn on cob, 50 ears; lettuce, for salads, 10 heads; lettuce, for garnish, 5 heads; peas, in pod, 25 pounds; potatoes, mashed, 15 pounds; potatoes, baked or boiled, 50 medium, or about 18 pounds; potatoes, creamed or scalloped, 12½ pounds; spinach, 12½ pounds; tomatoes, scalloped, 10 No. 2½ cans.

Salads, any meat, fish or fruit salad, approximately 6½ quarts; potato salad, 6½ quarts; mayonnaise, 1 quart; olives (2 each), 2 quarts; pickles, 2 quarts; tomatoes for salad (2 slices), 25 tomatoes.

Applesauce, for dessert (½ cup), 25 pounds; applesauce for relish, 12½ pounds; bread (1½ slices), 6 1-pound loaves; biscuits or rolls, 6½ dozen; butter (1 square each), 1½ pounds; butter for vegetables, 1 pound; cheese, 2 pounds; cream, light, for tea, 1 quart; cream for coffee, 1½ quarts; cream, to top desserts (2 tablespoons each), 1 quart whipping; crackers, 1 pound (approximately); cocoa, 2½ gallons (or 1½ cups dry cocoa); coffee, 1 to 1½ pounds; ice cream (bulk), 7 quarts; ice cream (brick), 8½ quarts; punch, 2 gallons; sandwich filling (1 full-size sandwich each), 2 quarts; soups, 2 gallons; sugar, lump (2 each), 1 pound; pies, 9-inch size, 9 pies; tomato or fruit juice, 10 No. 2 cans; tea, ½ pound (approximately).

"Quick" Breads, Doughnuts, Yeast Bread

Banana Bread

- ½ cup butter
- 1 cup sugar
- 3 mashed bananas
- 1½ cups flour
- 1 teaspoon baking soda
- Few grains salt
- 2 eggs

Cream butter, then add the sugar. Add bananas (mashed with a fork). Sift flour, baking soda and salt. Add beaten eggs. Mix well and pour into greased baking dish. Bake in a slow oven, 325 to 350 degrees F.

Mrs. T.H. Lane, New Westminster.

Sweet Dough Foundation

- 2 cakes compressed yeast
- ¼ cup lukewarm water
- 1 cup milk
- ¼ cup butter
- ½ cup sugar
- 1 teaspoon salt
- 5 cups sifted all-purpose flour (about)
- 2 eggs, beaten

Soften yeast in lukewarm water. Scald milk. Add butter, sugar and salt and cool to lukewarm. Add enough of the flour to make a thick batter (about 2½ cups), then add yeast and beaten eggs and beat well. Add enough more flour to make a soft dough. Turn out on a lightly floured board and knead until satiny. Place in a greased bowl, cover and let rise until double in bulk—about two hours. Then punch down and shape into rolls, tea ring or coffee cake. Let rise until double in bulk (½ to ¾ hour). Bake in a moderately hot oven (370 deg. F.) for 20 to 25 minutes for rolls or tea ring, 25 to 30 minutes for coffee cake. Makes three dozen rolls or two 12-inch tea rings.

Cinnamon Rolls: Use half the recipe for sweet dough foundation. After rising roll dough in a rectangle ½ inch thick, brush with melted fat and sprinkle with a mixture of ¼ cup sugar, ½ teaspoon cinnamon and one-third cup raisins. Roll like a jelly roll and cut in one-inch slices. Place close together in a greased pan, cut side down.

Swedish Rye Bread

        2 cups boiling water
        ½ cup brown sugar
        1 teaspoon salt
        1 teaspoon caraway seed
        1 teaspoon anise
        1 tablespoon shortening
        1 cake fresh yeast
        3½ cups enriched flour
        2 cups rye flour

Combine water, sugar, salt, caraway seed, anise and shortening; cool to lukewarm. Add yeast and, when dissolved, add enriched flour; mix to a soft dough. Allow to rise about 1½ hours. Add rye flour to make a stiff dough and knead lightly. Place in a greased bowl and cover with damp cloth; let rise about 2 hours, or until doubled in bulk. Knead and divide into portions. Cover and let rise 15 minutes. Mould two loaves and place in greased pans. Cover and let rise until doubled in bulk. Bake in moderately hot oven (375 to 400 deg. F.) for 35 minutes.

Overnight Pancakes

Melt 1 tablespoon butter, place in mixing bowl or jug. Add 1 egg, unbeaten, 2 tablespoons sugar, 1 cup of milk, ½ teaspoon soda, and enough flour for batter. Beat briskly until thoroughly blended. Keep in icebox or cooler overnight. In the morning add 1 teaspoon baking powder and beat in. Now they are ready for the griddle.

"Left-over batter may be used for Scottish pikelets, those tiny pancakes the Scots serve for tea."

Mrs. Geraldine Appleby, Vancouver.

Scotch Oat Cakes

        2 cups ground oatmeal
        1 cup flour
        ¼ teaspoon baking soda
        ¼ teaspoon salt
        ¼ teaspoon sugar
        2 teaspoons baking powder
        ¼ cup lard or other shortening

Mix dry ingredients. Work in the lard with just enough cold water to make a soft dough. Roll thin. Cut into three-cornered pieces and bake in a hot oven until a light brown.

"In these days of rationing, when everyone's butter and sugar are scarce, I find these oatcakes a real saving in the above-mentioned precious ingredients. They can be cut with a round cookie cutter, with jam as a filling."

Mrs. A. Fulton, Vancouver.

Doughnuts in Rhyme

One cup of sugar, one cup of milk,
Two eggs beaten, fine as silk;
Salt and nutmeg (cinnamon will do),
Baking powder, teaspoons two.
Lightly stir the flour in,
Roll on pieboard, not too thin.
Cut in twists or balls or rings,
Drop with care the doughy things
Into hot fat that briskly swells
Evenly the doughy cells.
Watch with care the time for turning,
Fry them brown just short of burning;
Place them on a plate to cool—
I wish you luck with this old rule.

Mrs. G.A. Johnson, New Westminster.

Cookies and Squares

Strawberry Jam Bars

        2½ cups flour
        2 teaspoons baking powder
        ¼ teaspoon salt
        ½ cup brown sugar
        ½ cup white sugar
        ¾ cup butter or shortening
           Milk
           Jam

Mix dry ingredients and rub in shortening. Then add milk to make a soft dough. Roll into a rectangle about ⅛ of an inch thick. Cut into strips, 3 inches wide, and spread jam (scantily) down the centre. Fold edges of pastry to meet in the centre. Press together lightly and cut into bars. Turn bars over and bake 12 to 15 minutes at 400 deg. F.

Mrs. S.M. Sigurdson, New Westminster.

"Soldiers' Favourite" Cookies

1 cup sugar
¾ cup shortening
2 eggs
1 teaspoon cinnamon
2 cups flour
1 teaspoon soda
½ cup chopped nuts
2 cups quick-cooking cereal
1 cup raisins
5 tablespoons water

Cream sugar and shortening and add the well beaten eggs. Add the cinnamon and flour, into which soda has been sifted. Add the cereal, and lastly the raisins which have been stewed in 5 tablespoons water. Use enough of this liquid to make a dough which will drop from a spoon. Drop onto a greased cookie sheet and bake in a hot oven (500 deg. F.) for about 10 minutes.

"Soldiers' Favourite cookies are truly swell. I often send some overseas to my brother. He says the whole camp enjoys them."

Miss Hazel M. Homer, Haney.

Mincemeat Matrimonial Cake

½ cup shortening
1½ cups flour
½ teaspoon salt
1 cup brown sugar
1 teaspoon soda
1¾ cups rolled oats
Mincemeat

Rub first five ingredients together until crumbly. Add rolled oats and mix well. Pat half the mixture into a shallow greased pan, and spread with a layer of mincemeat. Sprinkle with remaining crumb mixture, patting into place. Bake at 325 degrees F. for 25–35 minutes. Cut in squares while still warm.

"I think most people like matrimonial cake but now that dates are things of the dim past we have not been able to bake it. This year, when mincemeat was plentiful, I tried making it with the mincemeat filling and my family decided it liked it even better than with the date filling."

Mrs. Robert Mollard, Westview.

Top-of-the-Range Cookies

1 egg
½ cup milk
¼ teaspoon flavouring
⅓ cup white sugar
¼ teaspoon salt
2½ teaspoons baking powder
1 cup flour
1 tablespoon butter (melted)

Beat egg until light. Add milk, flavouring, sifted dry ingredients and melted butter. Mix. Drop by spoonfuls into deep fat, fry until light brown and cooked through. Drain on paper and roll in sugar.

"You can make these cookies on top of the stove. People living in one-room apartments, with just a gas burner to cook on and a longing for a taste of home-made cookies, will find this recipe useful."

Mrs. A. Janes, Vancouver.

Vinar Tarta (Icelandic)

½ cup butter
1 cup sugar
1 egg
1 teaspoon baking powder
½ cup cream
Vanilla
Flour enough to roll thin

Bake this in 5 thin sheets (using round layer cake pans). Stack them, spreading well-cooked prune filling between the layers. Never cut this when it is fresh but let stand. When ready to serve, cut into small pieces, about ½-inch by 2½ inches.

"I have given this to many as I have travelled about, and they all thought it delicious and something entirely new."

Mrs. O.F. Bjornson, Port Alberni.

Ice-Cold Desserts

Chocolate Sauce for Ice Cream

- 2 squares unsweetened chocolate
- 6 tablespoons water
- ½ cup sugar
  Dash of salt
- 3 tablespoons butter
- ¼ teaspoon vanilla

Add chocolate to water and place over low flame, stirring until blended. Add sugar and salt and cook until sugar is dissolved and mixture very slightly thickened, stirring constantly. Add butter and vanilla. Makes about 1 cupful.

Big-Family Lemon Snow

- 1 cup sugar
- 1 quart water
- 4 tablespoons cornstarch
- 2 lemons
- 2 eggs
- 1 pint milk
  Vanilla

When sugar and water are boiling, thicken with cornstarch, mixed with a little cold water. Cook a few minutes. Then add juice of 2 lemons. Take off stove and add stiffly-beaten whites of 2 eggs and set aside to cool. Make a **Custard** of the 2 yolks with 1 pint milk, a tablespoon of sugar and vanilla.

"This is for a large family—there are nine of us, and it does nicely."

Mrs. Florence Charlton, Vancouver.

Grouse Mountain Fruit Juice Whip

- 3 cups fruit juice
- ½ cup cream of wheat
  Sugar to taste

Bring juice to boil. Slowly sprinkle in cream of wheat, stirring constantly until it begins to thicken. Cook 15 minutes or longer and add the sugar, stirring well. Cool in ice-box. Whip well with egg beater or electric mixer when cool. Serve with cream or whipped cream.

"My mother has been making this very good pudding for years—I think it originated in Finland. We live on Grouse Mountain and have canned a lot of blueberries. We make pies out of these and we use the left-over juice for the pudding. Blackberry juice is especially good for the purpose. The pudding can also be made out of strawberry, loganberry, raspberry or plum juice. Sometimes we rinse out jam, jelly or honey jars for added flavour."

Mrs. Elmi Hebron, Lynn Creek.

Quick Ice Cream

- 1 cup cream
- 3 tablespoons icing sugar
- 2 eggs

Beat cream stiff, add icing sugar and beaten egg yolks. Mix well. Beat egg whites stiff and fold carefully into cream mixture. Add ½ teaspoon vanilla or ¼ cup crushed peppermint candy stick. Place in tray and stir once after it has been freezing 10 to 30 minutes. Return to freezer and freeze another half to three-quarters of an hour.

"Now that ice-cream powders are hard to get, I find this recipe works just as well, and is economical, too."

Mrs. H.B Moore, Westview.

Marianne Linnell (left) serves coffee and treats to guests at the Edith Adams Cottage.

Appetizing Meat Dishes

English Bubble and Squeak

"Cut some of your Sunday roast meat into small pieces. Dust them with salt and pepper and fry in boiling fat. When of a nice brown colour, drain in a hot sieve. While the meat is draining, chop up a boiled cabbage and put it into a greased frying pan. Press it down closely and cover with a plate that fits. Put it over the fire for a few minutes, then uncover. Mix into it 1 ounce of butter and dust well with salt and pepper. Cover the pan again and, when the cabbage is heated through, place upon a hot platter and arrange the meat around it. Carefully lay poached eggs upon the cabbage (as many as are required). Serve very nicely with a boat of nicely-made gravy."

Ethelyn Rosalie Campbell, Victoria.

Mint Sauce for Lamb

¼ cup cider vinegar
¼ cup water
1 tablespoon sugar
¼ teaspoon salt
Dash of pepper
¼ cup finely chopped mint leaves

Combine vinegar, water, sugar, salt and pepper. Bring to the boiling point. Pour over the finely chopped mint leaves. Cool.

How to Make Gravy

For each cup of gravy desired, you will need 2 tablespoons of flour and 2 tablespoons of drippings from the roast. Stir the flour into the drippings and brown slightly. Slowly add the required amount of liquid, which may be water, meat stock or part milk. Cook, stirring constantly, until thickened. Season with salt and pepper.

Nice Way to Cook Tough Meat

Cut the beef in slices and lay at the bottom of a deep basin. Chop a medium-sized onion fine and sprinkle over meat, also salt and pepper and any kind of spices you like. Just cover with cold water and a tight-fitting lid. Let it cook slowly 3 or 4 hours in the oven. Thicken gravy and serve hot.

Mrs. A. Lane, Nanaimo.

January Faggots

1 cup cold mashed potato
1 pound raw ground beef
½ cup chopped raw ham or bacon
1 onion, chopped fine
2 stalks celery, chopped fine
1 egg
1 teaspoon sage
½ teaspoon mustard
Salt and pepper to taste

Mix ingredients until well blended. Form into 2-inch bundles (2 inches thick and 2 inches square). Place in an open baking pan. Pour over them 1 cup tomato juice and bake in a hot oven, basting frequently until richly brown. When baked, remove from pan and make a thickened sauce of the liquid left. Pour this over the faggots and serve with mashed parsnips and Swedish crisp bread. Serves 4 generously.

"This is nice, too, served with an Old Country Yorkshire pudding. It's an original and very tasty dinner dish and, somehow, seems very appropriate for winter weather. Although I made up the recipe myself, my mother, who is from England, says it reminds her of the Old Country faggots they used to have when she was a girl."

Mrs. Judith P. Biggs, Vancouver.

Denver Oysters (Liver)

"Take 24 small pieces of any kind of tender young liver, each about the size of an oyster. Dip in water, milk or cream, then roll in flour. Now here's the trick. Dip again into well-beaten egg and roll again in crushed cracker crumbs which contain a like amount of flour. Fry to a crisp golden brown and serve with applesauce or lemon, and a crisp salad."

Mrs. Violet Dynes, Port Coquitlam.

Fish

Codfish Cakes

      2 cups shredded salt codfish
      2 cups mashed potatoes
      1 tablespoon butter or drippings
      1 beaten egg
  ½ to ⅔ cup milk
      ½ teaspoon baking powder
         Dash of pepper

Freshen salt fish by soaking in cold water for one hour; drain. Cover with boiling water and simmer for 30 minutes; drain. Combine fish and remaining ingredients; beat until light. Cover and allow to stand for about two hours. Mould mixture in round cakes ½-inch thick. Brown in hot fat. Makes about 12 cakes.

Tender-Crisp Fried Fish

      2 lbs. fresh fish (halibut or cod)
      ¾ cup flour
      2 teaspoons salt
      ½ teaspoon paprika
      1 egg, slightly beaten with ¼ cup milk
      1 cup sifted crumbs
      ¼ cup cooking oil or fat

Cut fish into serving pieces and dip in flour which has been mixed with the salt and paprika. Dip fish in egg mixture, then in crumbs. Fry in hot oil or fat, over low heat, until a golden brown on both sides. Serve with lemon wedges. Serves six.

Clamburgers

      1 tin clams
      1 egg
         Seasoning to taste
         Cracker or bread crumbs

Put whole clams through fine mincer. Form into patties; dip into seasoned egg, then into crumbs. Brown on greased griddle. Serve in toasted bun with salad or vegetables as a luncheon or picnic dish. If cooking facilities are available at picnic grounds, Clamburgers may be prepared beforehand and transported in wax paper.

Mrs. A. Talbot, Essondale.

Buttered Trout

Prepare the fish, empty and clean them. Salt them and roll in flour. Heat some butter in a frying pan. Put in the trout and fry until a golden colour over a gentle plate, and sprinkle with chopped parsley. Moisten with a little melted butter added to the butter used in cooking.

Baked Stuffed B.C. Salmon

      2 cups soft bread crumbs
      1 teaspoon salt
         Black pepper
      1 tablespoon minced parsley
      1 tomato, cut in wedges
      2 tablespoons diced celery
      3 tablespoons minced onion
      ½ cup melted butter or substitute
      1 four-pound baking salmon (or other fish)
      2 tablespoons lemon juice

Mix crumbs with seasoning, add parsley and tomato; saute celery and onion in the butter until light yellow. Pour mixture over bread crumbs. Stuff fish. Close opening with skewers or tie with string. Sprinkle fish with lemon juice and bake in 450 degree F. oven about 30 minutes, or until done.

Mrs. Dora Wilkinson, Vancouver.

Wild Game and Garnishes

Wild Goose

Young wild goose may be disjointed and prepared like a good-size young chicken, such as fricasseed, or the pieces dredged in seasoned flour and fried slowly until tender and a golden brown; or it may, of course, be stuffed with a poultry dressing and roasted. Place on a rack in an uncovered roasting pan and roast in a very hot oven (500 deg. F.) for 15 minutes. Reduce heat to 350 deg. F. for remainder of roasting period. Allow 25 minutes per pound for an older goose, and 15 minutes per pound for a gosling.

Roast Bear

Place roast in an uncovered roasting pan. Bake in a slow oven (325 deg. F.), allowing about 40 minutes to the pound. An hour before removing from the oven, sprinkle with salt and pepper.

Reindeer: Cook as you would venison.
Buffalo: Cooked similarly to beef.

Venison Steak or Chops

Rub the steak or chops well with oil and, if desired, a bit of garlic. Fry in a smoking hot frying pan until a rich brown on both sides. A thick steak or chop, rare, would require about 10 minutes. Season with salt and pepper, transfer to a hot platter and dot lightly with butter.

Game Meat Sauces

Currant Jelly Sauce: Blend together ¾ cup of currant jelly and 2 tablespoons of grated orange rind.

Spiced Apple Sauce: One pint apples (peeled, cored and chopped), ½ cup sugar, ½ cup water, pinch of salt, seasoning to taste.

Place apples in a deep baking dish; sprinkle with sugar, pinch of salt, grated orange or lemon rind, and a little cinnamon and nutmeg. Pour over the water and bake in a slow oven (250 to 300 deg. F.) for about two hours, or until a rich brown colour. Serve with game meat or birds.

Broiled Orange Slices: Peel and slice oranges, dot with butter, sprinkle with brown sugar and dust lightly with curry powder. Broil. Serve with game birds.

Stuffed Apples: Core apples and stuff with seasoned sausage meat mixed with half the quantity of bread crumbs. Bake until cooked and tender. Serve with game birds.

Oven-Fried Pheasant

Disjoint the cleaned bird as you would a chicken. Wipe the pieces with a damp cloth, season with salt and pepper and roll them in flour. Brown the meat in hot fat. Pour off excess fat and add a scant ¾ cup of top milk or cream; cover and cook in a moderate oven (350 deg. F.) until the meat is tender, about 1 hour, depending on the size and age of the bird. When the meat is tender, remove the cover and allow the meat to brown slightly. Remove from the pan, add additional milk to the drippings and thicken with a thin flour paste for gravy.

Braised Moose

Take a 4 to 6-pound piece of ripened meat. Trim off and wipe with damp cloth. Place over the top of meat strips of salt pork. Sprinkle with salt, pepper and a light dusting of cinnamon and cloves. Marinate in weak vinegar 2 or 3 days, in cooler or refrigerator, turning meat 2 or 3 times a day. Drain. Brown in drippings from salt pork in heavy frying pan, turning frequently, and then place moose meat in baking pan. Add ½ cup of water to drippings in frying pan. Bring to a boil. Pour over meat. Cover tightly and bake in a slow oven (300 to 325 deg. F.), allowing 35 minutes to the pound for total browning and baking. Turn meat every half-hour. When half-done, season with salt and pepper, adding 1 small onion and ½ bay leaf. Place meat on hot platter. Make pan gravy. Serves 6 to 8.

Roast Quail

Dress, clean and truss. Place on a rack in roasting pan. Brush with melted fat and sprinkle with salt and flour. Bake in a hot oven (400 deg. F.) for 20 minutes. Baste with melted butter or drippings several times during the roasting period.

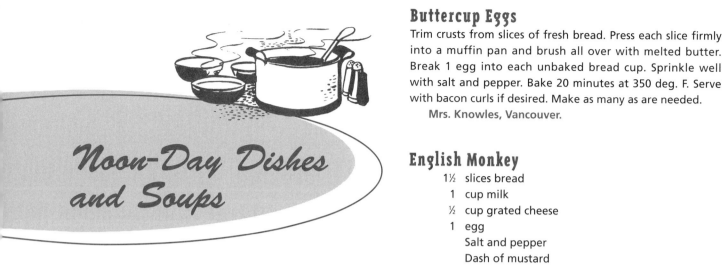

Noon-Day Dishes and Soups

French Toast

- 2 eggs
- ⅔ cup milk
- 1 teaspoon sugar
- ¼ teaspoon salt
- 6 slices bread (raisin, whole wheat or white)
- 2 tablespoons cooking fat

Beat the eggs slightly in a shallow dish; add milk, sugar and salt. Dip bread slices into mixture turning once. Heat fat in heavy frying pan; with wide spatula or pancake turner place bread slices in hot fat and brown on both sides. Serve immediately with syrup, honey, jam or jelly.

Soft French Toast: Allow bread to stand a few seconds in the egg mixture to absorb it.

Crisp French Toast: Dip bread quickly into the egg mixture.

Boxing Day Soup

- 1 carrot
- 1 stalk celery
- 2 slices onion
- Roast turkey bones
- 6 cups water
- ¼ cup rice
- 2 cans mushroom soup
- Salt, pepper

Slice carrot fine. Chop celery. Combine vegetables, turkey bones and water. Simmer, covered, for 2 hours. Strain. There should be 4 cupfuls of stock. Wash rice, add to stock and simmer until tender. Add mushroom soup (if condensed, add equal measure of water or milk), salt and pepper. Bring to boiling point. Serves 4 to 6.

Mrs. Stewart Burridge, Revelstoke.

Buttercup Eggs

Trim crusts from slices of fresh bread. Press each slice firmly into a muffin pan and brush all over with melted butter. Break 1 egg into each unbaked bread cup. Sprinkle well with salt and pepper. Bake 20 minutes at 350 deg. F. Serve with bacon curls if desired. Make as many as are needed.

Mrs. Knowles, Vancouver.

English Monkey

- 1½ slices bread
- 1 cup milk
- ½ cup grated cheese
- 1 egg
- Salt and pepper
- Dash of mustard

Break up bread and soak in milk. Melt cheese over hot fire, stirring all the time. Then add bread and milk to hot cheese, also unbeaten egg, salt, pepper and mustard. Stir over fire for five minutes until creamy. Serve on hot buttered toast. Serves four.

Mrs. Isobel Ashbee, Vancouver.

Cheese Dreams

Make sandwiches of cheese and cut in two. For four sandwiches beat 1 egg slightly, add ½ teaspoon salt, ½ teaspoon paprika, a few grains of cayenne and 1 cup milk. Dip sandwiches into mixture and saute in butter or bacon fat until brown on both sides and cheese is melted, or bake in hot oven until puffed and brown.

A Traditional Christmas

Roast Turkey

For each person allow one pound of meat (undrawn, feet and head on). This will allow for second servings and left-overs for another meal. Allow 1 cup of stuffing per pound of bird.

Time Table
(Weight drawn, minus head and feet)
7 to 10 lbs.—300 deg. F. oven, 30 min. per lb.
10 to 15 lbs.—300 deg. F. oven, 20 min. per lb.
15 to 18 lbs.—300 deg. F. oven, 18 min. per lb.
18 to 20 lbs.—300 deg. F. oven, 15 min. per lb.

Use uncovered roaster. Add no water. Do not baste. Start the roasting period about half an hour ahead of schedule. This will give you ample time for making gravy, removing the trussing cords and arranging the bird for serving. Place the trussed bird breast side down on the rack in a roasting pan. Cover with a clean white cloth moistened with melted cooking fat or oil. This cloth holds the fat and keeps the bird greased, doing away with the necessity for basting. Roast until half done, then place bird breast side up and replace cloth over top of bird. Remoisten cloth with melted fat if it is dry. Continue roasting until done. Remove the cloth the last 30 minutes should the bird not be browned enough. To know when the bird is cooked to the right turn, make this test: Press the thickest part of the drumstick between the fingers; if quite soft, the meat is well done. Or, if leg joints move readily, turkey is done.

Old-Fashioned Stuffing
   8   cups soft bread crumbs (about 1½ loaves day-old white bread)
2½ teaspoons salt
⅓ teaspoon pepper
   3   tablespoons finely minced parsley
½ cup finely minced celery
⅓ cup finely minced onion
   2   teaspoons mixed poultry seasoning (or to taste)
½ cup mild flavoured drippings (part butter if possible)

Combine all ingredients, working the drippings in with the finger tips. To 1 cup of this mixture add 1 slightly beaten egg and use to stuff the crop. The egg binds the stuffing and makes it easier to carve. A little stock or milk may be added to the remainder of the stuffing for filling loosely into the body cavity. Sufficient stuffing for a 10 or 12-pound bird.

Cranberry Sauce
   1   pound cranberries
1½ cups sugar
1½ cups boiling water

Pick over the berries, wash thoroughly and drain. Add sugar and water and cook without stirring until the skins burst (about 5 minutes). Remove from heat and allow to cool in saucepan. Turn into serving dish.

If you do not wish a thick sauce, simmer the sugar and water together for only 1 minute.

Old English Plum Pudding
(Family Recipe, 100 years old)
¾ pound chopped suet
   1   pound breadcrumbs
   4   cups flour
1½ pounds raisins
½ pound currants
   1   pound dates (or cherries)
¼ pound candied peel (chopped fine)
   1   pound can golden syrup
   2   ounces almonds (blanched and chopped)
   1   teaspoon mixed spice
½ teaspoon nutmeg
      Juice of 2 lemons and grated rind of one
   4   eggs, well beaten
½ cup of any fruit juice

Mix together thoroughly. Fill pudding bowls to ½-inch of top, tie down with damp cloth (loosely enough to allow pudding to swell). Tie corners of cloth up over top of bowls. Put into boiling water which comes almost to the top of bowls. Cover the boiler tightly and boil for 8 hours. When water boils down, add more boiling water. When done, take out and untie cloths and allow to dry. When dry, tie cloths on loosely and store in a dry place, preferably on a shelf, covered with a cloth. (Do not put in a covered tin, as it will cause them to mould.) When ready to use, steam again for 2 or 3 hours, and serve with your favourite pudding sauce. If kept dry, they will keep indefinitely.

Ellen Reeder, Eburne.

Stuffed Celery

Mash 1 small package of cream cheese and blend smooth with 2 tablespoons of cream or mayonnaise. Season with salt and pepper and add one-third cup of chopped stuffed olives and a dash of condiment sauce. Use as a filling for celery stalks.

Christmas Tree Croutons

Cut a tree pattern about 2 inches tall from pasteboard. Lay pattern on thin slices of bread and cut around edges with a sharp knife. Toast or fry golden brown. Cover thickly with minced parsley or chives. Place on top of individual soup servings.

Hard Sauce Stars

- ½ cup butter
- ½ teaspoon salt
- 2 teaspoons vanilla
- 2½ cups sifted confectioner's sugar

Combine butter, salt and vanilla, mix until blended. Add sugar gradually and cream until light and fluffy. Spread mixture in a shallow pan and chill thoroughly. Cut in stars with 2-inch star cutter. Makes 18.

It is best to spread mixture over the bottom of an inverted pan. Cut the stars and lift with a thin spatula or thin-bladed sharp knife.

Christmas Cookies

- ½ cup butter or shortening
- 1 cup sugar
- 2 eggs, well beaten
- 1 tablespoon milk
- ½ teaspoon vanilla
- 2½ cups cake flour
- 2 teaspoons baking powder
- ¼ teaspoon salt
- ½ cup ground nuts (almonds or filberts)

Cream butter or shortening, add sugar gradually, continuing to cream. Add eggs, milk and vanilla. Sift flour, measure and sift with baking powder and salt. Add to first mixture, with nuts, gradually stirring it in. Chill dough thoroughly (overnight in refrigerator if possible). Roll out quite thin on a lightly floured board. Cut in fancy Christmas shapes, such as stars, bells or wreaths. Bake in a moderate oven (350 deg. F.) for about 10 minutes, or until delicately browned. If desired, decorate with icing, green citron, candied cherries or dragees. Makes about 7 dozen.

Candy Canes

- 2 cups granulated sugar
- ¼ teaspoon cream of tartar
- ⅔ cup water
   Red and green food colouring
- ¼ teaspoon mint flavouring

Combine sugar, cream of tartar and water. Place over low heat, stirring constantly until mixture begins to boil. Cook without stirring to 265 deg. F. (hard ball in cold water). Remove from heat and wipe off the pouring side of saucepan with a damp cloth. Pour the hot syrup into a lightly buttered pan to form thin sheet; allow to cool undisturbed. When cool enough to handle divide in two parts, add red colouring to one half and green to the other and a few drops of mint flavouring to each. Pull like taffy until very firm and the candy loses most of its gloss. Stretch into ropes about ½ inch in diameter. Twine a pink and a green rope together. Cut in 3-inch pieces and twist until stretched to 5 inches. Curve one end and allow to harden overnight. Makes about 2 dozen canes.

Uncooked Mincemeat

- 1 pound currants
- ¾ pound raisins
- 2 pounds apples (finely chopped)
- ½ pound sultanas
- 1 pound brown sugar
   Juice of 4 oranges and 2 lemons, and finely chopped peel of lemons
- ¾ pound of suet (chopped)
- ½ pound mixed candied peel (finely chopped)
- 1 teaspoon mace
- 1 teaspoon allspice

Mix thoroughly and pack into sealers. Seal tightly. Keep in a cool place. When time comes to use, make pastry for a two-crust pie. Use 3 cups prepared mincemeat as the filling. Bake in a hot oven (425° deg. F.) for 40 minutes.

Ellen Reeder, Eburne.

Cocktails and Punches

Mint Julep:

Sprigs of mint, ½ teaspoon powdered sugar, ice, Bourbon whisky, cracked ice. Put 2 sprigs of mint in tall glass or pewter tankard, add sugar and crush gently with spoon or swizzle stick. Put in 2 lumps of ice and cover with Bourbon; fill glass with cracked ice and chill several hours to frost glass. Top with mint.

Gin Rickey:

Put cube of ice in medium-sized glass, add juice of ½ lemon or one lime and 1 jigger (glass measure, about 1½ liquid ounces) of gin, and fill glass with carbonated water. Stir and garnish with sprig of mint, if desired. Bourbon, rum, rye or Scotch may be substituted for gin.

Planter's Punch:

1 part lime juice, 3 parts Jamaica rum, 2 teaspoons powdered sugar and dash of bitters. Strain into a tall glass, half-filled with cracked ice, garnish with maraschino cherry, a sliver of pineapple, a slice of orange and a sprig of mint. Serve with a straw.

Hot Whisky Toddy:

1 lump sugar, 1 teaspoon hot water, 1 stick (½-inch) cinnamon, 1 twist lemon peel, 2 whole cloves, 1½ ounces rye whisky, hot water. Dissolve sugar in hot water; add cinnamon, lemon peel and cloves, and crush with swizzle stick or spoon. Add rye and serve in Old-Fashioned or 6-ounce glass, with silver pitcher of hot water on the side. Add small piece of butter, if desired.

Canadian Navy Cocktail:

1 part demerara rum, ½ part Montserrat lime juice, ⅛ part maple syrup, 1 part water.

New Year's Eggnog:

6 eggs (separated), ¾ cup granulated sugar, 1½ cups cognac brandy, ½ cup rum, 4 cups milk, 4 cups heavy cream, nutmeg. Beat egg yolks until very light, add granulated sugar and continue beating until well blended; slowly add brandy and rum, then the milk and cream. Beat egg whites until stiff; fold into egg yolk-brandy mixture. Grate or sprinkle nutmeg lightly over each glass. Approximate yield: 24 portions.

Daiquiri Cocktail:

⅓ jigger lime or lemon juice, ⅔ jigger Bacardi rum, 1 teaspoon sugar.

Highballs:

1 jigger of Scotch, rye, gin or brandy; ice. Fill with soda or ginger ale.

Tom Collins:

Juice of 1 lemon, 1 jigger gin, 1 teaspoon sugar. Fill with soda.

Punch for Party of Fifteen:

1 bottle rum, 1 bottle wine, 10 lemons, 2 oranges, 2 pounds sugar, 10 eggs. Dissolve sugar in juice of lemons and oranges and rind of 1 orange. Strain carefully into bowl and add by degrees the whites of eggs, beaten to a froth. Place bowl on ice for one hour, then stir in rum and wine.

Fruit Juice-Ginger Ale Punch

2	quarts strong tea
1½–2	quarts loganberry juice
1⅔	cups strained lemon juice
4	cups strained orange juice
2	quarts water
1	cup sugar
6	bottles (9 oz.) ginger ale

Mix tea, fruit juices, water and sugar, and chill ½ day. Just before serving, add ginger ale and pour over large piece of ice in punch bowl. Makes 8 quarts, or 60 small glasses.

Jellies

General Directions for Making Jelly

1. This method can be used for apples, crabapples, gooseberries, loganberries, grapes, currants and sour plums or such combinations as grape and apple, plum and apple, quince and apple, or red currant and raspberry.
2. Select clean, sound but slightly under-ripe fruit. Over-ripe fruit does not make good jelly.
3. Cut or crush, do not core or peel fruit. Add water to come just below top of fruit. Cook slowly until fruit is soft and mushy and juice is drawn out.
4. Drain thoroughly through a moist jelly bag. Do not squeeze bag if you wish a clear jelly.
5. Measure juice and sugar. Allow ¾ cup sugar to each cup juice.
6. Boil juice gently for 10 to 20 minutes, testing frequently for pectin.
7. Add heated sugar. Boil 3 to 8 minutes or until jelly sheets from spoon (220 deg F.).
8. Pour into hot sterilized jars. Let stand until set. Seal.

Pectin Test

To test for pectin with alcohol, measure 1 tablespoon fruit juice into a dish and add 1 tablespoon alcohol. If a jelly-like mass forms, a large amount of pectin is present and the sugar can be added. If the mixture remains unchanged in consistency, boil the juice a few minutes longer—until the test gives a jelly-like mass (do not taste mixture). Then add sugar.

Rose Hip Juice:

4 cups rose hips, 2 cups boiling water. Wash hips, remove ends, chop coarsely. Add boiling water. Cook 5 minutes and strain through a jelly bag. Add 1 cup of this juice (rich in vitamins) to 3 cups of prepared apple juice and proceed as for apple jelly.

Salal Berry Jelly:

Gather as many salal berries as you think you need, wash them and add enough water to cover. Cook for 10 minutes, crushing the berries with a wooden spoon while cooking to obtain their full flavour. Pour into a jelly bag and press out the juice, measure same and bring to the boil. Then add 1 cup of sugar to 1 cup of juice. Boil until the mixture jells. Pour into jars and seal.

Mrs. E.M. Read, North Vancouver.

Mountain Ash (Rowan) Jelly:

Stem fruit, wash in 3 waters. Cover with fresh water and boil until soft. Mash with masher and strain through a flannel jelly bag. Measure juice and boil 25 minutes. Now add 1 to 1⅓ cups sugar to 1 cup fruit juice (as measured). Stir as the sugar is sprinkled in. When juice is well on the boil, skim, and it is done.

Miss Josephine Rowa, Vancouver.

Geranium Crabapple Jelly:

"For those who like adventures in flavours, I believe this is one of my best tricks: Place a small, rose-scented geranium leaf in the bottom of each sterilized glass just before you pour in crabapple jelly. Seal as usual. After about a month open a jar and you will find that you have something special in flavour."

Mrs. A. McKenzie, Vancouver.

The Vancouver Sun's 11th Annual Cook Book

1946

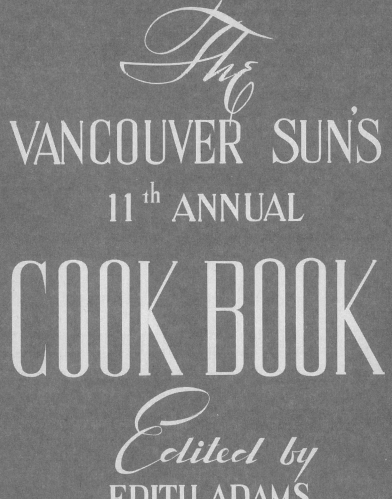

The

VANCOUVER SUN'S
11th ANNUAL

COOK BOOK

Edited by
EDITH ADAMS

Including: PRIZE WINNING RECIPES
CANNING, CALORIE CHART, ENTERTAINING

SUN READERS CAN AID WORLD'S STARVING MILLIONS

Never in modern times have so many people in the world faced starvation. Tens of thousands will die this year for lack of food. Great Britain has adopted the slogan "Dig Against Famine" in an effort to have its people grow more and more vegetables; defeated Germany has had its individual daily ration cut to 1000 calories; other lands, their people weak with hunger, look to Canada and the United States for food which does not come or comes in insufficient quantities.

By ceaseless economy in the kitchen, each British Columbia home can release food supplies for these unfortunate fellow human beings. Every loaf of bread, every can of vegetables, every pound of bacon, that is NOT used in Canada, can be sent abroad to save life. Buy less, stretch every ounce of food to its uttermost, waste nothing. That is the underlying purpose of this Eleventh Annual Cook Book of Readers' Recipes, published by The Vancouver Sun.

EDITH ADAMS,

Cookery Editor.

1946 Cakes

Quickest-Cake-in-the-World

- 5 eggs
- 1 cup sugar (approximate)
- 1 cup cake flour
- 1 teaspoon baking powder
- Vanilla
- Jam

Beat together the eggs and sugar. Then add flour, baking powder and a little vanilla. Pour into two equal-size cake tins and bake. Spread a little jam between the layers.

"This cake takes no butter and the only washing-up after mixing is a bowl and spoon. This is so simple and easy to make that the recipe should be popular with bachelors and children, as well as housewives."

Mrs. Harold Neave, Francois Lake.

Buttermilk or Sour Milk White Cake

- ½ cup shortening
- ⅔ cup sugar
- 2 eggs
- 2 cups flour
- ½ teaspoon salt
- ½ teaspoon soda
- 1 teaspoon baking powder
- ⅔ cup buttermilk or sour milk

Cream shortening and sugar. Add beaten eggs, then add sifted dry ingredients alternately with buttermilk or sour milk. Bake in moderate oven. (By substituting the white sugar for brown and adding 1 teaspoon cinnamon, ½ teaspoon nutmeg and ½ teaspoon allspice to the dry ingredients, the above recipe makes a grand spice cake. To make a chocolate cake of the above recipe, add three squares of melted chocolate or three tablespoons cocoa.)

"This makes a nice moist white cake and uses up sour milk or buttermilk."

Mrs. John Lukacs, Vancouver.

Blueberry and Applesauce Cake

- ⅓ cup shortening
- ½ cup sugar
- 1 egg (beaten)
- 2 cups flour
- 1 teaspoon cinnamon
- ½ teaspoon nutmeg
- ¼ teaspoon salt
- 1½ cups applesauce (slightly sweetened)
- 1 teaspoon baking soda (stir into applesauce)
- 1½ cups blueberries (floured)
- Any left-over stewed figs or prunes

Cream shortening, sugar and egg. Add other ingredients in order named. Bake in a moderately hot oven from 25 to 30 minutes. Sprinkle with confectioner's sugar and serve hot or cold.

"One day while in a mood to use up this, that and the other, I concocted the above cake. It's nice and moist. The family all proclaimed it a big success."

Mrs. J.H. Hobbins, Quesnel.

Mother's Pear Cake

- 2 eggs, beaten light
- 1 cup sugar
- ½ cup cold water
- ½ cup melted butter
- ½ cup chopped walnuts
- 1 cup sticky raisins (cut up)
- ⅔ cup chopped pears (canned)
- ¼ teaspoon each of cinnamon, allspice, cloves, nutmeg
- 1 teaspoon soda in a little warm water
- 1½ cups flour

Bake in a square tin in a medium oven (350 deg. F.).

For Icing:

Cream butter and icing sugar, add table cream and vanilla.

Mrs. B.M. Love, Vancouver.

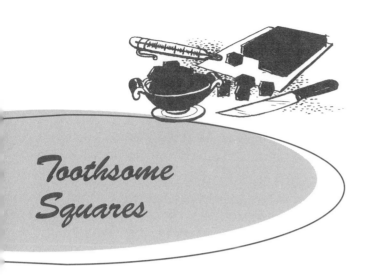

Toothsome Squares

Quick Date Squares

½   cup shortening (butter is best)
1   cup brown sugar
2   eggs
1   cup dates
½   cup walnuts or pecans
1   teaspoon vanilla
1½ cups flour
1½ teaspoons baking powder
½   teaspoon salt
½   teaspoon cinnamon

Melt the shortening, then add the sugar. Beat well. Add the eggs which have been well beaten, then add cut dates and nut meats, also flavouring. Stir well. Add the flour, baking powder, salt and cinnamon, sifted together. Stir well. Grease a flat pan and spread this mixture out as much as you can. Bake in a moderate oven 30 minutes, or until nicely browned. Cut into squares while hot. Powder with icing sugar, if desired.

"These are delicious."
Mrs. Hazel G. Campbell, Vancouver.

Raised Oven Doughnuts

4¾ cups flour
1½ cups milk
⅓   cup shortening
4   tablespoons sugar
2   teaspoons salt
2   teaspoons nutmeg
2   eggs, well beaten
2   cakes compressed yeast (softened in 4 table-spoons lukewarm water)
    Melted butter or substitute
    Sugar

Sift flour and measure. Bring milk to the boiling point and pour over the shortening, sugar, salt and spices in a large mixing bowl. Cool to lukewarm. Add sifted flour, eggs and softened yeast. Beat until well mixed. Cover and let stand in warm place until dough is double in bulk (about 50 or 60 minutes). Turn dough onto well-floured board, turning over two or three times to shape in soft ball. (Dough will be soft to handle.) Roll out lightly (to avoid stretching) to about ½-inch thickness. Cut with 3-inch doughnut cutter and place rings carefully, 2 inches apart, on greased baking sheet. (Doughnut rings may be twisted into figure 8's or cruller shapes.) Brush with melted butter, or substitute, and let rise in a warm place until double in bulk (about 20 minutes). Bake in hot oven of 425 deg. F. for 8 to 10 minutes. After removing from oven, brush top lightly with melted butter and roll doughnuts in sugar. Recipe makes approximately 3 dozen doughnuts.

"We like this recipe as the doughnuts are not greasy."
Mrs. Ray A. Weaver, Cranberry Lake.

True Wartime Cookies

4   tablespoons shortening
½   cup (approx.) jam or jelly (it won't matter if fer-mented)
¾   cup flour
¼   teaspoon baking soda
1   teaspoon baking powder
    Vanilla
    Salt
½   cup quick oats
¾   cup cornflakes
¼   cup raisins
¼   cup dates (nuts, etc., may be substituted)

Drop on well-greased cookie sheet and bake 10 minutes at 400 deg. F. Makes 2½ dozen cookies.

"No butter, no sugar, no eggs and no milk—this is truly a wartime recipe, and the cookies are delicious, too. Everything in them is economical and easily obtained."
Mrs. R.B. McKenzie, North Vancouver.

Jumbo Raisin Cookies

1   cup water
2   cups raisins
1   cup shortening
2   cups sugar
3   eggs
1   teaspoon vanilla
4   cups all-purpose flour
1   teaspoon baking powder
1   teaspoon soda
2   teaspoons salt
1½ teaspoons cinnamon
½   teaspoon nutmeg
¼   teaspoon allspice
1   cup chopped nuts (optional)

Boil water and raisins for 5 minutes. Cool. Cream shortening, add sugar, then 3 eggs, beaten well. Add vanilla and cooled raisin mixture. Sift dry ingredients. Add to raisin mixture and blend well. Chill. Drop by teaspoonfuls on a greased floured baking sheet. Bake in 400 deg. F. oven for 12 to 15 minutes. Makes 6 dozen cookies.

"These jumbo cookies require no butter, and both children and grown-ups love them."

Mrs. C. Escott, Vancouver.

No-Shortening Recipes, Butter Stretchers

Army Cook's Butter Stretcher

"Now that butter is getting harder to get, I have come across a new method to stretch out our short ration allowance. I think it is a real help-out on this problem. First, I got some good beef fat and rendered it down gently so as not to discolour the dripping. Then, to 1 pound of butter (cut up in small chunks) I added an equal amount of beef dripping and mixed up very well. That made 2 pounds and, when the mixture was set the difference from real butter was hardly noticeable. The beef dripping sure seemed to add taste and zest besides doubling the amount."

Barney Duncan, Army Cook, Vancouver.

Yuletide Butter

       1   pound butter
       1   pound fluffy vegetable shortening
       4   eggs
           Salt to taste

Soften butter and shortening. Beat with a rotary beater until soft and smooth. Add one egg at a time, and beat well after each addition. Salt to taste.

"If the eggs have real yellow yolks the butter will have a better colour and the flavour will be improved. Put in a cool place to set and you will be pleasantly surprised at the quantity and quality of the butter."

Mrs. William Peers, Chilliwack.

Home-made Lard for Pies

"This is an original recipe of my own for securing enough lard for two pies from 1 pound of pork sausage. First, fry the sausage slowly, pouring off grease from time to time. When all the grease is rendered, pour boiling water over lard. Allow to stand on stove until lard is heated through and stir.

Then remove from stove to cool. When lard is set, tip pan to one side and pour off water and sediment. Repeat once again, then remove lard and place in refrigerator to chill. The boiling water purifies the lard and removes all taste."

Mrs. Fred Clark, Vancouver.

Fluffy Home-made Shortening

"Save fat from all cooked meats. When you have collected about two cupfuls, melt it and strain through a clean cloth. Let stand and cool but do not set. Add one-eighth teaspoon soda and beat with electric mixer, increasing the speed as fat becomes thicker. When it is thick and white, let it set and you have some nice, fluffy shortening for pies, cakes and cookies. At this time, when shortening is so scarce, this answers the purpose very nicely."

Mrs. K. Russo, Vancouver.

Ice-Cold Desserts for Hot Days

Peach Milk Sherbet

          4   peaches
              Juice of ½ lemon
   ¼ to ⅓   cup sugar
          1   teaspoon gelatine
          2   cups milk
          1   egg
              Salt

Skin peaches and put through sieve or fruit press. Sprinkle with lemon juice and sugar (to taste) and let stand. Place gelatine in 1 cup milk and heat to dissolve. Separate egg and beat yolk into other cup of milk with a few grains of salt. Chill milk mixtures. Then beat both together. Beat egg white and beat into sieved peaches. Then add milk and beat all together. Put into refrigerator tray and set refrigerator for freezing ice-cream. Freeze to a mush and again beat smooth in cold bowl. Return to tray and freeze until firm.

Mrs. W.R. Trembath, New Westminster.

Caramel Ice Cream

1½ cups top milk or table cream
2 tablespoons white sugar
2 eggs
A sprinkle of salt
1 teaspoon plain gelatine
¼ cup golden syrup

Scald the milk in a double boiler. Melt the white sugar in a frying pan, stirring constantly until golden in colour. Add to the scalded milk. Stir until the caramel is dissolved. Pour over well-beaten yolks of two eggs. Cook in double boiler until the mixture coats the spoon. Take off the heat. Add salt and gelatine softened with a little water. Stir well and cool. Put in freezer until almost frozen. Beat egg whites stiff, adding syrup slowly. Beat frozen mixture till soft but not melted. Fold in egg-white and syrup mixtures. Return to freezer until frozen.

Miss M.E. Colman, Vancouver.

Banana Icebox Cake

1½ cups milk
2 eggs
2 tablespoons flour
½ cup sugar
1 tablespoon butter
3 bananas
12 graham wafers, rolled into fine crumbs

Scald milk. Mix beaten eggs, flour and sugar. Add to milk and cook in a double boiler until smooth and thick. Add butter and flavouring (vanilla or lemon). Cool. Line an oblong pan with waxed paper. First, put in a layer of crumbs, then a layer of bananas, then custard. Repeat until all bananas and custard are used. Then finish top with crumbs. Chill for 6 hours. Turn out and take off the waxed paper. If possible, serve with whipped cream. Enough for 6.

"This nourishing dessert can be easily made without a refrigerator on chilly nights."

Mrs. Stewart Burridge, Revelstoke.

Apricot Mousse

1 pint canned apricots
1 banana
¾ cup orange marmalade
1 teaspoon gelatine
1 cup heavy cream

Rub the apricots and banana through the colander, add the apricot juice and the marmalade. Add gelatine which has been soaked for 5 minutes in 1 tablespoon cold water, and thoroughly dissolve over hot water. This mixture should be very sweet. If not, add as much powdered sugar as may seem necessary. Fold into cream which has been beaten stiff. Pour into refrigerator trays and freeze without stirring.

Miss R. Grant, Chilliwack.

Make Use of "No Token" Meats

Rabbit en Casserole

Cut rabbit into serving pieces, season and brown in hot fat. Brown one medium-sized onion and make gravy with the remaining fat, adding a little sage or poultry dressing. Place rabbit in casserole. Pour gravy and onion over it and bake in oven at 375 deg. F. 45 minutes for a young rabbit and longer for an older one.

James Lawrence, Vancouver.

Chicken de Luxe

Place chicken (cut as for frying) in a casserole. Salt and pepper it. Add 3 not-too-large carrots (quartered) and two onions (quartered). Then fill the casserole to three-quarters full with milk. Place in oven. When done, thicken with the gravy and flour. Serve with potatoes.

"This is simple and delicious. Boiling fowl served this way is always tender and has a grand flavour."

Mrs. Sam Lamont, Penticton.

Scotch Eggs

7 eggs
1 pound sausage meat
Browned bread crumbs

Hard-boil 6 eggs and remove shells. Beat up seventh egg. Divide meat into 6 portions. Roll each egg in meat and cover completely. Dip in beaten egg and roll in browned crumbs. Fry in boiling deep fat. Reduce temperature to avoid burning. Drain on paper. Serve hot with vegetables or use on salad plate, splitting egg lengthwise. Beets and French-fried potatoes make good accompaniments.

Mrs. William Ellis, Vancouver.

Savoury Ham

Rub a paste of 2 tablespoons of dry mustard and 2 tablespoons water into both sides of a slice of tenderized ham, about 1¾ inches thick. (About 2 lbs. Size of slice may vary.) Place ham slice in shallow baking dish, cover with 1 cup milk and bake 45 minutes at 425 deg. F—or until ham is tender and top is nicely browned.

"Mustard, ham and milk are easily combined and the oven does the rest. This has become a request in our home—a time-saver with a grand flavour."

Mrs. R.C. Russell, Vancouver.

More Fish at Home—More Fish Abroad

Keirgary (Dutch)

- 1 cup raw rice
- ½ pound dry salt cod
- ½ can tomatoes
- 2 tablespoons vinegar
  Butter (size of walnut)
- ¼ teaspoon pepper
- ¼ teaspoon cayenne pepper

Boil rice until nearly done. Soak for 1 hour the salt cod (the kind that is packed in small wooden boxes). Break it up and add to the rice. Put in one-half can tomatoes, or its equivalent in fresh tomatoes, cut up. Add vinegar, butter and seasonings and cook in oven casserole or on top of stove, until done. Taste it for salt, as the fish may salt it sufficiently. "This is an appetizing dish for meatless days."

Mrs. C.M. Lyne, North Vancouver.

Creamed Mushrooms and Fish

- ⅔ cup sliced mushrooms
- 2 tablespoons butter
- 4 tablespoons flour
- ½ teaspoon salt
  Pepper
- 2 cups milk
- 2 cups flaked cooked fish
  Minced parsley

Saute mushrooms in butter. Blend in flour, salt and pepper. Add milk slowly. Cook in double boiler, stirring constantly until thick. Add fish and minced parsley. Heat and serve on toast.

"This makes a nice luncheon for Lent."

N.I. McDonald, New Westminster.

Crabmeat Pie

- 3 cups thick white sauce
- ½ pound grated cheese
- 1 teaspoon celery salt
- 1 medium green pepper (may be omitted)
- 2 medium cans crabmeat
- 1 small can sliced mushrooms
  Salt and pepper
  Pastry
  Cracker crumbs
  Butter

Make white sauce in double boiler. Blend grated cheese into sauce, stirring until smooth. Add celery salt and chopped green pepper, then flaked crabmeat and sliced mushrooms. Season. Cool. Pour this mixture into deep baking dish which has been lined with pastry (individual ramekins may be used). Cover with cracker crumbs and dot lightly with butter. Bake in oven at 400 deg. F. until brown. Serves 6.

Mrs. Reginald Sangster, Vancouver.

Bread Stuffing for Salmon

- ½ lemon or ½ cup cranberries
- 1 medium onion
- ½ cup any pickle (ground)
- 1 salmon liver, soaked 10 minutes in vinegar
- ½ cup chopped celery
- 1 level teaspoon poultry dressing
  Salt and pepper
- 4 tablespoons melted butter, shortening or cream
- 1½ cups bread crumbs

Grind lemon (rind and all), onion, pickles and liver. Add celery, seasonings and butter and mix well with bread crumbs. Pack into cleaned salmon. Sift flour and more seasoning over fish and bake slowly for 2 hours.

Mrs. Violet E. Dynes, Port Coquitlam.

Appetite Appeal for Vegetables

Spinach Puffs for Meatless Days

1½ pounds spinach or other greens (about 2 cupfuls, cooked)
½ cup thick cream sauce
2 eggs
½ cup bread crumbs
Salt and pepper
Few grains nutmeg
2 tablespoons mild-flavoured fat

Wash and cook greens and chop slightly. Add sauce, beaten eggs, bread crumbs and seasonings to greens. Melt fat in hot frying pan and drop mixture by spoonfuls. Brown on both sides.

"This is just the meal for meatless days."

Mrs. R. Thomas, Armstrong.

Breaded Green Marrows

"In our Victory garden we have a lot of small immature green marrows. This is how I serve them: I wash and dry them, leaving on the peel. Then I cut into slices, dip into egg and cracker crumbs and fry until golden brown. This is an attractive way to serve marrows—golden crumbly slices with green edges. I cook cucumbers the same way, except that I slice them lengthwise."

Mrs. F. Lawson, Kamloops.

Potato Suzettes

6 medium-sized potatoes
2 tablespoons melted butter
½ cup hot milk
1 tablespoon grated cheese
6 eggs
6 tablespoons buttered crumbs
Salt and pepper

Prepare as for stuffed potatoes. Bake first, scoop out potato. Mash and season. Refill the shells almost to the top. Break an egg into each opening, season with salt and pepper, and sprinkle with buttered crumbs. Bake long enough to set the eggs, as in cooking poached eggs. Brown lightly about 6 minutes.

Miss R. Grant, Chilliwack.

Green Onions on Toast

On toasted bread slices place small bundles of cooked green onions (as per asparagus). Pour over them melted cheese. Serve.

"Here is an 'a la' way to serve the homely bread and cheese and onion. It makes a nice snack for any time."

Mrs. F. Lawson, Kamloops.

Garden Peas with Mint

1 tablespoon butter
2 tablespoons flour
½ teaspoon salt
⅛ teaspoon pepper
1 cup milk
¼ cup finely chopped mint
2 cups hot cooked peas

Melt the fat, add flour, salt and pepper, and mix thoroughly. Add the milk gradually and bring to the boiling point, stirring constantly. Add the chopped mint and peas. Mix together and serve at once.

Miss Ruby Grant, Chilliwack.

Creamed Cauliflower de Luxe

Cook a medium-sized cauliflower in the usual way. Have ready about 2 cupfuls seasoned creamy white sauce. Add 2 chopped hard-boiled eggs, 1 tablespoon prepared mustard and at the last, a spoonful of chopped chives. Pour over cauliflower and serve.

Miss Elsie M. Birss, Vancouver.

Edith Adams' Twelfth Annual Prize Cook Book

1948

EDITH ADAMS' TWELFTH ANNUAL

Prize COOK BOOK

READERS'
TESTED RECIPES •
BASIC COOKERY •

By EDITH ADAMS

Director, Edith Adams' Cottage
Homemakers' Service
THE VANCOUVER SUN

THE SUN

For more than twenty years, Western Canada's most versatile home cooks have been sending their favourite recipes to Edith Adams, and this well-known food authority has been publishing one of them each day, with a dollar prize award, in her regular newspaper column. Women everywhere have liked the practical recipes and many of them, by popular demand, have been compiled into a number of Edith Adams' Prize Cook Books. This is the twelfth of the series and, with more than 550 readers' recipes and basic cookery recipes from Miss Adams' own file, easily becomes the largest of them all. Each recipe on the following pages will be found to have a certain "different" quality that will delight homemakers. Indeed, the entire book will serve as a good basis for practising that most satisfying of all domestic arts— home cooking.

Fish

Fraser River Salmon Royal
(Native Dish Contest Grand Winner)

Clean a salmon, fillet, and sprinkle with salt inside and out. Stuff with oyster stuffing and sew. Cut 5 gashes diagonally on each side of backbone and insert narrow pieces of salt pork. Arrange on a baking dish and sprinkle with salt, pepper and dredge with flour. Bake in a 400 degree F. oven 25 minutes to the pound. Serve with drawn butter or tomato sauce.

Oyster Stuffing:

Mix 2 cups soft bread crumbs with ¼ cup mild shortening. Add:

- ¾ teaspoon salt
- ½ teaspoon black pepper
- 1 tablespoon parsley
- 1½ tablespoons lemon juice
- 1 cup chopped oysters

Drawn Butter Sauce:

Melt 3 tablespoons butter, add 3 tablespoons flour and stir until well blended. Add 1½ cups boiling water gradually and stir until sauce is smooth. Then add ¼ cup butter in small pieces. Season with ½ teaspoon salt. Add 1 tablespoon lemon juice and 1 tablespoon chopped parsley.

Tomato Sauce:

- 1 medium size onion, chopped fine
- ¼ cup chopped celery
- 2 tablespoons shortening
- ½ teaspoon salt
- ⅛ teaspoon pepper
- 1 bay leaf
- 2 cups canned tomatoes
- 1 tablespoon finely chopped parsley
- ½ teaspoon nutmeg

Combine ingredients and cook for 5 minutes. Pour over skinned fish just before serving.

Mrs. S. Bingaman, New Westminster.

Two Meals in One

Prepare enough potatoes and carrots. Cook in water for 10 minutes and then add enough Alaska Black Cod for the meal. Cook approximately 10 minutes more or until vegetables are tender. Serve, saving liquid. Into this liquid, later, place a package of noodle soup mix. Cook the required time and serve with crackers.

"This is a wholesome arrangement, for nothing of value goes down the drain. And is it good!"

Mr. Todd Voikin, Vancouver.

Locarno Smelts

Clean, wash and dry 2 pounds of smelts. Dip in dry flour, shaking off surplus. Fry in shortening or oil until nice and brown on both sides. Arrange in layers in deep dish. Sprinkle each layer with chopped shallots or onions, sage, parsley, salt, pepper and a sliver of garlic. Finally, cover with vinegar and leave overnight.

"These keep almost indefinitely. With olives, etc., they're delicious served as appetizers."

Mrs. Margaret Ielmini, Vancouver.

Cooking a Skate

Place fish in a pan of boiling salted water, simmer 5 minutes, then pour water off and cover with milk, medium-sized onion (sliced or whole), 1 tablespoon butter, salt and pepper. Simmer until tender.

"I find that children are very fond of skate cooked this way and it is very nutritious. The milk can be served as a cream soup."

Mrs. Eric Springer, Vancouver.

The sign marking the entrance.

Meats

Cariboo Short Ribs of Beef
(Native Dish Contest Winner)

6 pieces short ribs in 3-inch lengths
3 tablespoons flour
1 teaspoon salt
¼ teaspoon pepper and paprika mixed
2 tablespoons fat
1 onion, chopped
¼ cup cider vinegar
2 tablespoons brown sugar
2 tablespoons Worcestershire sauce
1 cup water
½ teaspoon dry mustard
½ cup celery, diced

Have the ribs in 3-inch pieces. Combine flour, salt, pepper and paprika; rub the seasoned flour on the meat. Heat the fat and sear the floured short ribs. Lift into casserole. Add chopped onion to the fat in pan, cook and stir until golden brown. Add all remaining ingredients and heat to near boiling. Pour this over short ribs. Cover closely and bake until tender. Use a 325 degree F. oven and bake for about 2 hours. Serve with golden brown roasted potatoes.

Mrs. Jean R. Haines, Wildwood Heights.

Lamb Chops Supreme

Although I enjoy lamb chops very much, I have often wished there were some way of eliminating their characteristic, objectionable, greasy taste, so the other day I made a rather successful experiment. I took as much fat as possible from 4 lamb chops, cut the fat in small pieces and fried the chops in this under a lid. When done, I drained all the fat and wiped the pan out with tissue, replaced the chops, added 4 sliced crabapples, 2 tablespoons mint sauce (using quite a bit of mint leaf). To this I added vegetable water (potato or pea). I allowed this to simmer until the apples were cooked and the water had evaporated, leaving a thick sauce. The lamb was delicious, flavourful, and the sauce a good complement to the meat and vegetables.

Mr. Walter J. Camozzi, Vancouver.

Limey Bride's Sausage Batter

1 pound of sausage
1 cup flour
½ teaspoon salt
2 eggs
1 cup milk

Half cook meat in hot oven. Sift dry ingredients into a bowl. Combine 2 beaten eggs and milk and stir into flour mixture until batter is smooth. Pour batter over sausage and bake in hot oven (450 degrees F.) for 25 to 30 minutes.

"As a very newly arrived 'Limey Bride' I find your readers' prize recipes most helpful, and I wonder if any of your Canadian housewives would be interested in this very economical English supper dish. Few people in this district seem to know about it, and those who have tried it like it immensely. Incidentally, I would like to say how very kind everyone has been to me here in Canada, and I am very happy in your grand country."

Patricia A. LaVac, Vancouver.

Chicken Paprika, Vancouver Style
(Native Dish Contest Winner)

Cut 4-pound chicken (or any size, any age) into serving pieces. Roll in flour, brown on both sides in a little fat, add one medium-size onion, cook slightly. Add salt, pepper, to taste, 1½ tablespoons of red sweet paprika, 1 tablespoon chopped parsley and about 1 cup of water. Cook until tender, adding a little water as water evaporates in cooking. To make gravy, mix 2 tablespoons flour in 1 cup of cream and add to dripping. Add 1 teaspoon lemon juice drop by drop to the simmering gravy. The gravy can be made with water instead of cream; in that case, add a tablespoon of butter to the gravy.

Mrs. F.C. Atkinson, Vancouver.

Wild Game

Venison Steak Supreme

Select a leg cut of venison, 1½ inches thick. Melt ¼ cup of butter in a heavy iron frying pan and brown the meat on one side over a hot fire. Then add 2 tablespoons of oil to the butter and brown the other side. Spread 3 heaping tablespoons of tart currant jelly on the top side. Add a dash of cinnamon, and a tablespoon of chopped parsley to ⅔ pint of dry red wine. Add this to the meat. Cover closely and simmer slowly about 35 minutes, basting occasionally. Drain small tin of mushrooms and add them about 10 minutes before the meat is done. Serve immediately with buttered toast.

Venison should be hung up to 11 days in a medium cool place. The steak should not be soaked in brine or vinegar which would destroy the wild flavour but merely wiped with clean wet cloth to remove hair.

Mrs. M. Hunt, Vernon.

Sweet and Sour Deer Ribs

    3 lbs. deer ribs
    1 large tin tomato juice
    1 tablespoon salt
    ½ teaspoon dry mustard
    ¼ teaspoon black pepper (or to taste)
    3 tablespoons brown sugar
    ½ cup white vinegar
    3 tablespoons melted fat
    6 medium sized whole onions

Soak ribs in salted water overnight. Then drain well. Mix ingredients except onions and pour over ribs in roaster. Roast in a hot oven, 400 degrees F., until each rib has browned nicely, turning each one. Add onions and reduce heat to 350 degrees F. and roast (uncovered) one hour, stirring occasionally. When done, thicken gravy with flour mixed in a little cold water, about 3 tablespoons, and cook a few minutes more. You may use salt pork instead of fat mentioned if you mince it and dry lightly before using, and omit salt in recipe. One small chopped bud of garlic may be added if desired.

Mrs. J.R. Drake, Nanaimo.

B.C. Game Bird Pie
(Native Dish Contest Winner)

    1 pheasant
    1 blue grouse
    1 prairie chicken, OR
    3 quail

Skin, wash, cut up and cook in as little water as possible. Do not use skin. To the meat, after being removed from bones, add salt to season and ½ teaspoon black pepper. Cook separately 1 cup diced carrots and 1 cup onions, in as little water as possible. Combine meat with vegetables in an 8-inch casserole. Before covering with crust, add 1 heaping tablespoon flour with ¾ cup of cold water, mixing first to thin batter.

    Crust:
    1 cup flour
    1 teaspoon baking powder
    ¼ teaspoon salt
    1 heaping tablespoon shortening
    1 egg
    ¼ cup milk

Sift dry ingredients. Cut in shortening. Add beaten egg and milk enough to form a stiff dough. Roll to ½-inch thickness, or large enough to cover the casserole. Place inverted egg cup in centre of pie to hold up crust. Cook until crust is slightly browned in a 375 to 400 degrees F. oven.

Fred W. Heslewood, Vancouver.

Cariboo Grouse

Pluck and prepare as many grouse as available in the usual manner for fowl. Cut into convenient serving pieces. Dredge in seasoned flour, and saute carefully in butter, until well-browned on all sides. Place in a casserole, and barely cover with rich milk. Cook in a very moderate oven (350 degrees F.) about 1 hour. Serve with high bush cranberry jelly.

Mrs. O.B. Utterstrom, Mission City.

Egg Dishes

Mushroom Eggs au Gratin

8 or 10 medium-sized mushrooms
6 hard-cooked eggs
Salt, pepper
Paprika
2 tablespoons butter
2 tablespoons flour
1½ cups milk
2 tablespoons grated cheese

Peel and chop mushrooms and saute in 1 teaspoon butter for 5 minutes. Cut eggs in half lengthwise and remove yolks. Mash yolks and mix with mushrooms and seasonings. Then refill whites, press halves together and place in greased baking dish. Make white sauce by melting butter, stirring in flour and then milk, stirring constantly. Add salt and pepper. Pour over the eggs. Sprinkle with grated cheese. Bake at 375 degrees F. for about 20 minutes. Garnish with tiny sprigs of parsley to serve.

"This is a very tasty, nourishing luncheon or supper dish."

Mrs. C. Hayward, Vancouver.

Eggs in Curry-Cream Sauce

½ cup finely diced onion
2 tablespoons butter
4 tablespoons flour
1 teaspoon curry
1 teaspoon Worcestershire sauce
1 teaspoon salt
2½ cups milk
5 hard-cooked eggs, sliced
2 tablespoons parsley (optional)

Cook onion in butter over low heat until tender, add flour, curry powder, Worcestershire sauce and milk, slowly. Cook until smooth and thickened, stirring constantly. Add egg slices and parsley; heat and serve on chop plate with a border of cooked macaroni or rice.

Meat-Shortage Eggs

Butter
Grated onion
Grated cheese
As many eggs as required
Bread crumbs
Hot toast

Melt the butter in a casserole, then sprinkle a little grated onion on top. Add a layer of grated cheese. Then make divisions to place eggs as required into cheese nests. Cover with a layer of cheese and lastly, add a layer of bread crumbs. Put dots of butter on top and bake slowly, about 30 minutes. Serve on hot toast.

"This is a tasty way to serve eggs, especially now, with the high cost of meat."

Mrs. A. Hughes, White Rock.

Green Apple Omelet

Core and pare 8 large green apples and steam until soft enough to mash free from lumps. While still warm, add 2 tablespoons butter and 1 cup sugar. Beat 4 eggs until they form a close heavy froth and fold or beat these lightly into the apple mixture. Bake in a shallow, well-greased dish and serve as an accompaniment for roast pork or spare ribs. Add cinnamon or nutmeg as desired.

Vegetables

Canned Spiced Beets

    4   cups cooked beets
    2   cups white vinegar
    ¼   cup sugar
    ½   teaspoon salt
    ½   teaspoon white mustard seed
    2   teaspoons cinnamon
    ½   teaspoon whole cloves
    1   teaspoon celery seed

Place cooked, skinned beets in sterilized pint jars. Boil other ingredients for a few minutes and pour the spiced vinegar over beets. Seal.

Cucumbers in Sour Cream

    3   cucumbers
    3   tablespoons butter
    ⅔   cup sliced radishes
    ¼   cup sour cream
    ½   teaspoon salt
        Few grains pepper

Pare cucumbers, slice thin. Melt butter, add cucumbers and radishes. Cover. Cook rapidly 10 minutes. Uncover and cook until most of the liquid has evaporated. Add cream, salt and pepper. Heat. Serves four.

"Your Edith Adams Columns, also Pennywise's Shopping Guide, are a great help to us housewives."

Mrs. Enid Lane, Vancouver.

Potato and Cheese Loaf

    2   cups hot mashed potato
    2   cups mashed cottage cheese
    ½   cup stale bread crumbs
    ¼   cup minced onion
    ¼   cup melted shortening
    1   well-beaten egg
        Dash of salt
        Pepper and celery salt

Mix together thoroughly and turn into a greased loaf pan, lined with wax paper. Bake in a moderate oven (375 degrees F.) for 45 minutes.

"Serve hot as a main dish with tomato sauce or any green vegetable."

Miss B.P. Garner, Vancouver.

Osoyoos Tomato Fritters

    2   cups canned tomatoes
    2   tablespoons butter (melted)
    1   teaspoon salt
    ¼   teaspoon pepper
    ½   teaspoon sugar
    1   cup flour
    1   teaspoon baking powder

Mix thoroughly. Drop into boiling fat by small spoonfuls and brown on both sides. Serve hot with cold meat and a salad for lunch.

"We live in the southern Okanagan where tomatoes are grown by the ton, so we do try our wings when it comes to recipes."

Mrs. J. Armstrong, Osoyoos.

Judy Ruddell, Edith Adams supervisor, polishes the entrance light, 14 March 1966.

Tea Biscuits, Tea Loaves

Canadian Blackberry Roll

- 2 cups flour
- 4 teaspoons baking powder
- 1½ teaspoons salt
- ¼ cup shortening
- ⅔ cup sweet milk
- Melted butter
- 2 cups blackberries
- ½ cup sugar
- 1 tablespoon lemon juice

Sift flour, baking powder and salt. Cut in shortening, add milk to make a soft dough. Roll out, ⅛ inch thick, into a rectangle, 12 by 14 inches. Spread with melted butter. Combine blackberries, sugar and lemon juice. Cover dough with berry mixture. Roll like jelly roll; twist ends to form crescent. With scissors cut top crust of roll at 3½-inch intervals. Line bake pan with wax paper. Bake in hot oven of 425 degrees F. for 25 to 30 minutes. Serve hot with cream or milk as desired.

"Blackberries are hanging ripe and luscious on the bushes in the pastures and vacant lots, so here is my favourite recipe for our own Canadian Blackberry Roll."

Mrs. N.P. Frost, Abbotsford.

Tomato Surprise Biscuits

- 2 cups flour
- 3 teaspoons baking powder
- ½ teaspoon salt
- 3 tablespoons shortening
- 3 tablespoons grated cheese
- ½ cup milk
- 8 small ripe tomatoes

Sift baking powder and salt with the flour. Cut in the shortening. Add the cheese and sufficient milk to make a firm but easy-to-roll dough. Have ready the tomatoes that have first been placed for 1 minute in boiling water, then left to cool before skinning. Roll the dough out ½-inch thick and cut into squares. Place a tomato in the centre of each square and fold the dough around it. Make a hole in the centre. Bake for 20 minutes in a hot oven.

"These are very nice with a salad."

Mrs. Frank D. Ellis, West Vancouver.

Orange Bread

Cut the peel of 2 large or 3 small oranges very fine or put through the meat chopper. Boil with 1 cup of water 10 minutes. Drain off all but 2 or 3 tablespoons liquid. Add ¼ cup each of white and brown sugar and boil 10 minutes longer. Add 3 tablespoons shortening (beef dripping will do) and leave to melt. In the meantime, sift several times together 3 cups all-purpose flour (measured before sifting), 1 teaspoon salt and 6 teaspoons baking powder. Make a hollow in the middle of the dry ingredients, add 1 beaten egg, 1 cup milk and the hot syrupy mixture. Blend well. Turn out into the loaf pan. Allow to stand 10 minutes and bake in 350 degree F. oven for 1 hour.

"I seem to be using this Orange Bread a lot lately—my family enjoys it in lunch pails and for tea."

Mrs. P. Molberg, Vancouver.

Quick Raisin Bread

- 2 cups flour
- ½ teaspoon salt
- 4 teaspoons baking powder
- ¼ cup sugar
- ½ cup nuts
- 1 cup raisins
- 1 egg
- 1 cup milk
- 1 tablespoon shortening (melted)

Sift the dry ingredients together. Add nuts, raisins, slightly beaten egg, milk and shortening. Mix up quickly and turn into a greased loaf pan. Allow to stand for 15 minutes before baking. Sprinkle with sugar and cinnamon if desired.

"This loaf is lovely when fresh, and has often taken the place of cake or cookies at our house when sugar and shortening have been scarce."

Mrs. A. Aho, Vancouver.

Muffins

Plain Muffins

  2 cups all-purpose flour
3½ teaspoons baking powder
 ½ teaspoon salt
 ¼ cup sugar
  1 egg
  1 cup milk
 ¼ cup melted shortening

Sift flour, measure and sift with baking powder, salt and sugar. Beat egg lightly, add milk and melted shortening. Make a depression in flour mixture and pour in the liquid. Stir only enough to combine. Fill greased muffin pans two-thirds full and bake at 425 degrees F. for 20 to 25 minutes. Yield: 12 muffins.

Muffin Variations

Apple Muffins: Fold in ½ cup peeled, chopped apples or peel cooking apples about diameter of muffins and dip into a mixture of 1 part cinnamon and 4 parts sugar. Place slice of apple on each partially filled muffin cup. Bake as directed above.

Fruit or Nut: ½ cup raisins or currants, ½ cup chopped nuts, ½ cup chopped dates, figs, prunes or peaches may be added to the plain recipe.

Blondie's Health Muffins

 ½ cup cornmeal
 ½ cup rolled oats
 ½ cup graham or whole wheat flour
 ½ cup flour
  2 tablespoons sugar
3½ teaspoons baking powder
 ½ teaspoon salt
  1 egg
  1 cup milk
  3 tablespoons shortening, melted

Mix the dry ingredients, add beaten egg and milk. Add melted shortening. Bake at 400 degrees F. about 25 minutes. This makes 1 dozen medium muffins.

    Mrs. Amy Bumstead, New Westminster.

Instead-of-Porridge Oatmeal Muffins

 ¼ cup shortening
 ⅓ cup brown sugar
1½ cups bread flour
  4 teaspoons baking powder
  1 teaspoon salt
  1 cup quick-cooking oats
  1 egg
 ¾ cup milk
  3 teaspoons grated orange rind

Combine shortening and sugar. Add dry ingredients and milk-and-egg alternately. Lastly, add orange rind. Bake in a hot oven (about 425 degrees F.) for 20 minutes or until done.

    "These muffins have a delightfully 'different' flavour. Served for Sunday morning breakfast, they're more exciting than oatmeal porridge."

    Mrs. E.M. McLean, Kimberley.

Coffee Cakes, Scones

Spice Twists

¾ cup flour
1 teaspoon baking powder
2 tablespoons sugar
½ teaspoon cinnamon
2 tablespoons shortening
1 egg yolk
¼ cup milk
½ cup cereal bran
1 egg white, beaten
1 tablespoon water
¼ cup sugar
1 teaspoon cinnamon

Mix first eight ingredients together, then roll out. Brush the dough with the egg white, beaten with water, sugar and cinnamon. Cut in strips and twist together. Bake in moderately hot oven (425 degrees F.) about 15 minutes. Yields 15 3½-inch twists.

Mrs. Clarence Newby, Sardis.

Pear Coffee Cake

2 cups once-sifted cake flour
4 teaspoons baking powder
½ teaspoon salt
⅛ teaspoon nutmeg
¼ teaspoon granulated sugar
4 tablespoons shortening
1 egg, well beaten
½ cup milk
4 or 5 canned or fresh ripe pears
¼ cup brown sugar, lightly packed
⅛ teaspoon cinnamon
½ cup crisp rice cereal
2 tablespoons corn syrup

Measure and sift together twice the flour, baking powder, salt, nutmeg and sugar. Cut in shortening finely. Combine the well-beaten egg and milk. Form a well in the dry ingredients, add liquids all at once and combine lightly and thoroughly. Turn into a buttered and lightly floured 8-inch square cake pan and pat evenly. Peel, quarter and core pears and cut into thin wedges. Press into dough. Combine brown sugar, cinnamon and rice cereal and sprinkle over the pears. Drizzle with corn syrup. Bake in hot oven, 400 degrees F., about 40 minutes.

"This can be served as a coffee cake or it's very nice as a hot pudding with cream or sauce."

Mrs. L. Hibberd, Hollyburn.

Fluffy Tea Scones

2 cups all-purpose flour
½ cup sugar
½ teaspoon salt
4 teaspoons baking powder
½ cup shortening (part may be butter)
1 egg
1 cup cold milk and water
½ cup fruit (raisins, currants and a little peel)
1 tablespoon extra sugar

Mix flour, sugar, salt and baking powder. Then rub in shortening. Break the egg into the middle of mixture, beat a few turns with a large stiff fork, add some of the liquid, continue stirring, add remainder of liquid and stir again. The dough should be too thick to pour, and not thick enough to roll out. With large baking spoon place half in each of two buttered pie plates, and spread lightly to the edges (the surface will be rather rough). Sprinkle the extra sugar over the tops of the scones. Oven should be at 475 degrees F. when the scones go in. When it drops to 450 degrees, let it remain for 8 minutes when the scones should be slightly browned. Turn off the heat and let remain another 5 minutes or so.

"These are best when freshly baked."

Mrs. A.H. Williams, Vancouver.

Scotch Tea Scones

¼ cup butter
½ cup icing sugar
1 egg
1 cup sifted flour
2 teaspoons baking powder
¼ teaspoon baking soda
⅔ cup milk

Cream the butter and the sugar. Beat the egg until light and add to the creamed mixture. Combine well. Sift flour, baking powder and soda and sift into the creamed mixture alternately with the milk, stirring to keep the batter smooth. Have a griddle on low heat. Place the batter on the griddle using a heaping teaspoon for each scone. When the bubbles appear on the top turn the pancake over and cook to golden brown on the other side. Serve cold.

Plain and Chocolate Cakes

Starlight Cake

    2   cups sifted flour
    1⅓ cups granulated sugar
    ½   cup shortening
    1   teaspoon salt
    1   cup milk
    3½ teaspoons double-action baking powder
    4   egg whites
    1   teaspoon vanilla

Into a mixing bowl measure flour, sugar, shortening, salt, and ⅔ cup of milk. Beat vigorously with a spoon for 2 minutes, or 200 strokes, scraping the bowl frequently. Quickly stir in the baking powder, scraping the bowl frequently. Then add the egg whites, unbeaten; add remaining ⅓ cup of milk, and vanilla. Blend with spoon 2 minutes, or 200 strokes. Pour into two 9 inch or deep 8 inch layer cake tins greased and floured. The batter will be smooth and thin. Bake in moderate oven, 360 degrees F., about 30 minutes, or until done.

Lazy Daisy Cake

    2   eggs
    1   cup granulated sugar
    1   teaspoon vanilla
    1   cup flour
    1   teaspoon baking powder
    ½   teaspoon salt
    ½   cup milk
    1   tablespoon butter

Beat eggs and gradually add sugar. Beat until thick. Add vanilla. Sift flour, baking powder and salt and add to egg mixture, beating well. Lastly add the milk which has been brought to the boil with the butter. Beat well. Pour batter into greased cake tin and bake at 350 degrees F. for about 20 minutes.

While still warm, spread with the following mixture and brown in the oven:

3 tablespoons melted butter, 5 tablespoons brown sugar, 2 tablespoons milk or cream, 1 cup coconut or ½ cup chopped walnuts.

Sour Cream Cocoa Cake

    3   eggs
    1½ cups sugar
    ¼   teaspoon salt
    3   tablespoons cocoa
    1   teaspoon soda
    2   cups flour
    1   teaspoon baking powder
    1½ cups thick sour cream
    1   teaspoon vanilla

Beat eggs well. Add sugar, salt and cocoa, sifted together. Add soda dissolved in a little hot water. Add flour and baking powder alternately with cream and flavouring. Mix thoroughly and bake in 10 x 6 tin at 375 degrees F. for about 45 minutes.

Mrs. M.E. Nicholls, Vancouver.

Crazy Chocolate Cake

    1   cup sugar
    1   egg
    ½   cup milk, sweet or sour
    ½   cup shortening
    ½   teaspoon salt
    1   teaspoon soda
    1   teaspoon vanilla
    1½ cups flour
    ½   cup cocoa
    ½   cup boiling water

Put ingredients into mixing bowl in the order given (do not mix or stir until the boiling water is added). When water is added, beat vigorously until mixture is smooth. Pour into greased cake tin and bake at about 375 degrees F. Frost with your favourite icing.

Mrs. R.W. Travis, Nanaimo.

Judy Ruddell in the Edith Adams Cottage kitchen, 10 March 1966.

Sponge and Angel Cakes

Poor Man's Angel Food

- ½ cup cold water
- 4 eggs
- 1¼ cups sugar
- 1½ cups flour
- ¼ to ½ teaspoon salt
- ¾ teaspoon cream of tartar
- ½ teaspoon baking powder
- 1 teaspoon vanilla

Add cold water to egg yolks and beat until thick. Add sugar. Sift dry ingredients and add. Lastly add vanilla and beaten egg yolks. Fold in. Put in greased angel food tin. Bake at 325 degrees F. for 1 hour. Ice with icing sugar mixed with lemon juice.

A. Kerr, Vancouver.

Pride of All Sponge Cakes

- 1 cup all-purpose flour
- 1 teaspoon baking powder
- ¼ teaspoon salt
- 3 egg yolks
- 1 cup fine sugar
- ½ cup cold water
- 3 egg whites
- ¼ teaspoon cream of tartar
- 1 teaspoon lemon extract

Sift flour, baking powder and salt three times. Then beat yolks, sugar and water until bubbly. Beat egg whites with cream of tartar and flavouring. Now stir the dry ingredients into the egg yolk mixture, then fold in egg whites. Pour into an angel food pan and bake in a slow oven of 300 degrees F. for about 1 hour. If desired, ice with lemon icing.

Mrs. W.M. Eddy, New Westminister.

Jubilee Jelly Roll

- 3 eggs
- 1 cup sugar
- 3 tablespoons water
- ½ teaspoon lemon extract
- 1 cup sifted pastry flour
- 1 teaspoon baking powder
- ¼ teaspoon salt

Separate the eggs and beat the yolks until thick and light in colour. Add sugar gradually, then the water and flavouring and beat until very light. Add dry ingredients. Beat egg whites stiff and fold into egg mixture. Bake in jelly roll tin which has been greased and lined with waxed paper. Bake in a 350 degrees F. oven 20 minutes. Turn out onto a cloth which has been wrung out of cold water. Cut off hard edges. Spread with jelly or jam and roll up immediately. Sprinkle with icing sugar. Wrap in wax paper to keep moist.

"This jelly roll has won first prize at five different fairs." Mrs. L.E. Sanders, Burnaby.

Butterscotch Top Cake

- 2 eggs, well beaten
- 1 cup sugar
- 1 cup flour
- 1 teaspoon baking powder
- ½ teaspoon salt
- ½ teaspoon vanilla
- 2 tablespoons butter or shortening
- ½ cup milk

Beat eggs until thick, gradually beating in sugar. Sift flour with baking powder and salt and add to cake mixture with vanilla. Heat milk to boiling point and add butter, then stir into first mixture. Pour into 8-inch pan and bake at 350 degrees F. for 30 minutes. Remove from the oven and cover with the following:

- ½ cup crushed cornflakes
- 1 tablespoon melted butter
- ¼ teaspoon vanilla
- 3 tablespoons brown sugar
- 1 tablespoon cream

Spread over baked cake with a fork and broil at top of oven for 3 or 4 minutes til brown.

"Instead of cream I use canned milk which serves just as well."

Mrs. H. Irvin, Penticton.

Magic-Quick Chocolate Frosting
(Covers tops of two 9-inch layers)

- 2 squares (2 oz.) unsweetened chocolate
- 1½ cups (15 oz. can) sweetened condensed milk
- 1 tablespoon water

Melt chocolate in top of double boiler. Add sweetened condensed milk and stir over rapidly boiling water 5 to 10 minutes or until thick. Remove from heat. Add water. Cool. Spread on cold cake.

Frostings

Butter Icing

- ⅓ cup butter
- 1 egg yolk well beaten or 2 tablespoons milk, cream or fruit juice
- 1 to 1½ cups icing sugar
- ½ teaspoon vanilla

Cream butter thoroughly. Add well-beaten yolk or the liquid and beat well. Gradually blend in sugar until icing is of the right consistency to spread. Add vanilla and spread on cake.

Orange or Lemon: Make butter icing and use orange or lemon juice for the liquid. Add 1 or 2 teaspoons grated rind with the flavouring.

Mocha: Make butter icing using cold coffee for liquid. Add 1 square melted chocolate to creamed butter.

Caramel Icing

- 2 cups brown sugar
- 1 cup milk or cream
- 3 tablespoons butter
- 1 teaspoon vanilla

Place sugar and cream in a saucepan and bring to boil stirring until the sugar is dissolved. Boil to the soft ball stage (238 degrees). Remove from fire, add butter and vanilla. Allow to cool, then beat until thick and creamy. If it becomes too thick, thin with a little cream. This is a lovely icing with a banana cake.

Cream Cheese Chocolate Icing

- 1 cup icing sugar
- 2 tablespoons cocoa
- 2½ tablespoons white cream cheese, creamed until fluffy
- 4 tablespoons hot cream
  Few drops vanilla extract

Sift together icing sugar and cocoa. Cream the cream cheese until fluffy and add alternately to the icing-sugar-and-cocoa mixture with the hot cream, beating thoroughly after each addition. Lastly, add the vanilla.

Mrs. F. Garner, Vancouver.

Bars and Squares

Almond Wafers

- ¼ cup butter
- ½ cup icing sugar
- ¼ cup milk
- ⅞ cup bread flour
- ½ teaspoon almond flavouring
- ⅓ cup almonds

Cream butter and sugar and add milk very slowly. Beat well after each addition of milk. Add flour and almond flavouring. Mix well and spread with a spatula on a greased baking sheet. This mixture must be spread to almost paper thinness. Score in squares and sprinkle with chopped nuts, pressing them into the dough. Bake in a moderate oven, 350 degrees F., until a delicate brown, turning pan frequently to ensure even baking. When brown you may open the oven door and roll the squares, if rolled wafers are desired.

Mrs. J.B. Currie, Qualicum Beach.

Japanese Hardtack

- 2 eggs
- ½ cup sugar (half white and half brown)
  Butter, size of an egg
- 4 to 6 tablespoons flour
- 1 teaspoon baking powder
  Salt
- 1 cup nuts (I like almonds blanched and slightly roasted)
- 1 cup dates, chopped fine

Beat eggs until light, then add sugar slowly. Add soft butter, then flour mixture, nuts and dates. Leave in oven 15 to 20 minutes. Then cut in squares while still hot and roll in icing sugar to form small logs.

"These are nice for teas when you want something fancy."
Mrs. Muriel Ross, Vancouver.

Raspberry Bars a la Coconut

Line the bottom of a pan (8 x 8 or 8 x 10) with a rich flaky pastry. Bake in a hot oven, 425 degrees F. When cool, spread with a thin layer of raspberry jam and top with the following mixture:

Topping:

 Butter, size of an egg
¾ cup sugar
1 egg, well beaten
1 teaspoon vanilla
2 cups coconut

Cream butter and sugar, add egg, vanilla and coconut. Bake in a moderate oven, 350 degrees F., until brown. When cool, cut in fingers or bars.

Mrs. H.D. Phillips, New Westminster.

Yummy Lemon Squares

1¾ cups cracker crumbs (unsalted soda biscuits)
¾ cup flour
⅓ cup sugar
1 teaspoon baking powder
½ cup coconut (may be omitted)
½ cup shortening
2 tablespoons milk
1 egg

Mix dry ingredients and rub in shortening. Add milk. To make filling: 1 cup boiling water, ⅔ cup sugar, 2 tablespoons cornstarch, ¼ teaspoon salt, juice and rind of 1 lemon and 1 egg. Mix sugar, cornstarch and salt together. Add boiling water gradually and cook until mixture is slightly thickened. Add lemon juice and egg. Put two-thirds cracker mixture on the bottom of the greased cake pan. Pour filling over mixture. Sprinkle remaining one-third mixture over the top. Bake at 325 degrees F. for 45 minutes.

"I always serve this to company and find it grand for teas, bridge parties or as a dessert with custard sauce or whipped cream."

Mrs. W.H. Lloyd, Vancouver.

Cookies, Candies

Cry Baby Cookies

2½ cups sifted all-purpose flour
1 teaspoon soda
¼ teaspoon salt
½ teaspoon cloves
½ teaspoon cinnamon
½ cup sugar
¼ cup melted shortening
½ cup molasses
½ cup milk
½ cup chopped raisins

Measure first five ingredients into a sifter and sift. In a large mixing bowl combine sugar, shortening and molasses. Stir in the flour mixture alternately with milk. Beat smooth after each addition. Add raisins. Drop by teaspoonfuls on lightly-greased baking sheet. Bake for 12 minutes, or until well-done, at 375 degrees F. Makes about 2½ dozen 3-inch cookies.

"These cookies are what little folk want more of."

Mrs. Ken Palmer, Vancouver.

Jacquie's Oatmeal Cookies

1 cup shortening
⅔ cup brown sugar
2 eggs
2 teaspoons vanilla
2 cups flour
2 cups rolled oats
1 cup coconut
1 teaspoon baking soda
1 teaspoon baking powder
½ teaspoon salt

Cream shortening and sugar thoroughly, then eggs and vanilla. Work in other ingredients which have been stirred together. Roll into balls; flatten with a fork, after they have been placed on a greased baking sheet. Bake in a moderate oven, 375 degrees F. for 10 to 12 minutes.

"These have been in our family since I was a little girl."

Miss Jacquie Cross, Vancouver.

Home-made Fig Bars

- 6 tablespoons shortening
- ¾ cup sugar
- 2 eggs
- 2½ cups flour
- ½ teaspoon baking soda
- ⅛ teaspoon cloves
- ½ teaspoon salt
- ¼ teaspoon cinnamon
- ¼ cup sour milk

Filling:

- 2 cups cut figs
- 1 cup sugar
- 1 cup water

Cream shortening and sugar, add well-beaten eggs and beat up well. Sift together the dry ingredients and add to mixture alternately with sour milk. Roll the dough thin and cut into rectangles, 3 inches wide. Spread **Filling** (made by cooking figs, sugar and water until thick) down the centre. Fold each edge to centre to cover filling. Cut with knife into 2-inch lengths and place in greased pan, with the joined side down. Bake in moderate oven for 20 to 25 minutes.

Mrs. Pauline Kulyk, Vancouver.

P.N.E. Shortbread
(Took First Prize at Exhibition in 1947)

- ½ pound (1 cup) butter
- 5 ounces (⅔ cups) berry sugar
- 10 ounces (2 cups) all-purpose flour
- 2 ounces (½ cup) rice flour

Rub the butter into sugar. Then gradually work the flour and rice flour in with the hands. Knead until the dough is free from cracks. Bake in a round on a greased tin at 300 degrees F. until golden brown.

"This Scotch recipe has been in our family for years."

Mrs. F. Warburton, North Vancouver.

Filbert Balls

- ½ pound filberts (walnuts or any nut meats can be used)
- 1 cup brown sugar
- 2 unbeaten egg whites
- Pinch of salt
- 1 teaspoon vanilla

Put the nuts through the food chopper. Add brown sugar, unbeaten egg whites, salt and vanilla and combine very thoroughly. Shape the mixture into rather small balls and place on a greased pan. Place in oven at 375 degrees F. Bake until very delicately browned (about 15 to 20 minutes). The baked Filbert Balls may be dusted with icing sugar. Makes about 30 balls.

"These are something dainty to serve at 'showers' or afternoon tea where something sweet is appropriate."

Mrs. R. Hill, Vancouver.

Fruit Balls

- 1 cup dates
- 1 cup walnuts
- 1 cup coconut
- ½ cup sugar
- 1 teaspoon almond extract
- 2 egg whites, beaten slightly

Mix all ingredients together and put in cake tin and bake at 350 degrees F. until the top is light brown. Take from oven and stir well while still hot. Let cool. Roll into balls with the hands, and roll each ball in icing sugar.

Mrs. Ella Parkinson, Vancouver.

Peanut Brittle

- 1 cup peanuts
- 1 teaspoon vanilla
- ½ cup coconut
- 2 cups sugar

Spread peanuts in pan (not greased). Pour over peanuts the mixture of vanilla and coconut. Melt the sugar in a heavy frying pan. When all melted pour over the nuts. Be careful not to have the sugar browned. (It should be a golden colour.) Let stand until hard. Break up into pieces.

"My family like this very much and it's very simple to make."

Lois Simpson, Vernon.

Saturday Night Taffy Pull

- 3 cups white sugar
- ¼ cup water
- 3 tablespoons vinegar
- ¼ cup cream of tartar
- ½ cup melted butter (or less)
- ¼ teaspoon soda
- 1 teaspoon vanilla

Put sugar, water and vinegar in a saucepan and bring to the boil. When boiling add cream of tartar. Boil for a while, then add as much butter as you can spare, with the soda. Boil until the hard-ball stage or 290 degrees on the candy thermometer. Add flavouring. Stir constantly during the last part of cooking. Pour onto buttered plates. When cool enough to handle, pull.

"We have used this recipe for taffy for 50 years. Nowhere have I seen a better one."

Mrs. L.T. Beharrell, Matsqui.

Fruit Desserts, Custard Desserts

Blackberry Crumble

Put layer of blackberries into baking dish. Add a layer of green apples. Fill the dish and sprinkle over the top the following mixture: 1 cup brown sugar, ½ cup butter and ½ cup of flour, all crumbled with the fingers. Bake at 375 degrees F. for 30 to 40 minutes.

Mrs. A. Boucher, Vancouver.

Delicious Cherry Pudding

1 tablespoon butter or other shortening
½ cup sugar (scant)
1 egg
1 cup flour
2 teaspoons baking powder
2 cups fresh pitted cherries

Mix in the order given, leaving cherries whole. Put in greased pudding bowl and steam 1½ hours. Serve hot with top milk, cream or custard.

Mrs. Harold Martin, Abbotsford.

Rhubarb Crisp

4 cups diced rhubarb
½ cup white sugar
¼ cup flour
6 tablespoons brown sugar
¾ cup rolled oats
2 tablespoons butter

Dice rhubarb and mix well with the white sugar. Place in a greased baking dish. Combine flour, brown sugar and rolled oats, and cut in the butter. Spread this mixture over the rhubarb and bake in a moderate oven of 350 degrees F. until the rhubarb is tender and the top a golden brown. Serve with cream.

Mrs. F.E. Oakley, Vancouver.

Bramble Blancmange

2 pounds blackberries
¼ cup water
2 or 3 tablespoons sugar
Cornstarch

Stew blackberries with water until soft. Press through sieve to remove seeds. Measure (should be a pint). Put berry puree in saucepan, add sugar, stir until melted. Mix cornstarch (1 tablespoon to each pint of puree) with a little cold water, add to berries, bring to boil and boil for 3 minutes. Turn into mould and set. Serve cold with cream or custard. Serves 4.

"I make this jelly a lot for my mother and we find it very delicious."

Pat Westin, Burnaby.

Fluffy Tapioca Pudding

1 pint milk
½ cup sugar
Salt to taste
4 tablespoons minute tapioca
2 eggs
Vanilla

Put milk, sugar, salt and tapioca in a double boiler. Cook for 15 minutes. Add the well-beaten yolks of eggs and cook for a few minutes longer. Add flavouring. When cooked take off the fire and add stiffly-beaten egg whites, folding in gently.

"A very nice recipe."

Mrs. M. Ball, Victoria.

Fruit Pies

Wild Berry Pie

Take salal berries with some Oregon grapes to add colour and flavour. Wash fruit to float off loose blossoms, etc. To enough crushed fruit for a pie add juice of half a lemon, a little grated lemon peel and enough sugar to sweeten (about ½ cup sugar to 3 to 4 cups of fruit). Put between double crusts and bake like any other berry pie.

"This Wild Berry Pie is really good. Incidentally, it is easiest when picking the salal berries to leave them on the little branches they grow on and later cut them off with scissors. They don't crush that way. Oregon grapes are nearly always found where there are salal bushes."

Mrs. L. Davidge, care Mrs. Vera Parsons, Duncan.

Okanapple Pie
(Native Dish Contest Winner)
Pastry:

- 2 cups flour
- ¾ teaspoon baking powder
- ¾ teaspoon salt
- ¾ cup shortening

Filling:

- 6 to 8 apples
- ¾ cup sugar
- ½ teaspoon salt
- ⅓ teaspoon cinnamon
- 1 tablespoon butter

To make pastry, sift flour, baking powder and salt into a bowl. Press shortening into it with a spoon. Mix in enough cold water to make a firm dough. Roll out more than half for the bottom crust. Fit into a deep pie plate so juices won't be wasted in the oven. Put in an inch or more layer of sliced apples. Sprinkle with sugar, salt and cinnamon. Dot with pieces of butter.

Take remaining dough, roll for top crust. Prick at several places. Wet edges of lower crust with water. Place top crust on, and press down edges with thumb or fork. Sprinkle lightly with sugar. Bake in oven 425 degrees F. for 15 minutes, then turn oven temperature down to 350 degrees F. and continue baking until crust is a golden brown (about 30 minutes longer). The apples are done when the juice shows through punctures in the top crust.

To serve pie, top each piece with table cream, whipped cream, ice cream or a slice of cheese.

Mrs. Frank Tucker, Cloverdale.

Holiday Apple Pie

- 1¼ cups brown sugar
- 2 tablespoons cornstarch or flour
- ½ teaspoon salt
- 1 teaspoon cinnamon
- ½ teaspoon nutmeg
- ⅔ cup apple juice or water
- 1 teaspoon vinegar
- 2 tablespoons butter
- 5 cups apples, pared and finely diced
- ⅓ cup Brazil nuts, thinly sliced and toasted

Mix brown sugar, cornstarch, salt and spices in saucepan. Add apple juice, vinegar and butter and cook over moderate heat until thickened, stirring occasionally. Cool. Add apples. Roll ½ the pie dough and line a 9-inch pie plate. Flute the edge. Fill with fruit. Sprinkle nuts over top. Roll out remaining dough and cut in a circle that fits the filling but leaves about ½-inch space around the edge. Mark edges and cut slits. Place on top of filling. Bake in a hot oven, 425 degrees F., for 15 minutes, then reduce temperature of oven to 350 degrees F. and cook about 35 to 45 minutes longer.

"This apple pie tops any grandma used to make."

Mrs. Evelyn Battistone, Vancouver.

Angel-Berry Pie

- 6 egg whites
- 2 cups sugar, sifted
- 1 teaspoon vanilla
- 1 teaspoon vinegar

Beat egg whites to a stiff, dry froth. Add sugar a little at a time and beat in thoroughly. Add vanilla and vinegar. Beat again. Bake in a pan with a removable bottom for 1 hour and 10 minutes at 250 degrees F. Cool. Remove from pan onto large plate or platter. Slice fully ripe strawberries over the meringue. Cover with whipped cream which has been sweetened and flavoured with vanilla. Cut into six servings and top each with a whole strawberry.

"This is a Special Occasion Dessert for a birthday or an anniversary dinner."

Mrs. W.J. McKenzie, Vancouver.

Jams, Unusual Preserves

Jiffy Berry Jam
(For Raspberries, Blackberries, Boysenberries, Brambleberries and Loganberries)

Crush and boil for 3 minutes 6 to 8 cups berries. Remove from stove. Measure and add equal parts sugar to fruit. Boil again for 3 minutes. Remove from stove and beat with beater or wooden spoon for 3 minutes. Pour into hot sterilized glasses. Cover with paraffin and seal.

Cherry and Rhubarb Jam

To every pound of cherries, allow ½ pound rhubarb. Stone the cherries, put them through the mincer with the rhubarb, using the coarse knife. For every pound of fruit allow ¾ pound of sugar. Combine all the ingredients and let stand if desired for 2 to 3 hours. Then cook slowly, stirring frequently until thick.

"This is delicious and keeps well."

Mrs. C.E. Underwood, Vancouver.

Vitamin "C" Jam

    2   cups rose hips, fully ripe (best after frost has
        touched them)
    4   cups boiling water
    ¾   pound cooking apples
    2   pounds sugar

Wash hips and put into boiling water. Boil gently until soft. Mash with a wooden spoon. Strain through a jelly bag, letting drip overnight. Measure juice. Make up to 3 cups with water if necessary. Cook apples to a pulp. Rub through a sieve. Mix hip juice and apple pulp and bring to a boil. Stir in sugar and when dissolved, boil rapidly until jelly stage is reached. Pour into hot sterilized jars and seal. Hawthorn haws can be used for a similar jam.

"This Rose Hip Jam saves buying expensive citrus fruits during the winter, for 1 tablespoon of it will supply all the Vitamin C needed by one person for 1 day."

Miss Josephine Rowa, Vancouver.

Clover Blossom Honey

    10 cups white sugar
    3   cups water
    ½   teaspoon powdered alum
    80 blossoms white clover
    40 blossoms red clover
    5   roses, petals only, perfumed not too strongly

Boil sugar, water and alum for 5 minutes. Pour the syrup over the blossoms and let stand for 20 minutes. Strain through cheesecloth into hot sterilized jars. Adjust covers and store in a dry place. Makes about 5 pounds honey. The flavour improves as it ages. It's hard to tell it from real honey.

"I made this recipe last year and was sorry that I didn't make double the amount as everyone who tasted it couldn't believe it was made in such a way."

Mrs. B. Richards, Vancouver.

Peach Conserve

Skin and chop 6 peaches, add 1½ cups ripe chopped pears, 12 maraschino cherries, chopped; 2 tablespoons cherry liquid, 1 tablespoon lemon juice and 1 tablespoon grated orange rind. Mix in 4 cups white sugar, and let stand about 3 hours. Simmer until thick and put into hot sterilized jars. Half cup blanched, chopped almonds may be added to the conserve 20 minutes before the cooking time is completed.

Mrs. Jean R. Haines, Wildwood Heights.

Candied Orange Peel

        Peel of 2 oranges
    ½   cup sugar
    ¼   cup water

Cut the peel into sections, removing as much of the white pith as possible. Put into a lined pan, cover with cold water, and simmer slowly until tender—about 45 minutes. Drain and remove the rest of the pith, if any. Cut peel into strips, and return to pan with the measured sugar and water. From boiling point, simmer steadily for 20 minutes or so, when the peel should be semi-transparent. Lift onto a plate or wire tray to cool; roll in sugar, and store in a screw-top jar.

Parsley Jelly

Wash and stem the parsley. Place in a pan with enough cold water to cover when parsley is pressed down. Add a pinch of powdered alum (may omit). Boil 30 minutes, turning the parsley a time or two. Strain through a cloth and then boil the juice about 20 minutes. To every 4 cups of juice, add the juice of 1 lemon. To every cup of fluid, add 1 cup sugar. Boil to 223 to 224 degrees F. Test on saucer. When done, pour into jelly glasses and, when cold, cover with paraffin.

"Now that parsley is ready, it's a good time to make Parsley Jelly. This is how I make it—it's very nice."

Mrs. Etta Miller, Burnaby.

Red Pepper Jelly

    20 sweet red peppers
     4 hot red peppers
        Vinegar
     4 lemons
     3 pounds granulated sugar

Remove seeds from peppers, chop fine, cover with boiling water and boil for 10 minutes. Drain off the water and cover with vinegar. Add sliced lemons and boil for 30 minutes longer. Remove the lemon, add the 3 pounds sugar and boil until thick. Put into hot sterilized jars and seal immediately. Makes 5 pints.

  "I receive so many compliments when I serve this with a roast for Sunday dinner that I consider it well worth making."
  Mrs. Frank A. Jones, Penticton.

Any-Season Mincemeat

     1 pound apples
     ½ pound grapes
     ½ pound raisins
     ½ pound currants
     ¼ pound brown sugar
     ¼ mixed peel
     ¼ teaspoon cinnamon
        Grated rind and juice of 1 lemon

Peel and chop apples. Skin and stone grapes. Put pulp in a bowl and press well with a wooden spoon. Thoroughly mix with all ingredients. Put in a jar and fasten down tightly. That is all. For a richer mincemeat use less apples and more grapes.

  "This is an excellent mincemeat—so quick and easy that a small amount can be made at any time, all ingredients being available at any season."

Pat Pederson (left) and Brenda Thompson (right) make preserves in the Edith Adams Cottage kitchen, 10 August 1990.

Pickles and Ketchups

Chow-Chow Supreme

    4 quarts sliced green tomatoes
    1 quart chopped onions
3 or 4 sweet red peppers, chopped fine
    1 cup dairy salt
    1 quart chopped apples
    1 tablespoon turmeric
    3 cups vinegar
    3 cups white sugar
    1 cup whole mixed pickling spices

Put tomatoes, onions and peppers in a crock, add salt and cover with ice water. Let stand overnight. In the morning, drain thoroughly and put all in a large kettle. Add chopped apples, turmeric, vinegar and sugar. Tie spices in a cheese-cloth bag. Bring pickles to a boil and simmer 45 minutes. Remove spice bag and pour immediately into hot, sterilized jars and seal.

   Mrs. A. Watson, Vancouver.

8 Quarts of Dills

    13 cups water
     5 cups cider vinegar (can use white)
     1 cup salt (not iodized)

Boil all together and allow to cool. Pack small cucumbers in hot sterilized jars. Into each quart jar put 1 clove garlic, 1 pickling pepper and 3 or 4 pieces of dill. Pour the cooled liquid over the cucumbers and screw the tops of the jars down tightly.

   "These are delicious, crisp dills and are always a 'Must' at canning season in our home."

Peach and Pear Pickles

    4 pears
   4½ onions (medium)
   10 ripe tomatoes
    2 cups sugar
    1 teaspoon whole spice (in bag)
    1 red pepper, chopped fine
    2 cups vinegar
    1 teaspoon salt

Chop up fruit, onions and tomatoes. Add balance of ingredients. Cook slowly about 2 hours. Put into jars.

   "One of my favourites."

   Mrs. L.R. Mohs, Fort Smith, Northwest Territories.

Green Tomato Ketchup

    6 large green tomatoes
    1 stalk celery
    2 apples
    1 onion
    1 cucumber
    2 tablespoons sugar
   1½ teaspoons salt
    ¼ cup vinegar
       Allspice, cinnamon and cayenne to taste

Cut up tomatoes, celery, apples, onion and cucumber. Add 3 cups of water. Boil until soft. Press through fine sieve. Boil down if liquid is too thin. Add sugar, salt, vinegar and spices to suit taste. Seal in sterile bottles.

Crabapple Ketchup

    8 cups crabapples, peeled and quartered
    2 cups sugar
    2 teaspoons pepper
    2 teaspoons cloves
    2 teaspoons cinnamon
    3 large onions
    2 tablespoons salt
       Enough vinegar to cover

Stew apples until tender in as little water as possible. Press through sieve. Add sugar, spices and onions. Mix together. Add salt and vinegar to cover. Boil about 1 hour over low heat. Pour into sterilized jars and seal.

   "We all like this spicy ketchup with our meals. Most of the ingredients can be found on our pantry shelves."

   Mrs. Fraser McLeod, New Westminster.

Edith Adams' Thirteenth Prize Cook Book

1950

edith adams'
thirteenth prize

cook book

readers'
tested recipes
basic cookery
by **edith adams**

director
edith adams' cottage
homemakers' service
the vancouver sun

35c

"Good homemaking" and "Edith Adams" have become almost synonymous in the consciousness of British Columbia women. Since The Vancouver Sun established its homemaking adviser in her own friendly Cottage in January, 1947, hundreds of thousands of requests for information and advice have come to her by telephone, letter and personal interview. Women have also shared with her their own recipes and housekeeping lore, and in this Thirteenth Prize Cook Book, Edith Adams has culled some of the most popular recipes from The Sun's newspaper columns in which she first published them. But this Cook Book is more than a collection of good recipes. It's also a summary of balanced, low-cost menus (with recipes) for the four seasons of the year. Advising women on how to give their families good meals in the face of high food costs has become one of the most important phases of The Sun's homemakers' service.

The art of entertaining graciously in one's own home is another very real interest of women, Edith Adams has discovered, and in this book she outlines the various forms such entertaining may take, adding good recipes for easy preparation. Last of all is "Getting Ready for Christmas," summarizing the spirit which makes Edith Adams Cottage one of the friendliest spots in Western Canada during the four busiest weeks of a homemaker's year—her preparations for the Yuletide season.

Breads

Vitamin Bread

2 packages granular yeast
1 cup lukewarm water
1 teaspoon sugar
3 cups white flour
2 tablespoons malt extract
1 tablespoon molasses
2 cups potato water
12 cups whole wheat flour
2 tablespoons wheat germ
2 tablespoons salt
3 cups liquid

Dissolve the yeast in the lukewarm water and add the sugar. Set aside until well risen and foamy. Make a sponge of the white flour, malt, molasses, potato water and yeast. Beat well and set aside until well risen. Then add the whole wheat flour, wheat germ, salt and 3 cups liquid. Knead well and set in a warm place away from drafts. Knead down and let rise for three times. Shape into loaves and let rise in the pans until increased by about one third. Bake in a 400 deg. F. oven for 45 minutes.

Variations: Substitute part of the whole wheat flour with rye, barley, or graham flour. Omit the molasses and use white flour for white bread or rolls. To make crusty rolls sprinkle with ice-water before baking.

"This makes six 20-ounce loaves."

Mrs. Reginald Smith, Vancouver.

Savarin

2 packages granulated yeast
1 cup flour
1 cup milk
1 cup butter
1 cup sugar
3 eggs
Grated rind of 1 lemon
1 teaspoon salt
3 cups flour
Almonds or pecans

Dissolve the yeast according to the directions on the package. Add 1 cup flour and milk and let rise. Cream the butter and sugar, beat the eggs in one at a time. Add the lemon rind and salt. Add the flour and beat until the mixture is light and smooth. Butter two ring moulds and sprinkle with chopped nuts. Half fill with batter and let rise to the top. Bake in a 375 deg. F. oven for 45 minutes or until nicely done. Ice when cool.

Mrs. J.R. Lukach, Vancouver.

North Van Best Buns

1 package granulated yeast
½ cup water
1 teaspoon sugar
¾ cup milk
¼ cup shortening
¼ cup sugar
1 teaspoon salt
1 egg
3½ cups flour

Sprinkle yeast in ½ cup lukewarm water in which 1 teaspoon of sugar has been thoroughly dissolved. Let stand for 10 minutes. Scald milk, pour over shortening, sugar and salt in mixing bowl. Cool to lukewarm. Add yeast mixture and well beaten egg. Gradually stir in flour to form a soft dough. Beat thoroughly. Cover and let rise in a warm place until double in bulk. Turn out on a floured board and roll to ½ inch thickness. Cut with 2½ inch cutter and place on a greased cookie sheet. Cover and let rise until double in bulk. Bake at 375 deg. F. for 20 minutes.

Currant Buns: Add ½ cup currants to batter. For **Cinnamon Buns** roll out, sprinkle with brown sugar and cinnamon, roll like a jelly roll and cut up. For **Fruit Loaf**, add ¼ teaspoon nutmeg, ¼ pound fruit cake mixture, ¼ cup raisins and ¼ cup currants. Yield: 2 small loaves.

Mrs. R.B. McKenzie, North Vancouver.

Honey Pumpkin Bread

½ cup white sugar
½ cup soft honey
½ cup mixed butter and shortening
1 cup cooked pumpkin
2 cups sifted pastry flour
½ teaspoon cinnamon
1 teaspoon baking soda
½ teaspoon salt
½ teaspoon nutmeg
1 cup chopped dates or raisins
½ cup walnut pieces

Cream the sugar, honey and shortening together and add the pumpkin. Mix well. Sift the dry ingredients together and add the dates and walnuts. Mix the batter together well. Turn into a greased, floured loaf pan and bake in a moderate oven at 350 deg. F. for 1½ hours.

Mrs. C.B. Elliott, Vancouver.

Sweet Condensed Milk Recipes

Basic Cookies

1⅓ cups (15-oz. can) sweetened condensed milk
½ cup peanut butter

Mix these two together and add any ONE of the following 6 ingredients:

2 cups raisins
2 cups cornflakes
3 cups shredded coconut
2 cups bran flakes
1 cup chopped nuts
2 cups chopped dates

Drop from a teaspoon on a greased baking sheet and bake in a moderately hot oven, 375 deg. F., for 15 minutes or until brown. Remove from pan at once.

Unbaked Christmas Cake

4 cups rolled graham wafer crumbs
½ teaspoon salt
½ teaspoon cinnamon
½ teaspoon cloves
½ teaspoon nutmeg
½ teaspoon allspice
4 cups chopped marshmallows
1 cup raisins
2 cups chopped dates
1 cup currants
½ cup glazed cherries
1 cup chopped nuts
1⅓ cups sweetened condensed milk (1 tin)

Roll graham wafers very fine, and mix in salt and spices. Add marshmallows. (To cut marshmallows dip scissors in boiling water.) Add chopped fruit and nuts with condensed milk and mix all together thoroughly. Press into a loaf pan lined with wax paper. Chill for 2 days before cutting.

Mrs. H. Eidemm, Vancouver.

Opera Roll

2 cups sugar
½ cup cold water
⅔ cup light corn syrup
2 egg whites
1⅓ cups (1 can) sweetened condensed milk
½ cup butter
Nuts

Boil sugar, water and ½ cup light corn syrup together until it forms a hard ball in cold water, 250 deg. F., on candy thermometer. Then pour slowly into stiffly beaten egg whites. Beat hard at intervals until cool. When it begins to cool, shape with hands into rolls. When rolls are hard and dry make toffee.

Make toffee by boiling sweetened condensed milk, remaining corn syrup and butter together to the hard ball stage. Stir constantly as it burns easily. When hard ball stage is reached take each roll on a fork and submerge in toffee mixture. Remove and roll in chopped nuts. The remaining toffee can be boiled 15 minutes longer and poured into a buttered pan.

Chocolate Coconut Glossies

8 squares (1 package) semi-sweet chocolate
⅔ cup sweetened condensed milk*
¼ teaspoon salt
1 teaspoon vanilla
1½ cups shredded coconut

Heat chocolate over boiling water until partly melted. Then remove from boiling water and stir rapidly until entirely melted. Add milk, salt, vanilla and coconut and blend. Drop from teaspoon on waxed paper. Cool until firm. Makes about 3 dozen.

*For best results, have milk at room temperature.

Casseroles

Mushroom-Cheese Casserole

- 1 tablespoon dripping
- 1 tablespoon finely chopped onion
- 1 tablespoon flour
- ¼ teaspoon salt
- ⅛ teaspoon pepper, paprika and nutmeg (mixed)
- 1 cup milk
- 2 tablespoons butter
- 1 pound sliced mushrooms (fresh or canned)
- 2 tablespoons pimento, diced
- 1 cup grated hard cheese
- 4 tablespoons bread crumbs

Melt fat in pan, add onion, cook till golden brown. Blend in the flour and seasonings. Add milk; cook and stir until smooth. In the meantime, heat the butter and add the mushrooms, which have been peeled and sliced; cook and stir until tender. Add to the sauce, then add the pimento. Put the mixture into an oiled quart casserole. Cover with the grated cheese, then sprinkle with bread crumbs. Bake in oven, 375 deg. F., for about 15 minutes, until cheese melts and bubbles.

Served with a green salad, this is a delectable dish.

Jean R. Haines, Wildwood Heights.

Sausage-Noodle Casserole

- 8 ounce package noodles
- 1 pound sausages
- ½ green pepper, chopped
- 1 medium onion, chopped
- 1 can mushroom soup
-   Bread or cracker crumbs

Cook noodles according to directions and drain. Chop sausages into 1-inch pieces and brown in frying pan with pepper and onion. Alternate layers of noodles and the sausage mixture in a greased casserole, ending with a layer of noodles. Pour the soup over and top with buttered

crumbs. Bake 30 minutes in a 350 deg. F. oven. Serves 6. (Pepper may be omitted and cheese cracker crumbs used for a different topping.)

Mrs. M. Linn, Nanaimo.

Pork Chops en Casserole

Take 6 medium pork chops and salt and pepper them. Dip them in beaten egg and roll in bread crumbs. Sear a delicate brown in hot fat. While these are searing, make a sauce as follows:

- 1 can tomato juice (or ½ can tomato soup and ½ water)
- ¼ cup vinegar
- ½ teaspoon allspice
-   Salt and pepper
- ½ cup brown sugar
- ½ teaspoon cloves

Boil this for 3 minutes. Then take seared chops, place in a greased casserole, pour the cooked sauce over the chops, cover and bake at 350 deg. F. for 1 hour.

Mrs. Phyllis A. Cook, Victoria.

Egg and Asparagus Casserole

- 3 tablespoons butter or margarine
- 3 tablespoons chopped green pepper
- 1 tablespoon grated onion
- 2 tablespoons flour
- 1 cup milk
- 1 teaspoon salt
- ⅛ teaspoon pepper
- 1 pound fresh asparagus, cooked
- 3 hard-cooked eggs
- ½ cup buttered crumbs
- ½ cup grated cheese

Melt the butter; add the green pepper and onion and cook until golden; add flour and blend. Gradually add milk and cook until smooth and thick, stirring constantly. Add seasoning. Alternate rows of asparagus and egg slices in a greased 6 by 10 inch baking dish. Pour the sauce over. Top with buttered crumbs and cheese. Bake in a moderate oven, 350 deg. F., 20 minutes.

Lillian Spencer, Seattle, Washington.

Your Dinner Party

Hospitality is traditional. The breaking of bread and the passing of salt has always created a bond between host and guest.

Basic to all entertaining is planning. Planning includes the choice of the menu, making the shopping list and arranging the work schedule, selecting the theme of the party and choosing the decorations and correct table appointments. The schedule should also include a period of time for the hostess to rest and to dress with care so that she may be relaxed and poised when she greets her guests.

Invite guests who are compatible. The hostess should lead conversation to subjects of interest to her guests and away from the usual topics of cost of living and the difficulties of running a home. Stimulating conversation is just as enjoyable as good food and just as necessary for a successful party. The hostess who practises such a routine soon wins a reputation as a charming hostess.

Degrees of Formality
There are three types of table service. Russian, English or Compromise.

The Russian style is used for formal meals. Only flowers, silver and china are placed on the table at the beginning of the meal. The several courses are passed by the waitress, served to the left side of each guest. Each guest helps himself. Sometimes the plates are served from the kitchen and brought to each guest.

The English style of serving is used at small dinner parties or with the family. The host carves and serves the meat and gravy. The hostess serves the soup, vegetables, salad, dessert and coffee. The served dishes may be passed to each guest by the maid or they may be passed from person to person.

The Compromise style is a combination of the Russian and the English services. Usually the appetizer is placed on the table before the meal. The salad, vegetables and dessert are served from the kitchen; while the host carves and serves the meat. The hostess pours the coffee at the table. This type of service is mostly used for family meals.

Cloth and Napkins
A perfect table setting depends on the artistic arrangement of table decoration and the correct arrangement of table appointments. A white linen cloth is classic for formal dinner but embroidered linen or lace may also be used. The cloth should have one lengthwise crease and should hang evenly on all sides about 15 to 18 inches below the table top. Lace will hang even lower. Silence cloth should be used not only to protect the table top, but to make for quieter service. Napkins should match the cloth. Lace demands white damask napkins. Dinner napkins are usually 36 x 36 inches with a ⅛ to ¼ inch hem.

Luncheon cloths should be of lace or coloured damask (never white). Or you may use lace or other placemats, leaving the rest of the table bare. Napkins should match the cloth and should be 15 x 18 inches. The conventional tea cloth is white, but coloured ones may be used. Linen, lace or embroidered tea cloths are in good taste. The tea napkins are 12 x 12 inches in size.

Placing the Silver
The centrepiece should be placed in the centre of the table along with the candles and compotes. Place the necessary number of plates, with the pattern facing the guests, at equal distances on the table, allowing 24 inches for the cover. Lay the silver with the lower edge of the plate, and the tips of the handles of the silver parallel to each. Place the knives to the right of the cover plate with the cutting edge towards the plate, the spoons are on the right of these. On the left are all the forks, except the cocktail fork, which is laid to the extreme right of the knives. Silver is placed conveniently, starting from the outside for the first course and working towards the cover plate. From left to right the usual arrangement is fish fork, meat fork, salad fork, soup spoon, cocktail fork or grapefruit spoon. Only 3 knives and 3 forks are placed when setting the table. Additional silver will be placed during the dinner. The water goblet is placed above the blade tip of the dinner knife, with champagne glass to the right, and the claret glass in front between these 2 glasses. The sherry glass should be placed in front of the claret glass. The napkin is folded and placed on the cover plate parallel with the silver.

Place cards and individual nut dishes are placed above the cover.

The formal luncheon table is set as for the dinner with cover plate, 3 forks, 2 knives and small spoon. The lunch napkin is folded twice. The bread and butter plate with butter spreader is part of the cover.

Formal Service

Formal dining cannot well be undertaken unless there is adequate service (one waiter or waitress for each six or eight persons) and the necessary appointments are available. Written invitations are extended. Full evening dress is demanded. Certain rules are essential for formal service. No food is served until all guests are seated. Goblets are used, not tumblers. Salt and pepper are not placed on the table. A hard dinner roll is served but without butter. The dessert silver is placed on the table when the dessert is brought in. Candy, fruits and nuts can be part of the table decoration. Flowers and baskets of nuts and candies often provide favours. Place cards are hand written.

Service plates are always used. The plates must be of the same set, but a different set can be used for each course. Using the service plate makes for better service. The service plate is lifted each time and then replaced when the soiled plates are all cleared away. The guest is never left without a service plate except between the course which precedes the dessert and the serving of the dessert. (The service plate is lifted with the right hand and the course is placed with the left hand.) The food is offered with the serving silver to the left of each guest. The dish is held flat in the hand unless the dish is so heavy it requires both hands to support it. No second servings are offered. The finger bowls are offered with the dessert plate and silver. Demi-tasse is placed immediately after the dessert has been removed and no cream is served. Cigarettes and liqueurs are offered at this time. The gentlemen are served in the dining room while the ladies are served in the living room, or, as is usual now, both may be served in the living room.

Informal Service

The informal dinner affords more variety in dishes and method of service. Two courses are the minimum and four the maximum. It is not necessary to have a waitress. The English or the Compromise style of service can be used.

Cigarettes are on the table throughout the meal. Coffee may be served at the table or from the coffee tray in the living room. The hostess pours the coffee and passes the coffee to her guests. Cream is served.

Etiquette for Dinner Parties
A Good Hostess Must Plan

Successful parties are the result of careful planning and organization. Once you have decided on the kind of party, the date and the number of guests you wish to invite you can issue invitations by telephone or by informal note. The exception to this rule would be the formal invitation which must be printed and in the third person. When you are making your guest list be sure to choose people who are compatible. It is not necessary to keep to age levels as long as interests are related.

Plan a menu which you can cook successfully. If you're using a new dish, practise on the family first. Perhaps you can build a party around one special dish of yours. Remember the food fads and diets of your guests, too, if you would be a thoughtful hostess. Make a shopping list from the menu and do your shopping ahead of the preparation day, so that menu changes can be made if certain ingredients are unobtainable. It is a wise plan to make an early work schedule for yourself so that the house will be clean and shining, with you relaxed to enjoy your guests.

Setting the table the day before and covering it with a cloth will aid last-minute preparations. Flowers can be arranged on the day of the party and set in place before the arrival of guests.

Menus for Formal Dinners

Grape Sherry Cup

Oyster Bisque

Standing Rib Roast

Mashed Potatoes

Brussels Sprouts and Chestnuts

Avocado and Grapefruit Salad

French Dressing

Baked Alaska

Demi-tasse

•

Cocktails

Hors d'oeuvres

Melon Ball Cup

Filet Mignon

Browned Potato Balls

Sauteed Mushrooms

Buttered Broccoli

Brandied Peaches

Mixed Green Salad with French Dressing

Baked Alaska

Demi-tasse

Mushroom Puree

Wash and stem ½ pound fresh mushrooms. Scrub to remove the skin if necessary. Slice. Add to 6 tablespoons of melted butter and 2 teaspoons of lemon juice and cook until the mushrooms are tender. Then mash with a fork. This puree will be smooth and thick.

Filet Mignon

Cut a whole beef filet into 6 slices. Trim. Season with salt and pepper. Place in frying pan with melted butter. Brown on both sides. Cover with the mushroom puree. Arrange the filets in a baking pan. Cover with buttered paper and place in moderate oven, 350 deg. F., for 10 minutes. Transfer the mignons to a heated serving platter. Garnish with grilled tomato slices, topped with a poached egg, surrounded with an anchovy filet. Serve with the remaining mushroom puree.

Brandied Peaches

        4   pounds peaches
            Cloves
        4   pounds sugar
     3½   cups water
        1   egg white
        2   cups white brandy

Pare the peaches with silver knife and insert 2 cloves in each whole peach. Make a syrup of the sugar and water. Skim. Add the egg white beaten to a froth. Skim again. Then add the peaches one at a time. Cook until tender. Remove to platter and cool. Boil the excess syrup 10 minutes or until thick. Remove from fire. Add brandy. Pour over fruit placed in jars. Seal. Store for 1 week before using.

Pineapple Poinsettias

     ½   cup shortening
        1   cup sugar
        2   eggs
        2   tablespoons thick cream
        1   teaspoon vanilla
     2½   cups sifted bread flour
     ¼   teaspoon soda
     ½   teaspoon salt

Mix together thoroughly the shortening, sugar and eggs. Stir in cream and vanilla. Sift together and stir in bread flour, soda and salt. Chill dough, roll ⅛-inch thick. Cut in 3-inch squares. Place on lightly greased cookie sheet. Cut with sharp knife from corners of each square almost to centre, making 4 triangular sections, joined in centre, in each square. In centre place 1 teaspoon pineapple filling. Pick up left corner of any triangular section and fold down over centre filling, leaving the right corner flat to form a petal. Fold the three remaining left corners down over centre, press gently in centre to hold 4 points together. For a festive touch, press half a candied cherry in centre and sprinkle with red sugar. Bake 8 to 10 minutes in moderate oven, until delicately browned.

Pineapple Filling:

Mix together in saucepan: 1 cup sugar, 4 tablespoons flour. Stir in 1½ cups well-drained crushed pineapple (No. 2 can), 4 tablespoons lemon juice, 3 tablespoons butter, ¼ teaspoon nutmeg, ¾ cup pineapple juice. Cook slowly, stirring constantly until thickened. Cool.

Mrs. James Kirk, Stave Falls.

Chicken Saute with Almonds

    2   young chickens, cut in pieces (2¼–2½ pounds
        each)
        Salt
        Pepper
    4   tablespoons butter
    ½   cup almonds, peeled and sliced
    1   shallot or onion, chopped fine
    1   glass dry white wine
        Chopped parsley

Season chicken with salt and pepper. Fry slowly in butter. When light brown, add almonds and chopped shallots and fry until golden brown. Then, add wine and cook 20 to 30 minutes. Add chopped parsley and serve.

Duchess Potatoes

    2   cups hot mashed potatoes
    2   tablespoons butter
    ½   teaspoon salt
    2   eggs, separated

Combine mashed potatoes, butter, salt, and beaten egg yolks. Using a pastry bag, create swirls or other shapes. Place in buttered baking dish and brush with egg whites. Brown in hot oven, 450 deg. F. Yield: 6 servings.

Pork Roast

Wipe a 4 to 5 pound fresh pork butt with a damp cloth. Sprinkle with salt and pepper and place the roast on a rack in an open roasting pan with the fat side up. Roast in moderate oven, allowing 45–50 minutes to the pound. Yield: 10 servings.

Your Luncheon Party

Women Like Luncheons

Luncheon parties hold top honours with women as a delightful way of entertaining for visitors, playing hostess for one's club or repaying social obligations to other women. Its keynote is often its gay informality. Imagination will create unusual settings, floral centres and delicious food combinations that appeal especially to feminine appetites. The table is set as for an informal dinner but candles are never used. If her dining table will not accommodate the number of guests, the hostess will set up card tables throughout her rooms or in the garden during summer months. Casserole dishes, tempting salads and rich desserts are all excellent for a woman's luncheon party.

Chicken Mousse

    1½ tablespoons gelatin
    2   cups chicken broth
    2   egg yolks
    1   teaspoon salt
        Dash pepper
    ½   cup heavy cream
    ⅓   cup mayonnaise
    1   cup diced cooked chicken
    ½   cup diced cooked ham

Soften the gelatin in a quarter of a cup of the cold broth. Heat remaining broth and add slowly to the beaten egg yolks. Add seasonings and cook over boiling water until of custard consistency. Add gelatin and stir until dissolved. Strain and let stand until it starts to congeal. Whip the cream and fold the mayonnaise into it. Fold this mixture into the gelatin mixture, then fold in the diced meats. Pour into a mould and let set overnight. Finely chopped almonds, or pimento added make nice variations.

Tossed Luncheon Salad

1 clove garlic, cut into halves
1 head lettuce
1 bunch chicory
3 tomatoes, quartered
3 stalks celery, diced
1 cucumber, sliced
2 green pepper rings, finely diced
6 green onions, sliced
1 avocado, sliced
   French dressing
3 hard-cooked eggs, sliced

Rub the salad bowl with the cut surfaces of the garlic. Have the lettuce well washed, dried and crisp, then tear it rather than cut it as you put it in the bowl. Add the other vegetables. Marinate the avocado slices in French dressing. Toss the salad with the dressing and garnish the top with the hard cooked egg slices and the avocado. The salad should be served as soon as possible after the dressing is added as the oil wilts the vegetables.

Chicken Livers en Brochette

1 pound chicken livers
½ cup French dressing
½ pound bacon
6 small tomatoes
6 small boiled onions

Rinse the chicken livers under cold water then blot dry. Cut in squares about one inch by one inch. Marinate in the French dressing for one hour. Cut the bacon also in one inch squares. On a skewer place a small tomato, then alternate pieces of liver and bacon and place a cooked onion on the end. Brush with oil or melted shortening and place under the broiler for 5 minutes, turn and broil for an additional five minutes. Serve one skewer to a person.

Pat Pederson, home economist, tests a recipe in the Edith Adams Cottage kitchen, January 1982.

Luncheon Menus

Spiced Apple Juice
Boston Baked Beans
Boston Brown Bread
Cole Slaw
Celery Curls
Sherbet

•

Tomato Juice
Chicken Livers en Brochette
Potato Chips
Chef's Salad
Peanut Pie

•

Partially Defrosted Cantaloupe Balls
Sauteed Chicken with Curry Sauce
Green Beans and Glazed Carrots in Rice Mould
Lemon Ice-Box Cake

•

Fruit Cup with Mint
Creole Gumbo
Steamed Rice
Green Beans
Orange Bavarian Cream

Lemon Ice-Box Cake

½ cup butter or margarine
1 cup icing sugar
¼ cup milk
¼ cup sugar
1½ tablespoons cornstarch
3 eggs, separated
1 lemon, juice and rind
   Lady fingers
1 cup whipping cream

Cream the butter and the icing sugar together. Place the milk, sugar, cornstarch and egg yolks in the top of a double boiler. Stir until cornstarch is dissolved. Cook over boiling water until thick, stirring to keep it smooth. Add the lemon juice and rind and remove from the heat. Add the butter and powdered sugar and fold in the beaten egg whites. Line the bottom and sides of a mould or deep cake tin with lady fingers. Pour the filling in. Cover top with more lady fingers. Chill in the refrigerator for 24 hours. Unmould and garnish with whipped cream.

Potato Salad

3 cups cubed cold potatoes
½ teaspoon salt
¾ cup chopped celery
2 hard cooked eggs, diced
1 large onion, minced
1 cup mayonnaise

Combine the ingredients in the order listed, using enough mayonnaise to moisten. Garnish with radish roses and parsley. Serves 6.

Luncheon Menus

Consomme with Sherry

Chicken Mousse

Refrigerator Rolls

Fruit Salad

Pickles

Relishes

Blitz Torte

•

Jellied Tomato Bouillon

Shrimp and Pineapple Salad

Tea Biscuits

Assorted Relishes

Fruit Floating Island

•

Hot Tomato Juice

Cold Meat Platter

Potato Salad

Mixed Green Salad

Spiced Layer Cake

•

Cream Soup

Fruit Plate

Whipping Cream Dressing

Cheese Sticks

Hot Muffins

Chiffon Pie

Easter Nests

 ¾ pound sweet chocolate or chocolate bits
 3 cups whole flaked breakfast food

Melt the chocolate over hot water, never boiling water. Stir in the cereal and place on waxed paper shaping the mixture like a nest. Let chocolate harden. Fill the nests with coloured jelly beans or candy to represent eggs.

Chocolate Easter Eggs

 3 cups icing sugar
 1 egg white
 1 tablespoon water
 ½ teaspoon vanilla
 ½ package semi-sweet chocolate

Sift sugar in bowl, add egg white, water and flavouring. Knead until smooth. This should be stiff enough to hold its shape. Colour ⅓ of this mixture yellow, and flavour it with orange. Roll into small balls to make a yolk. Flatten out a piece from the white remainder large enough to wrap the yolk. Shape like an egg. Melt semi-sweet chocolate and dip eggs with a large fork until well covered. Place on wax paper to harden. Your child's name can be put on by drawing with a toothpick before the chocolate completely sets.

 Mrs. W.W. Anderson, New Westminster.

Simnel Easter Cake

 ⅔ cup butter
 ⅔ cup sugar
 1 teaspoon almond essence
 4 eggs
 1½ cups currants or sultanas (or you can mix them)
 ½ cup mixed peel
 1 teaspoon mixed spice
 2 cups flour
 1 teaspoon baking powder
  Almond paste

Beat butter, sugar, almond essence and eggs one at a time. Beat together thoroughly. Add fruit, spice and flour which has been sifted with the baking powder. Put layer of cake mixture in a greased and lined round cake tin. Then put a layer of almond paste, then the remainder of the cake batter. Bake in a slow oven, 300 deg. F. for 2 to 2½ hours. Make almond paste by using ½ pound ground almonds mixed with ¾ pound fine sugar and the beaten white of an egg.

 "I bought this recipe at a church tea where a member gave a slice of cake with each recipe sold. It is very nice."

 Mrs. A.E. Knowlden, Vancouver.

Easter

Flowers and bunnies, chicks and eggs, are age-old symbols of Easter tradition and deserve first place at your Easter holiday parties. Traditional symbols, combined with the Easter colours of yellow and purple, make table decoration relatively simple. There are traditional foods, too, that lend themselves well to menu planning for either formal or informal entertaining.

An Easter tree would make an unusual conversation centrepiece. Select a branch from your garden. Choose one with many sturdy twigs so that you can hang on them painted eggs, fluffy yellow chicks, candied Easter eggs or paper spring flowers. Perhaps a spring boutonniere for each guest would make the tree even more interesting.

Bunnies in the Grass

 1 package lime jelly
 4 (halves) tinned pears
  Few almonds
  Whipped cream, or custard

Make jelly according to instructions on package, and whisk just before it sets. Divide into four individual dishes; then place half a pear, rounded side up, in centre of each dish of jellied "grass." Press the almonds, split in half, into the fruit—one on each side of the pointed ends as "ears," and a third piece at the rounded end for a "tail." Decorate with rosettes of whipped cream or thick custard.

 Mrs. Jean R. Haines, Wildwood Heights.

Christmas Decorations, Breads, Cookies

Yule Logs

    2   pounds coarse salt
    2   pounds bluestone
    1   ounce each of chemical salts for colour (see below)
    2   gallons boiling water

Mix the above ingredients together in a wooden pail. The salts will corrode metals. Roll up magazines or newspaper tightly and tie with string. Place them in the solution for two weeks. Remove and allow to dry for 1 or 2 months.

Chemical Salts	Colour
Borax	purple
Potassium Chloride	purple
Cobalt	purple
Bismuth Nitrate	crimson
Strontium Nitrate	red
Sodium Chloride (table salt)	orange

Christmas Stollen

    1   package dehydrated yeast
    ½   cup lukewarm water
    ½   cup sugar
    ½   cup scalded and cooled milk
    ½   cup melted butter
    2   eggs, well beaten
    ¼   teaspoon salt
    4½ cups all-purpose flour
    1   cup raisins
    ½   cup dried currants
    ¼   pound candied fruit of any type
    ½   cup almonds or walnuts, chopped

Dissolve yeast in lukewarm water to which you add 2 teaspoons sugar. Scald and cool milk. Add yeast, sugar, butter, eggs, salt and half the flour. Beat to smooth batter. Cover and let rise 45 minutes. Add remaining flour, fruit and nuts. Beat the batter. Cover and let rise until double in bulk. Knead lightly on floured board. Divide into two portions and shape in loaves as a braided French loaf. Place on flat, greased baking pan. Brush with beaten egg. Let rise to double in bulk. Bake 375 deg. F. for 45 minutes.

Glaze: Boil together in small saucepan 2 tablespoons molasses and 2 tablespoons butter for 3 minutes. While the twist is warm brush it with the glaze.

Nut Topping: Mix ¾ cup icing sugar with about 1 tablespoon water until smooth enough to spread. Drop frosting with spoon twisting to create a design. Sprinkle with ½ cup chopped blanched almonds.

Danish Kringle
Dough:

    ½   package dehydrated yeast
    ¼   cup lukewarm water
    1   cup milk
    ⅓   cup sugar
    4   cups sifted all-purpose flour
    2   teaspoons salt
    ¾   cup shortening
    3   egg yolks

Filling and Topping:

    1   cup brown sugar, firmly packed
    1   cup chopped nut meats
    2   tablespoons flour
    2   egg whites, stiffly beaten
    1   egg white, lightly beaten
    ½   cup icing sugar
    2   tablespoons water

Combine yeast and ¼ cup lukewarm water. Heat milk to boiling. Add sugar. Cool to lukewarm. Mix flour and salt in bowl. Cut in shortening with pastry blender until it is as fine as cornmeal. Stir softened yeast and egg yolks into cooled milk, then add to dry ingredients. Beat well. This will be a soft dough. Chill 2 hours. Knead on lightly floured board until smooth. Divide dough in half to make 2 loaves. Roll out each half to 8 x 10 inch rectangle.

For filling, mix sugar, ⅔ cup of the nut meats, and flour, then fold into the 2 beaten egg whites. Spread half of this filling on each piece of dough. Roll up like jelly roll. Coil up or shape in crescent. Place on baking sheet. Let rise until double in bulk. Brush with remaining egg white. Bake in a moderate oven, 350 deg. F., about 40 minutes.

When slightly cool, frost with icing sugar mixed with water and sprinkle with remaining ⅓ cup chopped nut meats.

Yield: 2 coffee cakes (6 x 8 inches).

Pfeffernusse

- ½ cup butter or margarine
- 2 cups granulated sugar
- 2 eggs, well beaten
- 3 cups sifted all-purpose flour
- 1 teaspoon cinnamon
- ½ teaspoon nutmeg
- ½ teaspoon allspice
- ⅛ teaspoon pepper
- 1 teaspoon grated baker's ammonia
- ¼ cup chopped citron (optional)
- ¼ cup chopped candied orange peel (optional)
- ¼ cup chopped nut meats (optional)

Cream butter or margarine, add sugar, cream well. Add eggs, beaten, and mix well. Sift flour, measure and sift with spices. Add to first mixture, working in with hands if necessary. Add ammonia, which should be purchased at the druggist's as needed, for it loses its strength upon standing. Add fruits and mix thoroughly. Chill and then break dough into small pieces about ½ inch in diameter. Roll in ball and place on greased baking sheet an inch apart. Bake in moderate oven, 375 deg. F., for about 12 minutes. Makes about 20 dozen. These cookies should age before using.

Melting Shortbread

- 1 pound butter or part margarine
- 1 cup icing sugar
- 3 cups sifted all-purpose flour
- ½ cup cornstarch

Cream butter. Add sugar and work together thoroughly until creamy. Add sifted flour and cornstarch. Whip together until fluffy, and until mixture breaks. Either drop from a tablespoon or add a little more flour and knead until it can be rolled. Bake in a moderate oven, 325 deg. F., until light brown.

Mrs. C.E. Bolding, Vancouver.

Swedish Peppar Kakor

- 1 cup sugar
- 1 cup golden syrup
-   Butter, size of egg
- 3 egg yolks
- 6 tablespoons thick cream
- 1½ teaspoons ginger
- ½ teaspoon cloves
- 1½ teaspoons cinnamon
- 1 teaspoon soda
- 1 teaspoon baking powder
- 1 teaspoon salt
-   Flour

Bring sugar and syrup to boil, add butter the size of an egg, egg yolks and cream. Mix well. Add other ingredients and sufficient flour to make a stiff dough. Leave overnight, roll thin and bake. The thinner you roll them, the crisper they get.

"Swedish people usually have Peppar Kakor at Christmas."

Mrs. A. Edberg, Mission City.

Spritz Cookies

- 1 cup butter or margarine
- ¾ cup sugar
- 1 egg or 3 egg yolks
- 1 teaspoon almond extract
- 2½ cups sifted all-purpose flour
- ½ teaspoon baking powder
- ½ teaspoon salt

Work butter or margarine until soft. Cream with sugar until light and fluffy. Add beaten egg or yolks and almond extract and beat until smooth. Add sifted flour with baking powder and salt. Chill dough. Fill cookie press and force onto ungreased cold cookie sheet. Bake in hot oven, 400 deg. F., until delicately browned.

Index

This is an
Edith Adams' Cottage
publication